the
Happy
stepmother

the

Happy
stepmother

Stay Sane

Empower Yourself

Thrive in Your New Family

RACHELLE KATZ
Ed.D., LMFT

HARLEQUIN®

Author's Note: *To protect the privacy and confidentiality of the women who participated in my research, all names and identifying features have been changed. Some comments have been edited and condensed for the sake of brevity, but the gist of the sage advice offered to me by scores of courageous stepmothers has been retained. The author assumes full responsibility for the contents of this book.*

The Happy Stepmother

ISBN-13: 978-037-389225-9

© 2010 by Rachelle Katz

Library of Congress Cataloging-in-Publication Data

Katz, Rachelle.

The happy stepmother : stay sane, empower yourself, and thrive in your new family / Rachelle Katz.

p. cm.

Includes bibliographical references.

ISBN 978-0-373-89225-9 (pbk.)

1. Stepmothers. 2. Stepfamilies. I. Title.

HQ759.92.K374 2010

646.7'8—dc22

2009029471

www.eHarlequin.com

Printed in U.S.A.

Acknowledgments

When this project first took shape in my mind, I had no idea of the complexity and enormity of the task that lay ahead of me, nor did I realize how many wonderful people would support, guide and encourage me each step of the way. I am most grateful to family and friends for their patience, understanding and forbearance as I toiled for years to complete this book. Most notably, I want to thank my parents, Estelle and Leo, my husband, Ronnie, and my step-daughter, Jackie, for their unwavering love and unconditional support. My friends, Donna Linn, Dan Cohen, Barbara Bedick, Jill Bresler, and Jennifer Kotter read the manuscript at various stages, and offered many helpful suggestions. Their efforts extended beyond the usual bounds of friendship, and I am privileged to have them as my friends.

I have been fortunate to work with many talented, creative individuals who contributed their professional expertise to *The Happy Stepmother*. Joelle Delbourgo is the most competent and lovely literary agent; I am so grateful for her diligent efforts on my behalf. Working with Sarah Pelz, my editor at Harlequin Nonfiction, has been a gift I truly cherish. Because she combines intelligence and grace in all interactions, collaborating with her has been an absolutely joyous experience for me. I also want to thank everyone at Harlequin who worked so diligently on my behalf. I want to extend a special thanks to a most skilled and dedicated editor and friend, Pam Middleton, who embraced this project with as much enthusiasm as my own. Penelope Franklin edited the manuscript with incisive insights and demanded that I persevere until my best efforts were expended. I am so grateful for her guidance and wisdom. I also want to thank Betty Kelly Sargent and Phyllis Stern for their invaluable editorial help. I consider myself blessed with beginner's luck that collaboration on this project has been a joyous experience.

Last, I am eternally grateful to the wonderful women who responded to the Steps for Stepmothers online questionnaire and who participated in the online chat room for their willingness to disclose such highly personal information in the service of helping other stepmothers. I sincerely hope that the combined efforts and commitment of everyone who nurtured this book to completion will help many stepmothers lead happier, healthier lives.

Contents

Why I Wrote This Book

As a stepmother or a woman who may become one in the near future, do you find yourself amazed and concerned by the sheer number of challenges you face every day? Would you ever in a million years have imagined dealing with so many emotional upheavals and tedious chores, just because you fell in love with a man who already had children? Has your zest for life started to evaporate? If so, you are not alone. Many other stepmothers face the same emotional difficulties, but it doesn't have to be this way.

I have written this book for stepmothers who have not found their role to be easy and for women considering marrying men with children and who need reassurance and guidance about becoming stepmothers. Consider the following questions to see if *The Happy Stepmother* can help you:

- Do you find being a stepmother a struggle, or are you worried that it will be a challenge after your marriage?
- Do you have full-time care of your stepchildren and end up doing all the work, but get little appreciation and affection in return for your efforts?
- Do you feel worn out by the effort to "blend" your two families?
- Do you dread the time you spend with your partner's children?
- Do you feel jealous when your partner spends time alone with his children?
- Are you angry because you feel your needs are rarely considered?

- Do you dwell on stepfamily problems frequently during the day?
- Is it difficult to talk civilly to your partner about his children, and is this driving a wedge between the two of you?
- Does your partner expect you to discipline his children, but then criticizes you for being too tough when you do?
- Have you found yourself being mean, even cruel, to your partner and his children, and can't believe the words you hear coming from your own mouth?

If your answer is yes to at least one of these questions, *The Happy Stepmother* can help you take giant steps toward leading an emotionally healthy life.

As a stepmother, and as a psychotherapist with more than twenty-five years of experience treating many stepmothers, I've come to realize the extraordinary challenge this role can present. Studies from the U.S. Census Bureau indicate that 60 percent of second marriages end in divorce (compared to 50 percent of first marriages)! This figure is shockingly high, and should give pause to all of us who are thinking about marrying, or who are married to, men with children from a previous relationship. With only a four-in-ten chance of our marriages surviving, it is important for all of us to take the necessary precautions to avoid becoming another divorce casualty. *The Happy Stepmother* will help improve and strengthen your relationship with your partner.

Despite the challenges we stepmothers face, the role receives very little acknowledgment or support from others. Generally speaking, our culture does not recognize the love, kindness and compassion we give to our stepchildren. Our efforts to form close relationships with them, and to take care of their physical and emotional needs when they spend time with us, are largely overlooked by others. Instead, society perceives us as one step removed from the family, second best, or unfairly stepping into someone else's shoes. Without knowing us, others tend to assume that we are hostile and cruel to our stepchildren.

Often, stepmothers become scapegoats for many problems of the modern family. We are unfairly blamed when our stepchildren experience problems, such as dropping out of school or abusing drugs and alcohol. It is easier for society to blame us when stepfamily members fail to thrive than to thoroughly examine the multifaceted reasons that actually contribute to their various problems and to take the necessary measures to prevent their occurrence.

In fact, regardless of the actual circumstances of meeting and getting involved with our partners, we stepmothers are frequently perceived as "home wreckers," who deserve any misery that comes our way. This widespread societal belief affirms that we stepmothers are responsible for the failure of our partner's prior marriage, even though most of us met our mates long after their separation from their exes. When I told a colleague I was working on a self-help book for stepmothers, he wondered out loud why I would want to help home wreckers. I was shocked by his statement, since he was married to a woman whom he met years after divorcing his first wife, and who was a generous, loving stepmother to his children. Even though his personal experience contradicted the stereotype, it remained ingrained in his consciousness, an indication of its powerful nature.

In my therapy practice, I have worked with many lovely, bright, successful, accomplished women who, after getting involved with men with children, became depressed, frustrated shells of their former selves. Their self-esteem and morale plummeted after experiencing rejection, disrespect and an overall disregard for their emotional needs by partners and stepchildren. These women had been well liked and well respected by others, and believed that they would be treated similarly by stepfamily members in time. They were shocked and dismayed when this didn't happen. Gradually, they became worn down by their failure to break into the inner sanctum of the family and lost hope when their numerous attempts to bond with stepchildren were rebuffed.

Accustomed to having others listen to and respect their ideas, these women became frustrated when their suggestions were ignored by their partners. Unable to participate in important family decisions that affected their lives, they felt more and more trapped in circumstances that seemed beyond their control, and they were unable to find the contentment and peace of mind they so desperately needed. Observing their distress has confirmed my belief that many of us stepmothers are in dire need of assistance.

I also understand many of these problems from personal experience. When, eighteen years ago, I became a stepmother to a four-year-old girl, I knew it would not be easy to develop a warm relationship with her and become an integral member of a "blended" family. Still, I was surprised by the feelings of inadequacy I experienced.

I had not married impetuously. I was in my late thirties and had known my new husband for more than two years. And my situation was simple compared to that of many other women: My stepdaughter was well behaved, intelligent and easy to get along with, and her parents had set up a clear, fair visitation schedule that was strictly adhered to. I was willing to do everything I could to create a healthy, happy stepfamily. Yet, no matter how hard I tried to join the existing family unit, I felt like an outsider. Suddenly, too, it seemed that my time was no longer my own, my needs were placed last, and my discomfort was dismissed by my family and friends. Why, I asked myself, was I struggling?

My friends gently suggested that my difficulties as a stepmother were my own fault. They offered two hypotheses: Either I was having trouble because I did not have biological children of my own, so I didn't know what was expected of me, or I didn't really want to be a stepmother. This criticism annoyed me, because I thought that neither hypothesis was correct. I felt misunderstood. Was I off base, or were they?

For a long time, I wondered whether my problems stemmed from some selfishness and rigidity in my personality. But eventually, I had an important realization: I was *choosing* to sacrifice my time and energy to make others happy before taking care of myself. I decided to find out whether this martyrlike behavior was characteristic only of me, or if it was typical of the experiences of other stepmothers. This book began with that exploration.

In writing this book, I had one goal: to understand the variety of problems we stepmothers experience, in order to discover a set of solutions. To find out more about these issues, I first reviewed the research in the professional psychological literature. Then, to get input from stepmothers themselves, as well as to give them a much-needed community of peer support, I created a Web site, www.stepsforstepmothers.com, which includes a questionnaire for stepmothers and an online chat room—an interactive environment in which stepmothers can discuss their situations and offer mutual support (for more details see Appendix A). In addition, I interviewed fifty stepmothers by phone to gain a better understanding of their experiences.

Because I am a psychotherapist by profession—and not an academic—I based the online questionnaire on gathering information that I thought other stepmothers would find interesting and helpful. There are more than 120 multiple-choice questions that evaluate the quality of these women's relationships with partners and stepchildren, and probe their feelings about being stepmothers. Participants are asked to select the most appropriate response to each question from a seven-point scale. They are also given essay questions that explore particularly difficult experiences they have encountered, lessons they have learned, and tips they would offer to others in the same position.

The response to the Web site has been nothing short of phenomenal! In its first two years of operation, more than three thousand women filled out the questionnaire and registered to use the online chat room. It seems to have opened a crack in an emotional dam for stepmothers around the world.

The problems described by the stepmothers who responded to the questionnaire are far more challenging than I had ever imagined. They were facing issues ranging from daily irritations to serious crises, from dealing with stepchildren who refused to do their homework or help clean their rooms, to kids who were in trouble with the law or pregnant by age fourteen. Some of these women were annoyed by the refusal of ex-wives to follow pre-arranged visitation schedules, while others were dealing with crack-addicted ex-wives or ones who lived with convicted felons. Some experienced tension with partners who were unable to set consistent rules for the children, while others were involved with men who could not conduct conversations about their kids without becoming defensive, even abusive.

All these women had intended to create happy, loving stepfamilies and believed that over time they would succeed. But every single one of them complained of mental and physical exhaustion as a result of trying to achieve this goal. They all talked about feeling depressed, frustrated and dismayed by their inability to overcome stepfamily problems. While the underlying reasons for their struggles were distinctly their own, the effects on the stepmothers who completed the questionnaire were universal—self-blame, anger, disappointment, sadness and heartache. The tools in this book were designed to meet the unique needs of stepmothers like you, and offer you the understanding and support you deserve.

The Web site has given me much more information about the

lives of these women than I could ever have learned from working with a small number of clients in my psychotherapy practice. Still, you should consider the data I have gathered as anecdotal, based on the experiences of a particular self-selected group of stepmothers. I do not presume to understand the experiences of all stepmothers, but I do believe that those in my sample are representative of the lives of many, and that large numbers of us will be able to relate to their experiences.

After collecting the data from the questionnaire, the online chat room and the interviews, I realized that the specific problems we face are not nearly as important to our overall happiness as how we live our lives. With this in mind, I constructed a healing guide comprised of ten steps, to help you cope more effectively with your problems. This is what I have used for clients in my therapy practice, and it is my hope that these suggestions will enable you to change your thoughts, emotions and behaviors step by step in order to feel better about your life. Working on all these aspects together will give you a greater chance of success than if you focused on just one area of your life at a time.

How *The Happy Stepmother* Is Different from Other Books

Many books on stepparenting are available, but most are academic, written mainly to assist professional counselors. There are also some helpful books written for stepmothers by stepmothers, but they are also limited in scope, since they are based solely on one person's experience.

The Happy Stepmother has a broader focus. It is based on the collective voices and wisdom of many real stepmothers, and it also contains the most current knowledge available in the fields of family studies, communication and personal growth. The practical "how-to" suggestions here have been explored and tested in therapy and coaching sessions with many stepmothers. Developed by wise and respected mental health professionals, the techniques and exercises in *The Happy Stepmother* will help you achieve peace of mind when practiced with consistency. Although here they are tailored specifically to women's roles as stepmothers, they can also be extremely helpful in all areas of your life.

> *The Happy Stepmother* has three goals:
> 1. To provide direct help to stepmothers who seek greater peace of mind and serenity.
> 2. To educate you about the differences between the myths and the realities of stepfamily life.
> 3. To help change cultural perceptions to reflect the kindness, compassion and love that most stepmothers provide to their stepchildren.

I firmly believe that most stepmothers don't require professional assistance in order to handle the problems we face. In our culture, there is a growing awareness of the importance of emotional health if we are to lead productive and balanced lives. Fortunately, a variety of support groups are available to those recovering from addictions, healing from the loss of loved ones, and coping with serious illnesses, yet very few support groups exist for stepmothers. Our society, it seems, is not able to provide the help and compassion we so desperately need. This omission deeply troubles me, and I hope this book helps to fill that void and provides you with the tools you need to feel happier and more satisfied as a stepmother.

This book is not about blame. We are not to blame for the problems we encounter in stepfamilies, nor are our partners, their ex-wives, or our stepchildren responsible for these problems. The difficulties of stepfamilies are systemic, generally resulting from the traumatic effects of divorce, rather than from the actions of individuals. Yet, there is only one person who has control over your responses to the experience of being a stepmother—you! No one outside of you has the power to make you happy or is responsible for your personal satisfaction. This book is about empowering *you*, about helping you find ways to achieve harmony within yourself and within this difficult role.

Many women have benefited from the information and exercises contained in this book. For some, the transformation has been profound. Energy, joy and optimism have replaced feelings of depression, anxiety and frustration. Their confidence grew, and relationships with family members dramatically improved as they learned how to communicate directly and respectfully. For others, changes have been more subtle. These stepmothers felt less isolated as they dealt with family challenges, and more connected to a community of women who understood and shared their struggles. They developed more clarity and insight about their lives. As one stepmother said, "I made the decision to marry my partner after practicing the exercises you suggested. I no longer feel tortured because my partner's kids refuse to have a relationship with me. I understand that they have been told lies about me that I can't undo. I don't think about this anymore. While I am kind and compassionate to them, I now focus on pursuing meaningful activities and developing stronger relationships with those who care about me. Thanks for giving me this perspective to get on with my life."

By sharing the hard-won wisdom of other women and the research presented in this book, I hope to help you and many other stepmothers to discover balance and joy in your lives.

Chapter One

What Have We Gotten Ourselves Into?

While some stepmothers have a fairly easy time adjusting to their new roles, many of us find it far more difficult than we ever imagined. In a world filled with technology designed to help us enjoy more leisure time, many of us still forsake the simple joys—going to the movies, having lunch with girlfriends, reading novels—in order to take care of our stepfamilies. Very quickly after marrying our partners, too many of us have crossed the fine line into emotional imbalance by working too hard and becoming involved in situations where we receive little joy or reward. We are suddenly in deep water without a life jacket to keep us afloat.

Little guidance is available about the challenges we face—being a stepmother is truly a "forgotten" role in society. Have you ever complained about the problems you are having as a stepmother, and heard the comment: "Well, you knew he had kids when you married him"? Unfortunately, this is a statement that too many of us hear all too often.

Second marriages can be difficult in themselves, with or without stepchildren. Add children into the mix, and the situation is that much more complicated!

Why Are So Many of Us Having So Much Trouble?

As you might expect, the reasons for stepfamily problems are complex. One contributing factor is that many of us are just not prepared for this role and have no idea how demanding the job can be. Many of the respondents to the online questionnaire said that they simply had no concept of the depth and breadth of the problems they would encounter once married.

For many of us, affection for our new partners makes us turn a blind eye to potential problems down the road. We simply hope that our love will get us through. While most women understand that marrying a man with children won't be as easy as marrying a man without children, conventional wisdom suggests that time will help "blend" family members into a cohesive unit. We are led to believe that, eventually, stepchildren will grow to love and respect us, partners will overcome their guilt for hurting their children, and ex-wives will get over their anger and resentment. Even for those of us with prior experience—having been a stepmother in a previous relationship or having had a stepmother—this knowledge may not be of much use in our current situations.

66STEPMOTHERS SPEAK99

It's been a long road with my stepson. I have raised him for four years now. He was so sweet in the beginning. His mother and dad had been divorced for ten years before I met him. His father had raised him since he was three years old.

About a year after I came into his life, he started getting in trouble at school, but his behavior was manageable. Then he got kicked out of three schools. He got straight F's and refused to do his homework. At vocational school he was asked not to return because he was in trouble all the time. The list of troubles he has caused could fill a book. I wish I had known what he was going to be like when I met his father.

—TRIED 2 HARD

Problems can take months or years to develop in stepfamilies. Consequently, many of us are bound to be unprepared for the challenges we face, and are overwhelmed by their magnitude when they do occur.

Other stepmothers said that they *were* aware of potential problems in their stepfamilies, but they believed those difficulties would improve as everyone adjusted to the new family dynamic. Unfortunately, they were usually just plain wrong—the problems did not diminish. In fact, for many, the problems grew. Rather than improving, without intervention, stepfamily life tends to deteriorate or remain static over time.

There is a small group of women who did not know about their stepchildren when they got involved with, or married, their partners. Now that paternity tests are widely available, some women have discovered they were stepmothers months or years after they got married. Needless to say, these surprised stepmoms experienced a host of emotions, including shock and anger, when introduced to children they had no idea existed.

The conversations in the Steps for Stepmothers online chat room are powerful illustrations of the problems we as stepmothers experience and, to a large extent, these conversations have shaped my thinking about being a stepmother. Even the usernames on the message board are poignant. Many of these monikers, such as "Worn Out," "Want to Be Happy," "Stressed to the Max," and "At Wit's End" are vivid shorthand expressions of the painful experiences of these women.

Many of the stepmothers I have worked with in my psychotherapy practice have also felt unappreciated, overburdened and misunderstood by their families and communities. Before contacting me, many of these women had suffered in silence, for fear of being judged or ostracized, until their situations finally became intolerable.

There is a wide variety of problems that can make our lives as stepmothers miserable. Many stepmothers find that their partners act more like pals to their children than like fathers, with the result that stepchildren are undisciplined and spoiled. Some partners are afraid to set guidelines for their children to follow, along with appropriate consequences if those guidelines are ignored. Partners fear that if they are strict, their children will no longer be willing to spend time with them. To keep this from happening, they remain passive when their children act up. It is both difficult for stepmothers to witness and experience a child's misbehavior, and frustrating when they cannot get partners to understand the need to take corrective parental action. Other stepmothers must deal with intrusive, difficult ex-wives, who disrupt their households by calling at inappropriate times, change scheduled dropoffs and pickups at the last minute, and bad-mouth us to their children.

Many of us sadly realize that our attempts to bond with our stepchildren have failed, and we are left feeling ignored and disrespected. Some of us grow weary of dealing with stepchildren who seem unappreciative, uncooperative or spoiled. Some of us feel we have limited authority in our own households, because many decisions are made without our input or consent. Some of us—an unfortunate few—get to deal with *all* the above situations, and maybe more.

Would You Do It Again?

"If you knew what your life would be like as a stepmother, would you get involved with your partner again?" Stepmothers often ask this of each other in the online chat room, and I also asked this question in my survey. For many who responded to the survey, the answer was an unequivocal no. At times, do you also regret your decision to get involved with or to marry to your partner? To help you answer this question, consider the following:

Indications of Potential Problems

- You feel frustrated, aggravated, annoyed or angry about your stepfamily, and don't have appropriate outlets to deal with these negative feelings.
- You feel insecure about your place in the stepfamily. You feel like an outsider in your own home, despite concerted attempts to bond with your stepchildren.
- You are constantly tired, and don't have enough time to take care of yourself.
- You are unable to talk to your partner about his children without having a fight.
- Your partner is defensive and hostile when talking about his children.
- You avoid discussing certain topics with your partner's parents, children or ex-wife because you don't want to look bad in front of them.
- You don't have input into decisions about how money is spent in your stepfamily; your feelings and attitudes about money are not considered by your partner.
- You have issues with the custodial arrangements for your stepchildren, and do not have any input about their schedules.
- You are not allowed to discipline your stepchildren, and are expected to tolerate misbehavior.
- You feel that you take care of the needs of your stepchildren more than your partner or his ex-wife.
- You sometimes wonder if you made a terrible mistake getting involved with, or having married, your partner.
- You sometimes feel foolish for being trapped in your current circumstances.
- You sometimes wish you had listened to the warnings of family and friends, rather than following your conviction that your stepfamily would blend into a loving unit.

If any of these ring a bell, don't be dismayed—there is hope! While you may not be able to solve all the problems in your step-family, you can change the way you deal with them, making your life more satisfying and content. Before discussing some solutions that can help you, let's look at some of the problems you face as a stepmother in greater detail.

Chapter Two

Our Emotional Challenges and How the Ten Steps Can Help

Sadness, frustration, exhaustion, confusion, fury, thoughts of retribution, regret. Many of us experience these and other intense, negative emotions on a daily basis as a result of being embroiled in stepfamily problems we did not create.

Unfortunately, the numbers of us in this predicament are likely to grow rather than shrink, because trends suggest that many stepmothers will be spending more time with their stepchildren in the future. Within the last several decades, the structure of families has changed. Families have become more diverse, ranging from single-parent households to couples with children from various biological parents living under the same roof. Many more divorced fathers are being granted full-time custody of their children, while others enjoy more liberal visitation schedules. Divorced mothers are now less stigmatized if they give full-time custody of their children to their ex-husbands. Greater flexibility in child custody arrangements benefits biological parents, but for stepmothers, this may be a mixed blessing.

"STEPMOTHERS SPEAK"

Raising someone else's children is like working eighty hours a week without a paycheck or retirement benefits.

—Sleepless in Sarasota

More contact with stepchildren can be either a positive or a negative experience for us stepmothers. Spending more time together offers an opportunity to form closer relationships. On the other hand, more conflicts can arise, not only with stepchildren, but with biological mothers and partners.

The Emotional Challenges and Demands of Being a Stepmother

Many of us complain that our lives changed radically when we became involved with men who had children. The responsibilities of a stepmother can be so enormous that they prevent us from engaging in activities that we previously found pleasurable. We also may be surprised when, within a relatively short period, our personalities seem to have changed. Some of us who were once outspoken and forthright complain of becoming subservient and weak, and trying too hard to please others. Others, once physically and socially active, have become isolated from family and friends. Gradually, we find that our new status as wives and stepmothers has come to define our entire being. It may seem hard to believe that anyone can change so radically, but it does happen to many of us. Let's examine a few of the emotions we stepmothers have experienced. How many of these feelings do you relate to?

Anxiety

Anxiety is often triggered by an inability to control one's environment. Adults are accustomed to some measure of control, although, of course, none of us ever has complete control over our surroundings. When the level of control is diminished, internal stress develops. Headaches, stomachaches, disturbing thoughts, nightmares, an inability to concentrate and many other symptoms may result.

In the Steps for Stepmothers online chat room, many women complain about experiencing too much anxiety in their lives.

Although the degree of anxiety we experience may vary widely, there are some common underlying themes. Spending time with stepchildren can be extremely stressful. Some of us get anxious before our stepchildren visit because we anticipate conflict during their stay. Some of us fear that young stepchildren will be hurt in our care. Many of us just don't know how to behave, and our doubts fuel anxiety.

Anxiety can also be triggered when one of our basic needs remains unfulfilled. For instance, some of us become anxious when our emotional need to feel close to family or friends is thwarted. Despite years of trying to develop warm relationships with stepchildren, a number of stepmothers feel distant and uncomfortable in their presence. When this emotional need for familial closeness is unfulfilled, anxiety can develop.

“STEPMOTHERS SPEAK”

I feel so isolated and alone when my stepchildren visit.
I feel barely tolerated by them.

—PEGGY THE PARIAH

Emotional Fragility

Many of us become emotionally fragile after dealing with a variety of frustrating stepfamily experiences that drain us of energy and strength. When partners criticize and judge our feelings and perspectives about these events, we begin to feel emotionally threatened, concerned that we may be emotionally attacked for holding different views from theirs. For us to be misunderstood and mistrusted by the person we love is quite painful. We also may dread future stepfamily problems, not just because of how difficult they are to resolve, but because we anticipate they can be opportunities where we will become targets of emotional attack. Protecting ourselves from these encounters is exhausting and prevents us from feeling content and secure.

Jealousy

If you've experienced jealousy, you know how unpleasant it is. Jealousy is often accompanied by insecurity, confusion and doubt. You can feel consumed by the intensity of jealousy, as though it were eating you up inside. Jealousy can also be a confusing emotion, because you may be unsure about whether or not your feelings are based in reality.

Feeling jealous of an ex-wife is a particularly insidious emotion. Those of us who experience jealousy often feel inadequate because we believe that we love our partners more than they love us. Some of us feel that our partners still harbor feelings of love for their ex-wives. Or, we may worry that our partners won't allow

"STEPMOTHERS SPEAK"

How many of you are with a man you know would rather still be married to his ex-wife? My boyfriend's ex-wife cheated on him, and then filed for divorce. He was still very much in love with her. My only peace is in knowing that he would never go back to her because of her affair. But yet, I know I am his second choice. How do I live in peace with that?

—Worried Sick

themselves to fall in love as deeply as they did in the past, out of fear of being hurt again, and that they will be unable to form the deep emotional attachment that we crave. When we experience these fears, we feel trapped in a bind, since we can't force our partners to love us in the way we love them, nor can we stop ourselves from loving our partners.

Many stepmothers marry men who divorced because their ex-wives had been unfaithful to them. While the ex-wife's infidelity may have precipitated the separation, it did not necessarily diminish the love a partner felt for her. Even though many years may have passed since the divorce, many of these women believe that their husbands still have unresolved feelings for their ex-spouses.

"STEPMOTHERS SPEAK"

I know that my husband would never go back to his ex-wife because she had an affair. It still bothers me that I will never be his first for anything. He had all of his firsts with her and I have had most of my firsts with him. He is my first husband and I had my first son with him. It upsets me to think that he has been through all of this with someone else.

—Second Best

Jealousy is an irrational emotion, difficult to assuage even with a partner's reassurances. In order for it to be reduced or eliminated, you need to work through these feelings. Ways to build self-esteem, discussed in depth in chapter 9, are one invaluable source of help.

Anger

After months or even years of difficult experiences, it is not surprising that many of us grow angry at our circumstances. We may manifest this anger in a variety of ways, such as becoming irritated by minor annoyances or becoming uncharacteristically sarcastic, nasty or edgy. Our anger is unpleasant for us to feel and for others to experience. It is an unhealthy emotion to feel over an extended period, and can even cause physical problems.

This is a common scenario that many other stepmothers and I have experienced: We grow angry with our partners after repeated attempts to express our displeasure and frustration about a family situation. Instead of receiving acknowledgment and support for our insights and feelings, our partners rebuff them as minor or unwarranted. They become defensive and rigid, unwilling to make any changes to family situations that bother us. This disappoints us, which fuels our anger in an unhealthy cycle.

Some of us express our anger directly, while others try to stifle it. Either way, you will end up experiencing problems if you do not pinpoint and eliminate the source of your anger. In chapter 5, all of the suggested practices, including those of meditation, self-hypnosis and forgiveness, will help you let go of any negativity that you experience.

66STEPMOTHERS SPEAK99

I believed I would be able to have children of my own, but we can't afford to. I didn't know I was going to be sacrificing being a biological mother when I agreed to marry my husband.

—DEPRIVED OF MY DREAM

Depression

Many of us complain of feeling tormented, frazzled and depleted of energy and hope. All these are symptoms of depression, a mood disorder that prevents people from functioning at their full potential.

Unfortunately, many of us don't feel comfortable expressing painful feelings about our stepfamilies. We may fear that we will be judged as "wicked," or we may have been taught that it is improper to say anything negative. So we keep our feelings inside, where they fester, often leading to depression and desperation.

Depression is more serious than "feeling blue" for a limited period. After losing a loved one or experiencing a career or financial setback, it is common to feel sad, empty or uninterested in regular activities. But when such painful feelings persist for months and remain intense, then they may lead to depression. Symptoms of depression vary from one person to the next. Some people have trouble eating, sleeping and concentrating, and have little interest in activities that were once pleasurable, while others can be restless, anxious, and cry frequently. Some may dwell on feelings of worthlessness and hopelessness, and may even have thoughts of suicide. Depression is a painful emotional illness to experience, but it can be successfully treated by psychotherapy alone or with psychotherapy and medication. We as stepmothers do not need to tolerate these painful feelings, because help is available. The cognitive techniques described in chapter 4, along with the self-care exercises in chapter 5, are very effective in overcoming depression.

Stepmothers' Complaints— And It's *Not* About the Children!

You might think that most stepmothers' complaints would be about our stepchildren, but this isn't the case. In fact, only 25 percent of the complaints in the online chat room are about stepchildren.

The vast majority are about partners or their ex-wives. These complaints fall into five broad categories:

1. **Feeling unappreciated:** We feel unappreciated and that our needs are ignored by partners and stepchildren.
2. **Difficulty communicating with our partners:** We find it is difficult to communicate with our partners about their children.
3. **Guilt parenting and parental alienation:** Our partners often have difficulty parenting due to the aftereffects of divorce.
4. **Boundary violations:** We feel that our boundaries aren't respected.
5. **Difficult relationships with stepchildren:** We have to deal with our stepchildren's attitude or behavior problems.

Let's examine each of these complaints in greater detail.

Complaint 1: Feeling Unappreciated

It often happens that a man will view his new relationship as a "package deal," in which his partner is expected to take care of his children's needs as well as his own. Some men assume that their partners will automatically provide babysitting, cleaning and food-preparation services. When men remarry, some—either consciously or unconsciously—are seeking a family life similar to the one they had before, with a different woman in the role of wife.

This situation can get tiresome for us very quickly. We can easily develop resentments about being taken for granted and not receiving the understanding and support *we* deserve.

Many stepmothers report that they babysit, cook, clean for, and chauffeur their stepchildren, yet they don't receive any gratitude for their work. In fact, they say, the opposite happens: Spouses and stepchildren complain to us that whatever we are doing isn't enough.

A common complaint is that partners focus the majority of their time and attention on their children, so that we end up feeling like second-class citizens. In one extreme example, a woman complained that her husband insisted on allowing his six-year-old daughter to sleep in their bed. She was accustomed to sleeping with him, he said, and he didn't want to upset her. The new wife explained that three sharing a bed was physically uncomfortable for everyone, and emotionally unhealthy for the daughter. However, he remained inflexible.

It is common for divorced fathers to place the demands of their children first. Their hearts may be in the right place, but their actions can cause serious conflicts with their new wives. In addition, the excessive attention can end up spoiling their children, resulting in self-centered behavior that is hard for others, including their wives, to tolerate. This leads to another set of complaints expressed by many stepmothers.

Complaint 2: Difficulty Communicating with Your Partner

Why is it so hard to get along with a partner who has children from a prior marriage? One reason is the presence of children in the relationship right from the start, as opposed to months or years later. When the more natural progression is followed—dating, engagement, marriage and then children—a couple has time to get to know each other as separate individuals and to adjust to life together. Differences between partners can be dealt with gradually, and many can be resolved before children come along. As partners in stepfamilies, we are ironing out our relationships while at the same time dealing with problems with stepchildren.

Your partner is probably carrying his share of emotional baggage as a result of his divorce. Many men feel like failures after a divorce, blaming the breakup on their own personal deficiencies. These feelings of failure diminish their self-esteem. Depending on the circumstances, some divorced fathers may also feel betrayed and deceived by their ex-wives, which may affect their ability to trust others and become truly intimate again. Fear of losing his relationship with his children can also cause a father to act in uncharacteristic ways. For instance, normally strong men sometimes act as though they are weak around their children and ex-wives, since they may see this as a way to reduce conflict. Unless he has worked through these problems before you met, these negative emotions will inevitably affect your relationship with him.

Different expectations about the delegation of duties in a marriage can also cause fights within a couple. Although your partner may expect you to take care of his children, you may be more egalitarian in your views and believe both partners need to share household and parenting duties equally. Unless these philosophical differences are discussed and resolved, conflict will ensue.

Women who try to discuss such issues with their partners may notice that men and women have very different styles of communication. In general, men may prefer to avoid conflict at all costs, while women like to discuss problems until they are resolved. You may have found that when you bring up an issue involving a stepchild—for instance, your desire to have the stepchild go to bed at the same time each night—your partner becomes defensive about the irregular bedtime schedule his child follows, and resists further discussion about it. You continue to explain your point of view without success until your partner wonders out loud whether you truly care for his child. As much as you believe that structure is an important component for healthy development in children, you acknowledge a kernel of truth in his comments. You crave an hour of privacy to unwind and be alone with your partner before going to sleep and beginning another day. Not knowing how to respond to his comment, your silence ends the conversation. You hesitate to bring up such issues again, knowing that both of you will end up emotionally bruised, with little resolved.

Complaint 3: Guilt Parenting and Parental Alienation

Stepmothers in the Steps for Stepmothers online chat room claim that most of their fights with partners are about discipline, or more precisely, the lack of discipline their stepchildren receive. They are frustrated that their partners do not establish consistent rules for their children to follow. As a result, some stepchildren cause chaos in the household. This is particularly troublesome for women who have biological children, as well. It's hard for us to explain to our children why they must obey certain rules, while their stepsiblings are excused from them. When remarried fathers are lax parents, everyone in the stepfamily suffers.

Guilt Parenting

By far the most painful emotion divorced fathers experience is their overwhelming sense of loss and pain when they are forced to spend time apart from their children. In addition, they often feel profound guilt, knowing that their children may have been traumatized by the divorce, and intense fear that they will become estranged from them. This can lead to *guilt parenting*: a biological parent's inability to embrace all the responsibilities of parenthood, due to feelings of guilt. (When referring exclusively to fathers, guilt parenting is also called *guilty father syndrome*.)

> **"STEPMOTHERS SPEAK"**
>
> *My husband feels a lot of guilt associated with his children; I believe that he feels that he's let them down. Also, his ex-wife has said a lot of really nasty things about him to the children. I think he fears that he has to make up for this. It's funny—she walked out on him and yet the children feel that the divorce was his fault. I think my husband wears a hat that's too heavy for him to carry as a father.*
>
> —Worn Out

When fathers are concerned that the emotional bonds with their children may erode, they often change their behaviors and attitudes toward them. More than likely, they become more like playmates than parents. They fear angering their children and have trouble disciplining them, establishing rules or denying any requests they make. This is usually more of an issue for part-time fathers than those with full-time custody of their children.

Divorced fathers do not set out to spoil their children, but often, their feelings override their ability to set healthy boundaries. Living with a man who can't set limits for his children is difficult, to say the least. One woman told me that her husband would not stop her eight-year-old stepdaughter from doing cartwheels in the lobby of an elegant hotel. He explained that he did not want to squelch her creativity, and was seemingly oblivious to the disturbance the child was causing. His wife, on the other hand, was mortified by the cold stares of the annoyed hotel guests.

My husband was afraid to set rules and consequences for his daughter when she was young because he was reluctant to spoil the limited time they spent together and concerned that she would refuse to spend time with him in the future. He felt he needed to "walk on eggshells" in order to maintain his relationship with her. Every act of parenting became potentially relationship-threatening for him. You can imagine how painful this became for us both.

For instance, when my stepdaughter was about five years old, she was a picky eater. One morning she ate only a quarter of a bagel for breakfast, although she had promised to eat half. I asked her to eat the rest, and she started to cry, which disturbed my husband. He was afraid the rest of the day would be ruined, while I felt that asking my stepdaughter to eat the rest of the bagel would teach her about the need to keep her promises. In my mind, a few minutes of crying were worth a child's learning an important lesson. Sure enough, my stepdaughter ate the rest of the bagel, and was happy again five minutes later. It took my husband a little longer to overcome his anxiety over the incident.

Many divorced fathers fear that their ex-wives will alienate their children from them to retaliate for the divorce. Unfortunately, this fear is often grounded in reality. Relationships between fathers and their children can become fragile as a result of divorce. In her book, *We're Still Family: What Grown Children Have to Say about Divorce,* Dr. Constance Ahrons examined the relationships of divorced fathers and their children and found that one-third of these children felt that their relationships with their fathers had worsened after divorce.

According to Dr. Ahrons, father-child relations are strained when children feel they have lost their father's love and attention, believing it has been displaced by the presence of a new wife and her children. Children can commonly react to this feeling of loss by physically and emotionally withdrawing from their father. Constant fights between parents can also damage a child's relationship with his or her father. When children were exposed to these arguments, their loyalties to both parents were tested, and they tended to side with one parent, usually the mother.

Parent Alienation Syndrome

In some cases, despite their best efforts, fathers may be unable to maintain relationships with their children. This occurs primarily in cases of child custody disputes. Parent alienation syndrome (PAS) happens when a child turns against one parent as a result of manipulation by the other one. Dr. Richard A. Gardner coined this term in 1985 after witnessing an increasing number of children voice strong objections to one parent for no apparent reason. (This is different from situations in which children reject parents because of sexual, emotional or physical abuse.) Parent alienation syndrome can result when parents are so angry and hostile toward their ex-spouses that they want to hurt them, regardless of the consequences to their children. Through bad-mouthing the other parent in front of the children or withholding scheduled visits, parents can brain-wash their children into believing the other parent is the enemy. In some cases, an ex-partner's hatred may be so intense that she makes false allegations of domestic or sexual abuse, just to prevent the other parent from having contact with the children.

Other parents may be overly enmeshed in their children's lives, and unable to tolerate the fact that their children can have relationships apart from them, including one with the other parent. In other cases, parents may be so narcissistic and self-centered that they believe they are entitled to do whatever they want, even disobeying court orders mandating that their children stay with the other parent. In rare cases, a small number of parents may be sociopaths, who lack both a moral conscience and the ability to empathize or have compassion for others. They do not care that their ex-spouses and children are suffering as a result of being cut off from each other.

As Dr. Gardner points out, there must be two participants for this syndrome to occur. In addition to being influenced by a parent, children can also contribute to the alienation process by allying themselves with one parent, becoming angry at the other parent for unfounded reasons, and refusing to speak to or visit that parent. Children may claim that no one has influenced their thought process, and that they came to these conclusions independently. They don't show normal ambivalence about the estrangement, and their animosity extends to the other parent's family and friends.

Parents who are victims of parent alienation syndrome are naturally confused when their ex-spouses and children lie and make false accusations about them; they don't have any logical explanation for this estrangement. In fact, PAS isn't rational; it stems from psychological disturbances that can be difficult to counteract.

Many divorcing fathers have heard horror stories about children becoming alienated from parents, and do their utmost to avoid experiencing it. This is one reason that guilty father syndrome is so prevalent; fathers prefer to spoil their children rather than be estranged from them.

Overidentification

Some stepmothers complain about partners who treat fatherhood as the most important job in their lives. This is a variation of the guilty father syndrome. Some men work so hard to maintain their relationships with their children that they overidentify with the role of father. In other words, being a father becomes more meaningful to them than being a husband, son, other relative or friend. Their lives become wrapped around their children, so much so that everything else pales by comparison. Even their careers and hobbies are secondary to fatherhood. They may refuse to participate in other activities or relationships for fear that they might jeopardize their relationships with their children. Their lives tip out of balance.

"STEPMOTHERS SPEAK"

I feel as if I am the maid, the nanny, the housekeeper, the bookkeeper, the accountant, but rarely the girlfriend! I can't get my boyfriend to commit to spending two hours a week with me alone, without stepchildren who are old enough to be by themselves. He said he would try, but he is a parent first! He takes his son to the mall on Friday night and to the dance on Saturday night; he takes his daughter to chorus and basket-ball on Saturday. I ask for two hours and I get, "I'll try."

—Something's Terribly Wrong

Some men may be unwilling or unable to fully commit to a woman because they embrace fatherhood as their main priority. By placing the feelings of their children before their own, they may even sacrifice their own welfare. One woman recounted that her boyfriend's fifteen-year-old son had told her, "You're just another one of Daddy's stupid involvements. You know why they are all gone? Because I tell Daddy that they are mean to me, and he gets rid of them. You're next." Two weeks later, she was stunned when the child's prediction proved accurate. Her boyfriend told her that the relationship wasn't working out for him because he needed to be with a woman who cared about his son. He knew that she didn't, because the boy had told him that she wasn't nice to him.

Another woman shared a slightly different experience. Her boyfriend used his son as an excuse for not moving in with her. He told her, "My son really needs me to be there for him. I know you are great with him, but what if he needs me? I don't think we should do this now. Maybe when he is older—okay?" This may simply sound like the voice of a concerned parent, until we learn that the son in question was eighteen years old!

When fathers place their relationships with their children above everyone and everything else in their lives, we must often decide to forsake certain activities or participate in them alone. This may be acceptable for some of the independent-minded among us, but it places many other stepmothers in a no-win situation.

Questions to ask yourself about your partner:

(1) *Is he an effective parent? Is he capable of providing a structured routine for his children to follow? Is he capable of disciplining them when they misbehave?*

(2) *Does he suffer from guilty father syndrome? Is he a pushover, giving in to every demand your stepchildren make?*

(3) *Does he consider your wishes by discussing changes in your stepchildren's schedule with you?*

4. *Does he support you, rather than undermine you, in the presence of your stepchildren?*

5. *Are you expected to go along with whatever your partner wants to do as far as your stepchildren are concerned?*

6. *Can you comfortably discuss and negotiate which events you want to attend with your partner, even if they are scheduled at the same time as his children's events?*

Complaint 4: Boundary Violations

Most of the ways in which we are hurt by stepfamily members can be classified as boundary violations. Quite simply, these are inappropriate behaviors that cross the invisible line preserving a person's space. They are the emotional equivalent of having someone step on your toes. At the very least, boundary violations can be annoying; at worst, they can erode our self-esteem.

Parents should teach children to respect boundaries at a very young age, both by explicit instruction and by example. "Don't interrupt Mommy when she's on the phone" is one example of establishing a clear boundary for a child. Still, some families have clearer boundaries than others. Some people develop sound intuition about what is appropriate, while others are not so aware of the need for boundaries, despite what they may have been taught.

The underlying message communicated by people who violate boundaries is that their needs are more important than yours—that your feelings and opinions don't matter, or are inconsequential in comparison to theirs. Boundary violations can have a major impact on anyone's life—when people don't receive the respect they deserve, depression and feelings of unworthiness often follow.

Does your partner talk about the problems you are having as a couple with his mother or his ex-wife? Does he make arrangements with his ex-wife to see his children without consulting you?

Do your stepchildren share with their mother all the details of their time spent in your home? Do they rummage through your drawers without permission? All these are examples of boundary violations. Some of these may bother you, while others may not. People vary in how keenly they sense their own boundaries.

Ex-Spouses and Family Boundaries

For many divorced people there is a difference, consciously or unconsciously, between a legal decree of divorce and the actual emotional separation. The time it takes to become emotionally divorced varies from person to person. Some accomplish this separation long before their divorce decree is finalized; others can take a lot longer, and a few never fully separate from their partners emotionally, even after marrying someone else. We all know of couples who have been divorced for years, but are still actively involved with each other—who maintain contact above and beyond the co-parenting of their children. The desire to be taken care of by a former partner may not necessarily disappear because of a divorce.

Do you think that your partner has emotionally separated from his ex-wife? Is she emotionally separated from him? If one of them is still emotionally bound to the other, you stand a greater likelihood of experiencing painful boundary violations.

Oftentimes, stepmothers are frustrated by the favors ex-wives ask for. Some former spouses still rely on their ex-husbands for all sorts of help: fixing cars, cleaning roof gutters, preparing tax returns, installing new machinery or teaching them to operate technological devices. We naturally don't want to share our partners with ex-wives beyond the appropriate levels of interaction they have with each other as co-parents.

Many stepmothers also become frustrated and angry when our partners won't tell their ex-wives to stop calling at inappropriate times, or to be more conscientious about scheduled pickups and dropoffs of the children. We stepmothers feel as though we are left holding the bag when we are expected to accommodate interruptions or changes in plans without question.

Some ex-wives commit another type of boundary violation, more mean-spirited in nature to stepmothers; we become the targets of their hostility. Bitter about the direction their lives have taken, some exes may not have recovered from being divorced, and direct their anger and frustration toward us by criticizing us and our biological children at every opportunity, usually behind our backs. It may not matter to them that what they say about us is not accurate or fair; their criticism is a misdirected attempt to vent some of the frustration they are experiencing in their lives.

If you are subjected to such verbal assaults, you might not have the opportunity to respond, especially if they are made out of earshot. Even if you could defend yourself, it probably wouldn't do any good, a reality that can leave you feeling frustrated and angry, particularly if it prevents your stepchildren from forming a close relationship with you.

I experienced this myself and know firsthand how painful and frustrating it can be. One day, while my husband and I were taking a walk with my four-year-old stepdaughter, she looked up and spontaneously shouted, "Mommy says that you are a witch!" I was taken aback, but finally managed a response, "Oh, and what do you think?" She answered, "No, I don't think so." I changed the subject, but realized that if my husband's ex-wife wanted to say bad things about me, I wasn't going to be able to stop it. The best I could do was be myself and be the best stepmother I could be. Nevertheless, this meant I had to accept the possibility that, despite all my best efforts, my stepdaughter might grow to dislike me because of what her mother said about me, rather than loving me as a thoughtful and generous stepmother.

I was sad that I had so little control over a relationship that mattered so much to me, but I understood that not having control was also a fact in many other aspects of life. In order to be happier and make peace with the situation, I made a conscious choice to focus on what I *could* control and to live in the present, rather than worrying about what might, or might not, occur in the future.

Boundaries and the Extended Family

Extended family members can also be affected by a couple's divorce, and may have difficulty coping with the emotional pain it brings. They may even have trouble accepting the fact that their child or sibling has divorced and remarried. You may feel surprised and dismayed when in-laws make it difficult for your new family to work.

Most often, problems occur when in-laws choose to remain close to their former daughters- or sisters-in-law. Their warm and loving feelings for these women are often unaffected by divorce. They may choose to continue such relationships because this gives them closer contact with their grandchildren, or nieces and nephews, and they may even view this continuity of relationships as a way to limit further suffering on the part of the children. The desire to maintain a connection to a former in-law is not in itself an issue, but the manner in which the connection is maintained is key. Handled appropriately and with grace, it is irrelevant to our role; but handled poorly, it can cause us great emotional pain.

Certainly, problems with in-laws are not unique to stepmothers. What differentiates us is that, unlike mothers or other wives, we're especially hesitant to express our frustrations. Many of us feel we have to tread lightly, since we perceive our role in the family as fragile. We often fear that if we speak up, the entire family will perceive us as "wicked," or that we might be rejected and ostracized.

When in-laws invite a former daughter-in-law to a family function without first consulting their new daughter-in-law, they may be unnecessarily inflicting pain or they may not realize that reminiscing about the past with ex-spouses can be hurtful to new wives, who were not there to share those events. While concern for the emotional welfare of children is important, in-laws should also consider what's best for their grandchildren. Would the absence of one parent be potentially more disturbing to children than the awkwardness and tension of having both parents *and* the new stepmother present?

Complaint 5: Difficult Relationships with Stepchildren

Some stepchildren are difficult to please. They reject meals, refuse to participate in scheduled activities or disrupt the flow of the household. These attitude and behavior problems may stem from innate personality characteristics, or may be related to trauma they experienced when their parents divorced. Divorce may not be the only disturbing event in their lives. Children may have had to endure their parents' marital problems prior to the divorce, not to mention a host of unrelated stresses.

A recent study by Dr. Lisa Strohschein illustrates how children are affected by tensions in their parents' marriage, even before the breakup. Dr. Strohschein studied approximately 2,900 children for four years, and found that those who lived in highly dysfunctional families experienced more depression prior to and following divorce than other children did. She also found that children from highly dysfunctional families often exhibited antisocial behaviors—such as lying, cheating and bullying—which diminished once their parents divorced.

In households with high tension, the separation of parents can relieve stress for children. While divorce is almost always a healthier alternative for children than living with parents who fight frequently, kids can still be scarred for years afterward.

Bonding Problems

We complain about the messiness of stepchildren, their laziness about doing assigned chores, and their whining and complaining— yet these are universal issues associated with virtually all children. There is one complaint of stepmothers, however, that is markedly different from those of biological parents, one that can cause tremendous pain. This is the inability to bond with stepchildren, even after years of trying. Sadly, this is often the case. In a longitudinal study of divorce, Dr. E. Mavis Hetherington found that only 20 percent of young adults felt close to their stepmothers. The complaints of many of us accurately reflect the realities of our relationships with our stepchildren.

From the moment we meet them, some of us have trouble getting close to our stepchildren. Others of us believe that we have good relationships, only to find out later that our stepchildren actively dislike us, even complain about us to others.

It's often impossible for us to know how our stepchildren really feel about us. Even though some children may like their stepmothers, they may feel pressured to criticize them as a way of displaying loyalty to their biological mothers. Other kids may treat their stepmothers well, although they don't like them.

Society expects us to bond with stepchildren. When this doesn't happen, the natural reaction is to feel ashamed. We are embarrassed, and believe that we are to blame for the lack of a close relationship. After all, we reason, we are the adults and *should* be able to deal with this.

Of course, we all stand a better chance of having good relationships with stepchildren if we are kind and compassionate to them. Yet, stepchildren didn't choose us as stepmothers, so such relationships are really like a roll of the dice. For some of us, unfortunately, no amount of niceness can help. Our stepchildren are simply determined not to form an intimate relationship with us, and they cannot be forced to change their minds.

If you relate to any of these complaints, join the club. You are part of a large group of women who are trying to be the best stepmothers possible, yet are frustrated and react emotionally to their situations. Too many of us tolerate misery and pain, until we face divorce or a comparable crisis in our lives. Problems for stepmothers can crop up at any time during a marriage. No one is immune from experiencing some type of trouble in this role, regardless of how much we try to avoid it. But help is on the way, starting with the next chapter.

Celebrations: Cheery or Gloomy?

Christmas, Hanukkah, Kwanzaa, Thanksgiving, and other such holidays are times when we often feel like outsiders, even after years of marriage. Holidays that bring families together can be painful reminders for us when we are not treated as integral family members. Isn't it ironic that such occasions, which center on celebrating love and compassion, can cause some family members so much grief and pain?

Gift-giving, a traditional part of many holidays, may also be a source of rejection and discomfort for many of us. When everyone is gathered to open presents, some of us may find that our in-laws and stepchildren have neglected to include us. Imagine our discomfort when we are the only ones who are not receiving gifts! This is a very visible and hurtful form of rejection.

Mother's Day can be a particularly sad occasion for many stepmothers. This is the holiday that brings out the most complaints among women in the Steps for Stepmothers online chat room. While most of us realize that we have a different role from biological mothers, we still need recognition for all the work we do for our stepchildren. A token acknowledgment, such as a card, flowers or a small gift would be welcomed. Many of our partners are unaware of the significance this has for us, and may not even wish us a "Happy Mother's Day" or express their gratitude in other ways for how we take care of their children, and this adds to our feeling ignored and unappreciated.

These complaints are examples of just some of the problems facing many stepmothers. Can you relate to any, or all of them?

The Ten Steps

If you are like so many other stepmothers who have placed themselves last on their list of priorities, no wonder you feel drained and empty. While we want our lives to improve, many of us have no idea how to make the positive changes that will help us.

As a psychotherapist, I recognize that dealing with one specific problem is generally inadequate to help a person achieve overall peace and contentment. Working on yourself in a more comprehensive way, however, increases the likelihood of long-lasting improvement. My aim is to help you lead the most satisfying life possible, rather than simply resolving one particular issue. Instead of a laundry list of problems with accompanying solutions, I have developed a series of ten steps that, taken as a whole, will lead you closer to the emotional balance you seek. Together, as a group, they form a multifaceted approach that can help you focus your thoughts, emotions and actions.

The Ten Steps will give you an array of cognitive and emotional techniques, as well as a list of concrete actions, to help you stop feeling like a victim of unfortunate circumstances. By following these suggestions, you will be able to refocus your attention and energies in many positive ways. As a result, you will gain a better understanding of the problems caused by divorce, and you will be able to put the particular issues you encounter in your stepfamily in perspective. This will help you modify any unrealistic expectations you may have. To further your growth, you will learn techniques to reframe negative thought patterns and, in the process, gain a new level of inner peace and personal serenity. You will also learn new ways to communicate with your partner, stepchildren and other family members, all of which will protect and preserve your cherished boundaries.

These Ten Steps are user-friendly, simple, direct and easy to follow. They are organized in a logical progression so that you can remember them easily. With each step you take, the momentum for greater success builds. Taken as a whole, the Ten Steps will not only help you deal with your issues as a stepmother—they will also help you grow and develop to your full potential as an adult. If you follow the Ten Steps faithfully, I know you will gain more contentment, compassion and joy in your life.

Remember that, as in most aspects of living, there are no simple answers or quick fixes here. The techniques in this book are not a magic potion that will instantly resolve your difficulties. Genuine change will require real effort on your part. On the other hand, simply gaining some insight into your situation, and that of other women, will help you breathe a big sigh of relief, and give you the courage to begin. So, take some well-deserved time for yourself, begin practicing the Ten Steps and get ready for a big change in your life!

Following are the Ten Steps. Over the next ten chapters, we'll explore each step in more detail:

The Ten Steps
- **Step 1:** Understand the Facts
- **Step 2:** Revise Unrealistic Expectations
- **Step 3:** Your First Priority: Self-Care
- **Step 4:** Make Your Relationship Your Second Priority
- **Step 5:** Balance Love and Money
- **Step 6:** Set Clear Boundaries
- **Step 7:** Provide and Receive Respect and Compassion
- **Step 8:** Disengage, When Necessary
- **Step 9:** Make It Fun!
- **Step 10:** Create a Support Network

The Benefits of a Journal

Modifying your expectations will take time and effort, just like any other substantial change you make in your life. Writing down your thoughts is an excellent way to help you define and understand your attitudes. Then you can think more easily about how you can revise your expectations to be more attainable and realistic. I highly encourage you to get a notebook to record your responses to the ideas and questions in the following chapters. Over time, you will be able to go back and see how your attitudes and feelings have changed.

The more active you are in thinking about your expectations, attitudes and emotions, and in trying out new behaviors, the greater the chances that you will make positive changes in your life. Of course, there's no guarantee, but it is safe to say that the less you do, the less you will accomplish. Keeping a journal has been extremely useful to the stepmothers I have worked with because it helps keep them on course with their goals. Like counting calories on a diet, your daily recordings of progress are a constant gauge of your efforts.

Not everything in the following pages will work for every stepmother. Do what feels right for you at a pace that feels comfortable.

Here's to a successful journey!

Chapter Three

Step 1: Understand the Facts

We all enter into a new relationship with the hope that love will overcome any problems we may encounter. Unfortunately, it does not work out that way. Issues with stepchildren, partners and ex-wives may loom over us, our time and our thoughts, keeping us from contentment.

I have found that, for many stepmothers, unhappiness stems from unrealistic expectations about stepfamily life. In particular, many women simply don't know enough about the realities of divorce and the trauma it inflicts on parents and children. In this chapter, I will discuss stepmothers' expectations and how they can color our thoughts and feelings. Then I will present some facts and figures about the effects of divorce, which will help you to evaluate whether your expectations of your stepfamily are realistic. In the following chapter, I will make a number of practical suggestions to help you adjust your expectations so they are more in line with your actual circumstances.

Examining our Expectations

Our expectations play a large role in how we experience the present and anticipate the future. When our lives don't live up to our expectations, this creates frustration and misery. For instance, when we expect more romance from a relationship than actually exists, we may feel disappointed. When we expect more financial or emotional rewards from a career than are really there, we may become disgruntled. When we believe our everyday lives should be easier than they are, we may grow saddened and weary.

Oftentimes, our assumptions about what is normal in stepfamilies are based on myths, hopes and dreams rather than facts, and this can keep us from experiencing contentment, and leave us vulnerable to repeated disappointments.

The following questions will help you examine your own expectations.

- Do you expect that others will see you as kind and compassionate, rather than as the "wicked stepmother"?
- Do you expect your stepchildren to "act their age"?
- Do you expect that your stepchildren will love, respect and appreciate you?
- Do you expect your partner's ex-wife to act mature, responsible and thoughtful toward you?
- Do you expect to perform all maternal duties, such as cooking, cleaning and ensuring your stepchildren's health and safety, when they are in your care?
- Do you expect to love your stepchildren as much as your partner loves them?
- Do you expect that your biological children and your stepchildren will get along with each other?
- Do you expect that after some years of marriage, your stepfamily will blend into a loving, integrated unit?

While each of these assumptions is quite reasonable, they may lead you astray if your stepfamily cannot live up to them. Let's examine these expectations in more detail, and compare them with your stepfamily situation. You may then find that you need to adjust your assumptions to bring them into harmony with your reality.

Unrealistic expectation 1: *I will be recognized as kind and compassionate rather than as the "wicked stepmother."*

A more realistic expectation: *I know that society stigmatizes stepmothers, and I will strive to counteract the stereotype of the "wicked stepmother."*

What is the difference between these two statements? The first one assumes that we control how we will be recognized, while the second acknowledges that some assumptions are beyond our control. Cultural stereotypes are powerful. We all suffer a little from the negative effects of the "wicked stepmother" stereotype, even if we are kind, loving and respectful to our stepchildren. This stigma creates problems for us by hurting our self-esteem, causing confusion about the nature of our roles as stepmothers and making us feel that we have to convince others that we aren't like that.

Every stepmother who has taken a seat on my office sofa has begun our conversation by saying something like, "I'm not the wicked stepmother. I have tried so hard to make things work. I don't understand why I'm having so many problems." This statement expresses the pain of these women, and it also demonstrates the power of this long-held stereotype.

Before you do anything else to surmount your personal frustrations, you need to examine how you may be affected by the stigma often attached to the role of stepmother. While you may not see what relevance this has to your everyday life, it is a crucial first step toward improving your situation.

The Stereotype

The stereotype of the evil stepmother has existed for thousands of years. The saying "better a serpent than a stepmother" is attributed to Euripides, a Greek playwright who lived more than 2,400 years ago. More familiar to us are some of the fairy tales collected by the

Grimm brothers, such as "Cinderella" and "Snow White and the Seven Dwarfs," which express the point of view that stepmothers are wicked. Folktales serve a greater function than merely entertaining children; they reinforce the moral lessons that a society wants its members to learn. Unfortunately, the message that stepmothers are "the bad guys" still persists in the twenty-first century, even though the lesson no longer seems relevant. What a shame for us that impressionable young children are still reading these stories!

Fairy tales are not the only way our culture portrays stepmothers as evil—this negative stereotype also shows up in movies, television and popular fiction. Dr. Stephen Claxton-Oldfield and Bonnie Butler surveyed movies from 1990 to 2003 with stepmothers as characters, and found that *none* portrayed stepmothers in a positive light. In fact, over one-third of the stepmothers were shown as "murderous or abusive," and even more were portrayed as "money-grubbing or unwanted."

In addition to emphasizing that they are not wicked, stepmothers want me to know that they are not home wreckers, who forced their partners to abandon their wives and families for them. Only twenty women of the three thousand respondents to the online survey admitted to being major players in their partners' divorces; the overwhelming majority said they had met their husbands long after they had separated from their ex-wives.

In rare instances, there are "wicked" stepmothers who reject their stepchildren and make no attempt to develop relationships with them, not giving them the respect and kindness they deserve. It's sad that a stereotype can prevail because of a few rotten apples. In fact, I have not come into contact with any of these women. The stepmothers with whom I have worked, and those in the online chat room, are trying to improve their relationships with stepfamily members, just as you are.

Overfunctioning by Stepmothers

Many of us try to compensate for the "wicked stepmother" stereotype by overfunctioning. We take on greater responsibilities in our
stepfamilies as a way to fit in and help blend our new families. We
work hard to prove that we are different, that negative stereotypes do
not apply to us. When we try too hard to overcome a label attributed
to us, our efforts may fail, and may even serve to perpetuate the
stereotypes.

Dr. Claude M. Steele showed this firsthand in his research on
the effects of stereotyping. He found that when members of a group
were aware of the negative stereotypes attributed to them, and tried
to counteract them, their performance suffered. In one stark example, Dr. Steele examined how a negative stereotype about
women's mathematical abilities affected their performance on a
math test by studying groups of men and women who had
similar scores on an initial exam. Prior to taking another test, the
groups of men and women were told the test was challenging. The
scores the second time around were no longer similar. The men did
better than the women. In their attempt to avoid conforming to the
stereotype of being poor math students, the women experienced
more anxiety than the men, and their scores suffered. Dr. Steele
found that when a person's social identity is attached to a negative
stereotype, that person will tend to underperform in a manner
consistent with the stereotype.

In a similar experiment, Dr. Joshua Aronson tested white
males who were very proficient in math. All the subjects did well
when they weren't told anything about the exam. When they were
told that Asians typically outperformed whites on this test, their
scores dropped significantly. Both this experiment and the one
conducted by Dr. Steele demonstrate that performance is not just
based on ability. Other influences, such as the expectations we have
of ourselves, play a role in determining our level of performance.

How does this research on stereotyping pertain to us? You and everyone else in society are aware of negative stereotypes about stepmothers. If you try to avoid conforming to such labels, you will react differently than if you did not feel threatened. You will work harder to overcome the stereotype, and, more likely than not, you will experience more anxiety. The more we try to prove that we don't fit the stepmother stereotype, the more trouble we'll have doing so. Stepmothers will continue to be adversely affected by the negative connotations of the "wicked stepmother" until society no longer has this stigma.

Fighting the Effects of Stereotyping

You probably don't think it's appropriate for anyone to use a derogatory term for a member of any ethnic group. Jokes that poke fun at certain races or nationalities may seem harmless, but they covertly reinforce stereotypes. The same goes for prejudices about other groups of people. Not all blondes are dumb, and not all over-weight people are jolly. Such remarks perpetuate belief systems that compartmentalize and inaccurately define who a person may be. So, in the same way, you should not allow others to use derogatory adjectives when describing stepmothers in your presence. Tolerating contemptuous and ignorant remarks about stepmothers is unacceptable, and can damage your self-esteem, even when the thoughts are expressed as a form of humor or endearment. You might consider saying, "I know you don't mean any harm, but that comment is offensive to me because it perpetuates a stereotype about stepmothers."

Remember, victims of stereotyping are influenced by the same cultural assumptions as everyone else in society. Are you willing to try an experiment to find out how often you refer to yourself, in particular, and to stepmothers, in general, in a negative manner? For the next several weeks, carry your notepad or diary with you. Be conscious of the times when you use adjectives that relate to your identity as a stepmother. Every time you think of or express a negative description (such as *wicked, evil, mean, horrid*), or a positive one (such as *loving* or *kind*), write it down. After three or four weeks, compare your lists of positive and negative adjectives. Did you use negative adjectives more often than positive ones? Do not underestimate the power of what you say to yourself, since it has a tremendous influence on your behavior and beliefs.

Self-perception is very important. If you see yourself as honest, you are much more likely to behave honestly. Of course, this is not true 100 percent of the time. In general, though, self-perceptions influence actions. Even self-deprecating humor can be harmful to self-esteem. While you may think that poking fun at your own foibles will diminish their impact, you may actually be giving them more weight than they deserve. For example, describing yourself as lazy may not only make others think you are lazy, but it may prompt you to start believing it yourself.

By changing your negative self-perceptions of the role of stepmother and making them more positive, you ensure that you are not opening a door for negative behavior. Your mind is extremely powerful—it can determine who you are and what your life will be like. By periodically examining your beliefs and adjusting attitudes and thoughts that are outdated or unrealistic, you can become happier and healthier, even before making any other changes in your life.

Unrealistic expectation 2: *Stepchildren are similar to other children and generally "act their age."*

A more realistic expectation: *I accept that my stepchildren may experience developmental, emotional and social problems from the trauma of their parents' divorce.*

Are your stepchildren spoiled? Do they disrespect you? Are you worried that they will not develop into responsible adults capable of holding good jobs and having healthy families? If so, you are not alone. Stepmothers are often disappointed that their stepchildren's behavior doesn't live up to their expectations. Consider that your expectations for your stepchildren may be unrealistic, and that may be the primary source of your frustration with them.

It's important to remember that many stepchildren feel overburdened by the emotions, cares and responsibilities they face following their parents' separation. Of course, each child responds to divorce in her own way, based on her personality traits and the particular circumstances surrounding the breakup. Some children react with sadness, fear, anger or confusion; others are relieved, show little reaction at all or have delayed responses. Children's reactions vary based on their age, the custody arrangement, their parents' adjustment and their family's economic situation.

The trauma of divorce foists emotional issues on children that they must deal with for years. According to one young man whose parents had divorced when he was five years old, "When you feel like you're a Ping-Pong ball swatted around by battling parents, it's hard to feel grounded." The sense of fragility and vulnerability that this man describes is common to many stepchildren.

We can expect children of divorce to experience personal problems. When they're young, they may feel sad, lonely and angry. They may have trouble making friends, withdrawing socially (preferring to play computer games or watch television, rather than socializing with peers) or clinging excessively to parents in the presence of others. They may have trouble concentrating, and their schoolwork may suffer. They may experience sleep disorders and physical complaints, such as stomachaches and headaches. They often feel robbed of their carefree childhoods, and may express their unhappiness and frustration by acting rude, lazy or withdrawn.

As they get older, many children of divorce struggle to "find themselves," appearing to be lost souls without direction. These traits can make living with them extremely difficult, particularly when we expect them to be as mature and well-behaved as others their age.

66STEPMOTHERS SPEAK99

As a stepchild myself, I know how hard it is to accept a new person into the family. Sometimes it is like oil and water. I really think that it takes many, many years for kids to get over a divorce and sadly, because of their loyalty to their parents, all of that anger gets taken out on the closest and easiest target—the stepparent. As stepparents, we just have to remember that they are in intense pain; their world has been devastated by the divorce. I was talking to my father the other day, and he commented that it was hard for him to remember being married to my mother. Even though I was eleven when they got divorced, I told him that I vividly remember all of it. Children get stuck in the line of fire between adults and have to survive with very little life experience. When my stepdaughter ignores me (which happens more often than not), I try to make her accountable for her actions, but I also try to remember what I felt like when I was her age. Disrespectful behavior is inexcusable, but it helps to know where it is coming from.

—Fairy Stepmom

None of us wants to feel alienated from our stepchildren, or to fight with them—particularly over minor issues. Yet this is the reality faced by many of us, because our stepchildren are struggling to cope with their own emotional traumas. This may be an unpleasant experience for us, and often a lengthy one, but it is one that we need to learn to accept and deal with.

Understanding Stepchildren's Problems

It is likely that some of the scars that your stepchildren bear from their parents' divorce will affect your experience with them. To better understand some of the negative effects of divorce, let's examine some current research that will help put our experiences in perspective.

Each individual handles life's challenges in his own way, but children share some common characteristics after their parents' separation. In her twenty-five-year study of children of divorce, Dr. Judith Wallerstein of Stanford University found that the negative effects of divorce last far longer than many mental health professionals had thought. Many of the children in her study were still experiencing problems in their mid-thirties, challenging the belief that children generally overcome the trauma of divorce a couple of years after their parents' separation.

Growing up is an obstacle course for everybody; however, being raised in a divorced family can be more difficult because it involves dealing with both loss and failure. Dr. Wallerstein says, "Children of divorce need more time to grow up because they have to accomplish more; they must simultaneously let go of the past and create mental models for where they are headed, carving their own way."

Chronological and Emotional Ages May Differ

One stepmother expressed her annoyance with her stepson's behavior in the online chat room:

I am at the end of my rope with my teenage stepson, who is
lazy and irresponsible. He blames everything from bad grades
to not cleaning his room on everyone but himself. He has an
excuse for everything and never tells the truth. He has to be
told to put his dishes in the sink, to clean his room, to do his
homework—absolutely everything. Even when he is asked to
do something, he doesn't do it, claiming he didn't hear you
or forgot. He is fifteen; should I have to hand feed a child at
this age?

    —Not My Kid

This boy shares one of the characteristics of the children
Dr. Wallerstein studied: he is emotionally immature for his age.
While his stepmother expects him to behave like a fifteen-year-old,
he is ill-equipped to do so, and has had to put significant energy
into just dealing with his parents' divorce, rather than into the
growing-up process children from intact families undergo.

While stepchildren may take longer to grow up in some ways,
they may also engage in risky behaviors while quite young.
Dr. Wallerstein found that children of divorce experimented with
drugs and sex at earlier ages than children from intact families.
Fully half the children she studied were involved in serious abuse
of alcohol and drugs, some by age fourteen. Girls, in particular,
tended to become sexually active at early ages.

Dr. E. Mavis Hetherington conducted research for over twenty
years on the differences between children from intact and divorced
families. In her book, *For Better or Worse: Divorce Reconsidered,* she
found that children of divorce are *twice* as likely to have serious
behavioral, academic and social problems as children from intact
families. Only 10 percent of girls and boys from intact families had
serious behavioral problems, compared to 26 percent of boys and
34 percent of girls from divorced families. Children from divorced

families had more difficulties in school, more problems with peers, more trouble getting along with parents, and more of them suffered from a negative self-image than children from intact families.

While statistics cannot predict the future, they do help put your situation in perspective. Understanding these statistics can help you better understand your child's behavior and reexamine your expectations.

While some children exhibit obvious problems after their parents' divorce—such as poor grades and disciplinary problems—more resilient children who do not display these problems often are suffering, as well. In *Between Two Worlds,* Elizabeth Marquardt shows that even "good divorces"—a term coined by Dr. Constance Ahrons in *The Good Divorce* for divorces with low conflict levels—cause problems for children.

Ms. Marquardt, herself the child of a good divorce, felt that growing up a child of divorce was challenging for her. Even though she didn't display any obvious problems, she often felt lonely and insecure and felt compelled to maintain strict boundaries with each parent. She had to mature at an early age, and assume responsibility for her own needs, because she didn't want to burden her parents with extra demands. She also felt forced to intuit on her own the different rules and regulations of each household, because she wasn't told directly about them.

Based on her experiences, Ms. Marquardt conducted a study of other children of divorce and found that her own personal experiences were similar to those of many other children of divorce, who frequently felt lonely, worried that their needs might not be met, and responsible for the emotional well-being of their parents. Children of divorce don't feel completely comfortable in either their mother's or father's home. Shuffling back and forth, they miss out on experiences in each, and must find a way to learn about the changes that took place in their absence.

Children of divorce may feel ill-equipped to deal with the pressures of life, yet they often feel more burdened by responsibilities than other children. They tend to think and worry a great deal about the serious issues in their lives. For instance, they may wonder if their parents will learn to cope with the trauma of divorce and ever be happy again. Issues of security and safety are uppermost in their minds.

When children feel responsible for taking care of a parent, their adolescence lasts longer. Independence is more difficult for them to achieve, and emotional separation becomes more difficult, too. Also, such children may repeat these rescue fantasies in adult relationships by choosing partners who have many problems to overcome. They may define themselves as caregivers, developing a lifelong pattern of neglecting their own needs.

Stepchildren: Neither Here Nor There

Many divorced fathers treat their children with "kid gloves." They generally do this for two reasons: They want to prevent any further emotional damage to the children, and they wish to avoid as much conflict as possible so the children won't become alienated from them, thus falling into the trap of guilt parenting.

Similarly, many stepmothers are afraid of alienating their stepchildren. The common strategies of nagging, yelling, threatening, cajoling and bargaining, which we customarily use to keep our biological children in line, are not applied as freely to our stepchildren. We often feel that these parenting techniques will cause our stepchildren to resent us—they turn us into the "wicked stepmother"—so many of us swallow our own wishes and needs and then simmer with resentment when stepchildren refuse to cooperate.

There is a downside to this treatment for stepchildren. When they are dealt with more gingerly than everyone else in a household, they tend to feel that they do not fully belong. Instead of being perceived as full-fledged family members, they are treated more like guests in a hotel. This experience may cause problems for kids in their future relationships. If children or teenagers aren't encouraged to share household duties, will they be able to cooperate with their partners in later life? When children don't learn the value of cooperating with family members, they miss a valuable lesson about commitment.

Stepchildren's Intimacy Struggles with Stepmothers and Others

Dr. Wallerstein found that children of divorce have difficulty committing to intimate relationships, and are more pessimistic about relationships in general than children from intact families. This finding is understandable, when we consider that only seven of the 131 children Dr. Wallerstein studied felt their parents' second marriages were stable and allowed for good family relationships. More than two-thirds of the children in her study grew up in families with multiple remarriages and divorces. When children of divorce witness parents having numerous relationships, they conclude that love is fleeting. Not only do they view relationships as temporary, but they also see them as filled with conflicts that cannot be resolved by compromise and negotiation. These children become jaded by the problems of their parents, before they are old enough to draw conclusions about relationships from their own personal experiences. Not only can this affect their ability to form stable adult relationships, but it can make it more difficult for stepmothers to forge a strong relationship with their stepchildren.

Divorce as a Symbol of Failure

Divorce often lives on for the child as a symbol of failure. As Dr. Wallerstein explains, "Even if the young person decides as an adult that the divorce was necessary, that in fact the parents had little in common to begin with, the divorce still represents failure—failure to keep the man or the woman, failure to maintain the relationship, failure to be faithful or failure to stick around. This failure in turn shapes the child's inner template of self and family. If they failed [the child reasons], I can fail, too." Failure is a powerful experience for a young person. Everyone experiences some form of failure as they mature, and all these experiences aren't necessarily harmful, because they can teach valuable lessons about life and build strength when problems are overcome. However, children and teenagers are more emotionally vulnerable than adults, and feel the negative aspects of failure more acutely.

Unfortunately for us, many stepmothers are on the receiving end of their stepchildren's negative attitudes. As mentioned earlier, less than 20 percent of the young adult stepchildren in Dr. Hetherington's study felt close to their stepmothers. Stepchildren who lived full-time with fathers and stepmothers and were close to their noncustodial mothers were the least likely to have close relationships with their stepmothers. This is especially so if there's ongoing competition between noncustodial mothers and stepmothers. Often in these instances, stepchildren feel forced to choose between their mother and their stepmother, opting to be close to their mothers at the price of maintaining an emotional distance from their stepmothers.

Consider this: How many relationships did your partner have between separating from his ex-wife and meeting you? Do you know anything about how many relationships his ex-wife has had? If both your partner and his ex-wife had several relationships following their divorce, do you think the findings of Dr. Wallerstein about commitment problems in children of divorce might apply to your stepchildren? If so, remember that as much as you try to develop a relationship with them, they may not be open to having one with you, believing that it is only a matter of time before you, too, will be gone from their lives. Their attitude is a consequence of divorce, rather than a statement about you.

Developing Compassion Toward Your Stepchildren

It's clear that children of divorce face many challenges. While the adjustment phase immediately following a divorce may be most difficult for children, they can also experience problems for many years afterward. To help struggling stepchildren overcome these issues, stepfamilies need to devote additional time and attention to these children, which can take precious resources away from other family members and have an impact on the family as a whole.

If your stepchildren exhibit behavioral or social problems, you may need to adjust your expectations to accommodate the longer time they may need to grow up. When you can accept someone's flaws, you don't expect as much from them, and, therefore, you won't be as frustrated and disappointed when they don't meet your standards. Accepting that your stepchildren may be one age chronologically but another age emotionally may help you to be less aggravated when they shirk their household responsibilities, get into trouble at school or seem to have problems coping with adolescent life. While it is completely natural for you to dislike their actions sometimes, understand that they are probably not intentionally trying to annoy or hurt you. Children are the innocent victims of divorce, and must deal with problems they did not create. You are, no doubt, just one of several targets of their negative behaviors and attitudes.

Take a few minutes to answer these questions:

What current expectations of your stepchild are causing you stress and frustration?

What factors prevent your stepchild from meeting your expectations?

What is a more realistic expectation for you to have at this time?

ONE STEPMOTHER'S STORY: CHLOE

Chloe had a demanding job as a successful advertising executive, and worked long hours. She cherished her leisure time and loved to keep busy on weekends. She came to therapy after being married for two years. Her husband had two children, an eight-year-old boy and an eleven-year-old girl, who both spent every other weekend with them, and ate dinner with them on Wednesday nights. Chloe had formed a close relationship with her stepson, who was sweet and funny, but over time Chloe came to dread being with her stepdaughter, who was sullen, whiny and spoiled. Chloe had once enjoyed her weekends, but now she often wished that she were at work, rather than being with her stepdaughter. She felt guilty about this, and was afraid to admit to her husband how much her stepdaughter's constant demands and tantrums bothered her.

I asked Chloe to write down her responses to the following questions.

What are your current expectations of your stepchildren that are causing you stress and frustration?

I want my household to be calm and peaceful. I want a cooperative, loving atmosphere to exist. I expect that all of our needs will be considered equally, similar to the way I was raised by my parents. I expect to be close to my stepchildren.

What factors prevent your stepchild from meeting your expectations?

My stepdaughter is immature, spoiled and selfish. She cannot tolerate it when her needs are not met, and will throw a tantrum or have a fight until she gets her way. My husband ends up giving in to her every whim to stop the noise.

...ccept that I have different feelings for my
...en. I love my stepson, but dislike spending any
... my stepdaughter. To avoid getting annoyed by
...daughter's tantrums, I need to limit the time I
spe... with her. I need to do activities by myself during
weekends when my stepchildren are with us. I need to find
a way to explain my feelings to my husband without
hurting him.

I reminded Chloe that any steps she took to improve
things were for her own benefit. She should not do this to
make a point to others, most notably her husband. As an
example, I explained that if she decided to take a class, this
was to be for her own good rather than a means of teaching
her husband a lesson. If, as a result of her absence, he
came to understand that his daughter's behavior was
problematic, she should consider that to be the icing on
the cake; but she was baking the cake to take care of her
own emotional needs.

Writing down your expectations can give you greater insight
and understanding. As you read on, you will find other exercises
that will help you explore more of your feelings and behaviors, add
to your self-awareness, and give you more options for the future.

> **Unrealistic expectation 3:** *My partner's ex is going
> to be mature, responsible and respectful to me and
> my stepfamily.*

> **A more realistic expectation:** *I accept that my
> partner's ex-wife may suffer long-term serious problems
> after the divorce.*

You may feel compassion for your stepchildren, and be able to forgive them for any problems they cause you. However, you may have

more difficulty mustering sympathy for your partner's ex-wife. Many of us feel that we have been unfairly treated by ex-spouses, and resent the additional problems they have contributed to our new families' lives. But try to keep an open mind. A level of empathy with the ex-wife can help you deal with or overcome some of your challenges as a stepmother.

The Problems of Ex-Wives

While many wives initiate divorce proceedings because they are unhappily married, few anticipate, or are prepared for, the loss of financial stability that ensues. The breakup of a marriage has economic repercussions for most families—often the income for one household must be stretched to maintain two. But the impact is much greater on ex-wives than on ex-husbands.

After divorce, the economic well-being of many women and their children plummets drastically. According to a U.S. Census Bureau report, household income can drop as much as 50 percent, particularly for custodial mothers who aren't employed full-time. In 2005, custodial parents with full-time jobs had a poverty rate of 6.9 percent; 60 percent of custodial parents who did not work or who received public assistance fell within poverty guidelines. Most of these families received child support, yet the amount was insufficient to shield them from poverty.

In 2005, the poverty rate of custodial mothers was 27.7 percent—much higher than the 11.1 percent of custodial fathers. It may not seem alarming that more than one-quarter of custodial mothers and their children live in poverty until you consider that of the estimated 13.6 million parents with custody of 21.2 million children under twenty-one years of age in the spring of 2006, five out of every six custodial parents were mothers. That's more than 3 million custodial mothers and several million children living in poverty!

Ex-wives are naturally surprised and dismayed when they experience an economic decline after a divorce. What is more, divorced mothers with full-time custody of children have limited options to regain their former financial status. Most don't have the time to boost their job skills, or supplement their incomes by spending extra time at work, so they are often trapped at a socioeconomic level far below the one they enjoyed while they were married.

Perhaps it is true that money cannot buy happiness, but it does provide for essentials, such as food, clothing and housing. What happens to women when their sense of financial security is shattered? This, compounded by the emotional stress of losing a partner and other relationships connected to the marriage, can be a devastating blow for them. Many experience feelings of anxiety, depression and anger. The separation, letting go of the fantasy of living happily ever after, the inability to adjust to changes in circumstances, and resentment, jealousy or feelings of betrayal may cause an ex-wife to be stuck in a malaise from which she has trouble surfacing. While she may have functioned independently and maturely while married, divorce may trigger a major emotional setback. Many women eventually recover from divorce, but some do not.

Divorce can also exacerbate distress for women who were suffering from emotional problems prior to the separation. If your partner's ex-wife tended to be irrational and unpredictable while they were married, chances are she still is—perhaps even more so. Some ex-wives may have had alcohol or drug problems while married and these are likely to worsen after a divorce.

Consider your partner's ex-wife:
Is she financially stable?
Does she have marketable job skills?

Is she emotionally stable? Does she suffer from any emotional problems, such as anxiety or depression, which prevent her from making wise decisions about her children's welfare?

Is she physically healthy? Does she have any ailments that prevent her from working or taking care of her children?

Does she have a support system that she can rely on for help when needed?

Does she have friends? Does she have satisfying hobbies or interests to fill her leisure time?

Does she, in fact, have any leisure time to recuperate from the demands of her responsibilities?

Ineffectual Parenting by Divorced Mothers

Balancing the demands of a job, home, child care and a social life may be very stressful for divorced mothers. When these women experience major stress, their parenting generally suffers. As Drs. Jenn-Yun Tein, Irwin Sandler and Alex Zautra describe in their article, "Stressful Life Events, Psychological Distress, Coping, and Parenting of Divorced Mothers: A Longitudinal Study," such stress leads to troublesome inconsistencies in parenting style. For instance, these mothers may be harsh at one moment, and absentminded at another. In addition to affecting their ability to discipline their children appropriately, divorce-related stress may also impact mothers' ability to provide the comfort and reassurance that children need.

When mothers are distressed, their children become distressed. Parents must provide structure, discipline, moral values and appropriate boundaries in order for children to feel secure and protected. Without consistent and firm parental guidance, children flounder. When mothers are inconsistent in their parenting or are neglectful, their children may misbehave, and become worried, insecure or lonely. They may act out their feelings through behavioral problems, which, in turn, aggravate their mothers more, creating an ongoing cycle of stress in the family.

The Problem for Stepmothers

How are you, as a stepmother, affected by these issues? If their mother is stressed or depressed, your stepchildren are more likely to exhibit behavior problems during the times they spend with their father and you. So the emotional status of your partner's ex-wife is significant for you. Anticipate that there will be more conflicts with your stepchildren if their mother is having serious adjustment issues. You may be expected to pick up the slack, perhaps even become a full-time caregiver to your stepchildren.

Ask yourself:

How do you expect your partner's ex-wife to behave?

In what ways is this expectation realistic or unrealistic?

What factors are preventing your expectations from being realized?

How can you modify your expectations?

ONE STEPMOTHER'S STORY: TONYA

Let me describe the experience of another stepmother, Tonya, with whom I worked.

Tonya had been married for three years to a man with eight-year-old twin daughters; she adored both girls. She came to therapy because she was angry that her husband's ex-wife called their apartment several times a day to speak to the twins during their scheduled visits. She was especially bothered when dinner was interrupted by phone calls from the mother. These calls sometimes lasted more than fifteen minutes; each child was asked endless questions, such as what she was eating and how she was feeling. Tonya did not want to express her annoyance in front of her stepdaughters, since she didn't want them to feel bad about their mother's behavior, nor did she want to give them any reason to dislike her. Several times, her husband had asked his ex-wife to limit these calls to one per day, but she ignored his requests.

I asked Tonya to answer the four questions in the list.

How do you expect your partner's ex-wife to treat you?

With respect, and that means honoring the time we spend with the twins.

In what ways is this expectation realistic or unrealistic?

The ex-wife is needy. She doesn't have many friends and is lonely without the companionship of her daughters. She can't stand to be apart from them for more than a couple of hours.

What factors are preventing your expectations from being realized?

The ex-wife is uncooperative and my husband has never been able to have his requests granted.

How can you modify your expectations?

I need to accept that my husband's ex-wife cannot change her intrusive behavior, and I need to take measures into my own hands. I will turn off the phone at dinnertime. I will buy cell phones as Christmas presents for the girls and have them use these to speak to their mother, rather than using our phone.

Tonya realized that only she could reduce her frustration. After taking these actions, her feelings of annoyance began to dissipate. She actually started to feel bad for the twins' mother, who was struggling to separate from her daughters. Tonya realized that this was going to be an on-going issue for the ex, especially as the twins got older and became more independent. While Tonya did not think it was her place to help her husband's ex-wife deal with her problems, she could feel compassion toward her.

Unrealistic expectation 4: *Stepmothers assume all maternal duties during times spent with their stepchildren.*

A more realistic expectation: *I realize that I have choices about what I do for my stepchildren.*

Over the past fifty years, child custody arrangements have changed dramatically. In the 1960s and '70s, divorcing mothers were granted custody far more commonly than fathers, based on the belief that maternal care was more essential than paternal care to the healthy development of children. Joint custody emerged as an option in the 1980s, and over time, judges have changed their stances; they now routinely grant custody to either parent, or joint custody, based on the particular circumstances of each family. According to the U.S. Census Bureau, 2.3 million men were single fathers in 2006—a significant increase from the 1970 figure of 400,000. Currently, 16.2 percent of single parents are men.

Many of us will be affected by the changes in custody trends, and most likely, you will have more contact with your stepchildren than did the stepmothers of the 1960s and '70s.

When divorced fathers remarry, their ex-wives may welcome the opportunity to give them full-time custody of their children. Mothers may not consider this an option as long as their ex-partners are single. However, once a new wife enters the picture, a divorced woman may see an opportunity to take time and space to heal. She may be eager to take a much-needed break from the demands of single parenthood and focus on building a career or establishing a new social life. There is an increasing statistical probability that you will someday live with your stepchildren on a full-time basis. Have you considered how your life would be affected if this happened?

Marriage is a big adjustment, and the addition of stepchildren to the household can make the transition even more difficult. Even if your stepchildren only reside with you every other week or every other weekend, their presence requires extra cooking, cleaning and child-care responsibilities in the home. Who will assume these extra duties?

Too Many Tasks

No law defines the parameters of a stepmother's responsibilities. Many people assume, however, that stepmothers should take over the traditional and customary duties of mothers. I know that I believed this was true when I became a stepmother. Most stepmothers jump to pitch in when they see that their stepchildren are hungry, need their clothes washed or need help with schoolwork. It may make sense to perform some tasks for your stepchildren, just as you would for other family members, but you will become resentful if you feel you must fulfill *all* maternal duties for them, especially if you don't feel appreciated for what you do. Stepmothers often express their frustration at not getting the recognition they deserve from their stepfamilies.

ONE STEPMOTHER'S STORY: JADE

Jade was furious when she first came to see me. She said that she was exhausted from cooking, cleaning and chauffeuring her stepchildren from one activity to the next, without even a "thank-you" from them or her husband. Her spouse worked on Saturdays and took it for granted that she would take care of his children while he was out. Jade was a freelance magazine writer with a home office, who frequently had to work on weeknights and weekends to meet deadlines. Her husband believed that her schedule was flexible, and felt she could always complete an assignment after she took care of his children. Money was tight, and they could not afford a babysitter. Jade said she was coming to me for help before she lost all positive feelings for her husband.

I asked Jade several questions:

Do you expect to be appreciated by your stepfamily?

I like being acknowledged for the work I do, and I like to thank others for what they do for me. My parents were very concerned about us having good manners, and I believe that they are important, as well.

What prevents your expectations from being met?

My husband has a different philosophy of life than I do. He believes hard work is a part of life, and there's no need to acknowledge the tasks that we do; they're nothing special.

What are more realistic expectations?

I'm not sure I can teach my husband—an old dog—new tricks, but I can ask my stepchildren to thank me after I do something nice for them. And I can make sure I thank them, to model this behavior for them.

Maintaining a household is a laborious job, composed of many different tasks. Have you and your partner discussed who, specifically, will do what? You might consider making a list of the various needs of your household as a basis for discussion. To avoid fights as a couple, it is helpful to talk about everyone's responsibilities before conflict arises. In a later chapter on your relationship with your partner, you will learn how to discuss these and other sensitive topics in a calm manner.

Who Does the Housework?

If you are experiencing personal exhaustion and resentment from too many household responsibilities, consider these facts. Dr. E. Mavis Hetherington found that American men remain reluctant to do their fair share of the housework, so the burden of household labor still falls on female shoulders. When she began her longitudinal study of divorce in 1972, only 30 percent of married women worked outside the home. Over the course of the study, the percentage increased dramatically: By the 1990s, over 70 percent of young mothers and 90 percent of childless wives had jobs, adding to the family income.

Despite this increase in paid labor, Dr. Hetherington found that women devote an average of thirty-eight hours a week to family-related tasks and household chores, including cleaning, laundry, shopping, cooking and taking children to the doctor and other appointments. In 1973, men contributed approximately ten hours a week to household chores, and by 2000, their labor had increased to an average of fifteen hours. Unfortunately, the additional five hours does not come close to offsetting the amount of time women spend working outside the home! After work, women still go home to cook and clean for partners and children.

Unless you love to do housework, you can benefit from contemplating the results of these studies. If you want to have good relationships with your stepchildren and your partner, don't automatically become the primary housekeeper. Make sure that household tasks are shared fairly from the beginning.

Don't Overdo It

Stepchildren should be assets, rather than liabilities, in your life. To have good relationships with them, you need to spend quality time with them and interact in meaningful, pleasurable ways. It is easier to develop caring, loving and friendly relationships with your stepchildren without the burden of parental responsibilities. You aren't shirking stepmother duties if you don't cook, clean and discipline your stepchildren. Those are your partner's jobs, even if you are staying home to care for your own biological children.

The circumstances of each of us are unique, but you have the right to determine the responsibilities you will assume according to your own needs, as well as those of your stepfamily. If you ever babysat, you have experienced the difference in roles. As a babysitter, your assistance is limited and defined—you care for children for a specified period by playing with them, feeding them and watching them. Your help is appreciated by their parents, but you aren't expected to be available all the time to care for all their needs. Your role as a stepmother might be comparable, and you could also liken it to that of a roommate, aunt, grandmother or friend.

In no way am I suggesting that you ignore or neglect your stepchildren. Your desire to care for them is admirable and, at times, your assistance will be necessary. Of course, you can help and support them. Just make sure you don't go overboard in your efforts, deplete your energies and start to resent your role.

Simplify Your Life

The main complaints I hear from stepmothers are about how tired they are, how much they have to do, and how little time they

have to devote to themselves. What many of us don't realize is that
we have choices about what we do. We can regain our vitality in
life by reprioritizing our responsibilities and eliminating certain
tasks.

There are only twenty-four hours in a day; each moment of
time is precious, and our energy resources are limited. To prevent
burnout, you need to safeguard your time by saying no more often to
unreasonable requests, and by choosing activities you really,
really like to do, while letting go of the others. Doing less does not
mean you will compromise your chances for success in life. In fact,
you will probably be more creative, productive and engaged with
others if you are well-rested.

In your journal, consider these questions:

- How do you spend your time?
- What activities do you enjoy? Which ones don't you enjoy?
- What do you expect to do for your stepfamily?
- What does your partner expect you to do?
- How do you feel about doing these tasks?
- Think about your emotional welfare. What activities are healthy for you? Which ones are not? What activities would you like to give up? Which ones would you like to add to your life?
- Are you confident and skillful when negotiating for yourself about these issues?

Remember Chloe? She believed that she needed to spend all her time with her husband and stepchildren if she was going to build good relationships with them. When she realized that her stepdaughter's moodiness was too hard for her to bear for entire weekends, she decided to limit the time she spent with her.

One day Chloe came to my office with a beaming smile. She handed me a small bowl, her first pottery project. She told me that she was taking a beginner's class on Saturday afternoons, offered at a school a few blocks from her home. She had always wanted to learn to use a potter's wheel, and was ecstatic that the school was so conveniently located. She was also taking a spinning class on Saturday mornings with one of her neighbors. She said that she was enjoying weekends again—both the times she spent away from and the times she spent with her stepfamily. Her husband was changing, as well; he was beginning to realize that he needed to be more firm with his daughter.

Chloe was still cooking some breakfasts and dinners for her stepfamily, and participated in many activities with them. What had changed for her was that she no longer felt she *had* to spend every minute with them. That had been a constraint she had imposed on herself. In fact, by spending time away from the family, she found she had more fun with them when they were together.

Unrealistic expectation 5: *Stepmothers and stepchildren should love each other as much as they love blood relatives.*

A more realistic expectation: *I accept my feelings for my stepchildren and the feelings that my stepchildren have for me as "good enough."*

Do you expect to love and be loved by your stepchildren? If so, you may feel that you are failing as a stepmother if this doesn't happen. Many of us feel guilty that we don't have the same degree of love for our stepchildren as our partners do. Yet that is natural. After all, they are the biological parents, and have spent far more time with their children than we have. We can care about their children, and even grow to love them, but it is unrealistic to expect that we will ever feel as strongly about our partner's children as he does.

Even though more than 80 percent of the respondents to my questionnaire said they loved their stepchildren, half of them said they still felt their love wasn't good enough. Natasha came to see me because she felt terrible that she did not feel close to her stepson. She told me that she had tried to bond with him, and was always polite and kind to him, but they just didn't share any common interests. He was withdrawn and difficult to talk to. She said that she often felt awkward in his presence, and his long silences were excruciating for her to bear.

I reminded Natasha that love is an emotion that you feel for some people, but not necessarily for others. Love can't be forced. If it exists, that's wonderful, but if it doesn't, that's also acceptable, as long as you provide kindness, compassion and respect. No more and no less should be expected of you. When you remove expectations that you *must* love your stepchildren, it may be easier just to be nice to them—and in a genuine way. This can lead, eventually, to love. Remember, there are no wrong feelings—just potentially wrong actions. It's okay to feel angry toward your stepchildren, but it isn't fair to act out your aggressive feelings on them, or openly express dislike or disdain. As justified as you may be for having angry feelings, it is never acceptable to act on them. It's just not right to be unkind or hurtful.

It is unfair for your partner and his family to pressure you to embrace your stepchildren as your own. It is equally unfair to ask a man to be less of a father to his own offspring. I have heard of women demanding that their partners disavow their relationships with their children. If you are having similar thoughts, consider these two questions: First, why did you become involved with a man who had children if you weren't willing to be a stepmother? And second, if you love this man, why aren't you more accepting of his children?

It is never acceptable to interfere with a partner's right to maintain other significant relationships. Just because he has a new life with you does not mean that your partner should ever leave his children behind. Imagine if the shoe were on the other foot, and your partner insisted that you could not be close to someone you love, such as your children, parents, siblings or friends. This demand is simply destructive and unhealthy; it is emotionally abusive, akin to a form of imprisonment. You would be better off being single than manipulating a partner, or being manipulated by one.

When Stepchildren Reject You

Most of us try our hardest to be kind, considerate and loving to our stepchildren. If our efforts are rebuffed, we will naturally feel extremely hurt. If you are accustomed to helping others and being warmly appreciated for your efforts, rejection by a stepchild may be your first experience of failure in developing a caring relationship.

Stepchildren may reject your attention and warmth for various reasons. Perhaps they feel that since they already have two parents, they don't want a third one in their lives. They may be afraid that their mothers will be hurt if they become close to you. They may not trust that your relationship with their father will last, and do not want to experience loss again. Or they simply may not share your interests or temperament, and find it hard to relate to you. Any of these obstacles could take a long time to overcome, and the situation might not change at all, despite your best efforts. Whatever the case, you need to accept things as they are for your own emotional welfare.

Take a moment and write in your journal:

- Do you expect to love and be loved by your stepchildren?

- What is preventing this from occurring?

- What is a more realistic expectation for you to have right now?

Unrealistic expectation 6: *After an adjustment period, stepfamilies "blend" into loving, integrated units.*

A more realistic expectation: *I understand that the "blended" stepfamily may be more a myth than a reality.*

What do women want when we marry or start living with men who have children? We share the same dreams as everyone else who is beginning a new relationship. Most of us hope for the best: a loving family whose members like and respect each other. But it often doesn't turn out this way. A "blended" stepfamily doesn't always happen in reality. It is an admirable goal, yet few stepfamilies actually achieve this, and they are the lucky ones.

The fact is that stepfamilies are composed of individuals with different past experiences, attitudes and beliefs, which may clash with each other, preventing cooperation and harmony. Sometimes people just don't have a lot in common. For other stepfamilies—where partners, stepchildren or ex-wives are bitter, angry, hostile or demeaning to each other—blending becomes impossible. Stepfamily members may not want to have bad relationships. They may simply be stuck in bad habits and negative attitudes that stem from past stresses and impede their ability to improve their lives and relationships. Rather than accepting the blame for this, we stepmothers must recognize that integration may not be possible at this time.

Human beings are capable of great transformations that seem, at times, almost magical in scope, but this can happen only when people are ready to convert negative behaviors into positive ones. So please recognize that the people in your life will change when they see the need to improve *their* lives—not yours—and when they are willing to work hard to create change.

Can Stepsiblings Be as Close as Brothers and Sisters?

If you have biological children, what kind of relationship do you expect them to have with their stepsiblings? Do you expect them to be close? When both partners have children from prior relationships, the task of integrating everyone into one household can be daunting. While you can expect stepsiblings to be civil and respectful to each other, you can't expect them to love or be close to each other. There are many factors, such as age differences, varying amounts of time spent together, and differing interests that can prevent stepsiblings from developing close bonds.

Other factors can cause resentment and jealousy among stepsiblings. For example, if your children live with you full-time, they may be with your partner more often than his biological children are. Your stepchildren may be jealous of the attention their father devotes to your kids. Children may also have difficulty sharing space with each other, especially if they are forced into smaller quarters than they were accustomed to before joining a stepfamily.

There are other inequities between stepsiblings that can prevent them from becoming close. Financial resources may differ between families, with obvious disparities surfacing between stepchildren. Inadvertently, grandparents, aunts and uncles may cause disharmony among stepsiblings by treating them inequitably. Stepchildren may get birthday gifts and parties from both parents, while a biological child has only one set of gifts and one party. Some stepchildren have two families to provide for them, while others are not as fortunate, having little or no contact with one parent. When such disparities occur in stepfamilies, it can be painful, both for the less fortunate children and for their parents.

Yesterday, my mother-in-law took my stepson shopping for school clothes. He came home from the mall with seven bags full of clothes and with sneakers that cost more than $100. She didn't buy one item for my three children. I know she's not obligated to buy my children clothes, but if she's going to buy an entire wardrobe for my stepson, don't you think she could have thrown in token T-shirts for them? My three children resent that they don't receive equal treatment, and I'm upset that I can't afford to buy them comparable merchandise to make things fair for them. My husband doesn't understand why I'm upset. Why would he? His son got all the benefit.

—TOTALLY OVER IT

When this type of situation exists between stepchildren, it is only natural that some repercussions will develop, and one likely possibility is resentment. While we can and should explain to our children that life isn't always fair, there's no guarantee that our children will understand and accept material differences among stepfamily members.

In some instances, a stepfamily can be disrupted when one child takes out frustration and anger on stepsiblings. Some children are unable to channel negative feelings in a constructive manner, and resort to verbal and physical violence. This behavior should never be tolerated or justified as "children being children." If you find yourself in this circumstance, seek immediate professional help from an independent mental health counselor or one from the child's school. Hoping that such an issue will disappear is not a solution, since such problems tend to grow worse when left untreated. A young person who displays violent tendencies needs help, and your other children need to be protected from danger.

Sexual Abuse in the Stepfamily

Sometimes one child in the family can cajole, entice, demand or coerce sexual attention from another stepsibling. This is unacceptable behavior, and the victimized child can be traumatized for years afterward.

Sexual relations between minor stepsiblings are as harmful, if not more so, than physical abuse. (Needless to say, the situation can be even more serious if an adult within the family is perpetrating the abuse.) If you have any reason to suspect that such behavior is taking place in your stepfamily, make sure you immediately do something about it, rather than burying your head in the sand. All children need their households to be safe, secure and comfortable, and protecting their sexual boundaries is one way that this can be ensured.

Signs of Sexual Abuse

Often, signs of sexual abuse are not physically obvious. Therefore, the abuse can go undetected for long periods unless adults are aware of some of the nonphysical signs an abused child may display. These include:

- INAPPROPRIATE INTEREST IN OR KNOWLEDGE OF SEXUAL ACTS
- SEDUCTIVE BEHAVIOR
- SUDDEN RELUCTANCE OR REFUSAL TO UNDRESS IN FRONT OF OTHERS
- MORE AGGRESSIVE BEHAVIOR OR, CONVERSELY, MORE COMPLIANT BEHAVIOR THAN USUAL
- SUDDEN WITHDRAWAL FROM FAMILY AND/OR FRIENDS
- SUDDEN FEAR OF A PARTICULAR PERSON OR FAMILY MEMBER

If you suspect abuse, seek professional advice. You can get help from a variety of sources, such as your child's pediatrician, teacher or school counselor, a police officer, a child protection service worker or a mental health professional.

Give It Time

Even in the healthiest of situations, children need time to adjust to new stepsiblings. You can encourage them to get to know each other, but you need to allow these relationships to develop naturally. Don't force stepfamily members to participate in events or outings that might be awkward and uncomfortable for everyone. Also, minimize competition between stepsiblings by avoiding comparing them to each other. When stepsiblings play games together, encourage them to be graceful winners and losers in competitive play. Encourage them to say no if they don't want to play certain games or do anything else that stepsiblings might pressure them to do.

Despite the best efforts of everyone involved, and the passage of time, stepsiblings may not become close to each other. In *We're Still Family,* Dr. Constance Ahrons found that less than one-third of her study's sample considered stepsiblings to be like brothers or sisters. Rather, they saw each other as cousins, distant relatives, friends or mere acquaintances. Try to accept that this may be the case in your family, even if it may not be an ideal situation. Respect and compassion for each other are the most you can expect from every member of your stepfamily.

In your journal, answer these questions:

- What kind of relationships do you expect your children and stepchildren to have with each other?
- What prevents this from happening?
- What is a more realistic expectation for you to maintain, given your stepfamily circumstances?

ONE STEPMOTHER'S STORY: CASSANDRA

Cassandra cried when she described her stepfamily to me. A year before, she and her fourteen-year-old son had moved from upstate New York to Long Island to join her new husband and his children. His eldest child was a daughter, a senior in college who lived on campus. His two teenage sons, a junior and senior in high school, lived with them. Cassandra's son had problems relating to and communicating with others. Although he had improved tremendously with help from a specialized school, there were still times when he couldn't express his feelings, became frustrated and sometimes resorted to fighting. There had been a few minor incidents with him and his stepbrothers during the past year, but in the last few weeks physical skirmishes had escalated, and her stepsons were ganging up on her son, taunting him and generally making his life miserable. Rather than acting as a peacemaker, her husband was siding with his sons. Cassandra told me that she was giving serious thought to leaving her husband and moving back upstate.

I asked her to respond to these questions:

What kind of relationship do you expect your children and stepchildren to have with each other?

I hoped everyone would get along, and like each other. My son has made so much progress. He now has friends and is doing well in school. I hoped my stepsons would get along with him.

What prevents this from taking place?

My husband and his sons do not understand my son's problems. They're not bad people; they just don't get that my son has a condition that prevents him from relating [easily] to others.

What is a more realistic expectation for you to maintain, given your stepfamily circumstances?

I need to protect my son from getting beaten up. I can talk to my husband about making sure his boys stay away from mine. If that doesn't work, I will have to move back.

Cassandra was in a tough spot. She had hoped that her
love for her new husband would conquer all stepfamily
problems, but realized that some issues are too large
to be overcome by love alone, and require professional intervention. She realized that her initial desire for the boys
to get along with each other had been unrealistic. A more
realistic goal was to work toward peaceful coexistence.

The Sadness of Weddings

The integration of a stepfamily may take a long time to achieve.
Unresolved issues along the way may be painful, perhaps experienced most poignantly during the wedding of a stepchild. This is a
significant, celebratory event for a family that, unfortunately, can
be filled with sadness and emptiness for stepmothers. Some of us
may feel as though we are minor guests at the wedding, even after
years of marriage, years of being kind and dutiful to our stepchildren.
For instance, our names may not appear on wedding invitations,
or we may not be asked to participate in the ceremonies along with
other family members.

Recognize that weddings are an opportunity for brides and
grooms to play out their fantasies, which may include divorced
parents acting as if they were a happy family—even though they
may have been apart for a long time. While this situation isn't fair
or just, it is a common experience for many of the women in the
Steps for Stepmothers online chat room to feel excluded.

Ask yourself these questions:
- Do you expect your stepfamily to be "blended"?
- What factors prevent this from happening?
- What is a more realistic expectation for you to have?

When your stepchildren are getting married, or your family is
celebrating another special occasion, you may need to change your

expectations that your stepfamily will act as a loving and blended unit. Understand that regardless of the number of years you have been married to their father, your stepchildren may be still experiencing conflicts resulting from their parents' divorce. Their way of handling these difficult feelings may not include being considerate of you. Once you adjust your attitude, you'll be able to let go of many of your frustrations.

Evaluate Your Expectations

It's time to evaluate your expectations to see if they are unrealistic, given your particular stepfamily. If so, you may need to modify some of them. Consider:

- Do you need to overcome your negative perception of stepmothers?
- Do you need to adjust your expectations of your stepchildren?
- Do you need to accept the way your stepchildren feel about you?
- Do you need to accept the way you feel about your stepchildren?
- Do you need to accept your partner's ex-wife for the person she is now?
- Do you need to reevaluate your duties in your stepfamily so you won't be tired and resentful?
- Do you need to accept that your stepchildren may not express appreciation to you for all the hard work you do for them?
- Do you need to accept that you may not love your stepchildren as much as your partner loves them?
- Do you need to accept that your biological children and stepchildren do not have to get along well with each other?
- Do you need to accept your stepfamily as it is?

As I've said before, you can evaluate and modify your expectations more easily if you write them down. As you do this, leave some space between your responses, so you can go back and add the factors that prevent your expectations from being reached. Then, write down a set of expectations that are more in line with reality. Once you have completed this exercise, you can move forward toward achieving more realistic expectations.

Chapter Four

Step 2: Revise Unrealistic Expectations

Cognitive therapy, founded by Dr. Aaron Beck in the 1950s, offers some effective methods for changing unrealistic expectations to more healthy ones. These techniques have proven very successful in helping many people overcome depression and anxiety. They enable us to develop more realistic perspectives, make healthier choices and obtain relief from negative emotions, by helping us examine distorted thought patterns and replace them with healthier ways of thinking. Self-soothing statements, substitution of positive thoughts for negative ones, assertiveness training and the repetition of positive affirmations are used to break negative patterns. I am certain you have used some of these cognitive techniques already, even if you weren't aware of it. Let me give you several examples.

Have you ever felt nervous before a test? To help yourself relax and focus, did you ever talk to yourself inwardly, saying, "I will do the best I can. That's all I can expect from myself"? You may also have told yourself something like:

"This is going to be okay."

"I have the strength to cope with this."

"I have dealt with much worse in the past."

We can use self-soothing statements to calm ourselves when we are anxious. They can help us reframe negative feelings to more positive ones, and cope more effectively with our everyday challenging experiences. When you told yourself calming statements, you were practicing cognitive therapy, and you can continue to use its lessons to enhance your ability to keep experiences and expectations in perspective and enhance your self-esteem.

When our expectations of ourselves as stepmothers are not met, our inner dialogues will be affected. For example, when we're feeling "down," we may have the tendency to "catastrophize" (imagining the worst possible outcome to an event) or overgeneralize. Have you ever said this or something similar to yourself after a fight with your partner: "I hate my life, and wish I could run away from it all"? This thought is a broad generalization, and rather than accepting it as totally accurate, you might try examining the statement carefully, naming the specific aspects of your life that you detest. Could it be that only some parts of your life contribute to your misery—not all of them? By shifting your perspective from global to specific, you narrow down the precise cause of your unhappiness and increase your ability to improve your circumstances.

Here's another example of how to reframe negative thoughts. What do you say to yourself after making a mistake? Do you blame yourself, telling yourself something like "I can never do anything right"? This is a self-punitive comment that hurts your self-esteem. Instead, consider saying, "Everyone makes mistakes at times. I am only human, and I will try to learn from this mistake so I'll avoid similar ones in the future." This cognitive shift normalizes the mistake and uses it as a lesson to learn from. This is far healthier for your self-esteem than criticizing yourself.

In addition to observing your inner speech, notice the way you communicate with others. Do you have a tendency to embellish your sentences with modifiers like *always* and *never*? Have you ever said something like "He *never* considers my feelings"? This is an example of black-or-white thinking, in which a person or an event are seen in absolute terms, as all or nothing. This way of thinking tends to be an exaggeration of reality. By changing one word in the sentence, your speech can more accurately reflect the facts and keep your thoughts in perspective. Replace the word *never* with the word *sometimes* and see the difference in the two sentences. "*Sometimes* he doesn't consider my feelings" communicates a very different message. If you use sentences with *always, everybody* and *nobody,* change them to statements that accurately describe the event or person being discussed. For many people, this change in self-talk can prevent negativity from building up.

In a similar vein, observe your speech to see how often you use the word *should*. For example, have you ever said: "I *should* be a better stepmother"? When people use *should* frequently, they tend to be self-critical, and they are often disappointed by their own behavior. The word *should* applies pressure on you to live up to standards that can rarely be met. Banish this word from your vocabulary and replace it with *could*. The statement "I *could* be the best stepmother in the world" gives you more leeway in how you behave, and how you judge yourself as a stepmother.

There are several other ways of thinking that can trip us up. Do you jump to conclusions about an event or a person before you know all the facts? I was once guilty of this. If someone did not return a phone call, I would assume I had done something to offend her. I would spend hours thinking about what I could have done wrong, and wonder if the relationship was over. When she called, I would find that she had been busy, and just hadn't had time to get back to me. I realized that I needed to patiently wait for an explanation rather than personalize the reason that someone did not call. What a relief this was! I was freed from constantly worrying about how to handle negative consequences that never took place.

Similarly, do you think you can read other people's minds? Do you try to predict future outcomes? While you may be intuitive, there is a good chance of making a mistake if you believe you understand the motives of others, without seeking objective verification.

It is important to ask why a person has done something before making your own assumptions or interpretations. For instance, Nancy, one stepmother I worked with, would get upset when her partner came home late after dropping off his children. She assumed he had spent time talking to his ex-wife. When he walked in the door, she was already angry with him, which ruined the rest of their evening. I suggested that she ask him what he had been doing. Most times, he had been stuck in traffic, and occasionally, he had been delayed because he was buying Nancy flowers. Nancy was wasting energy getting angry about something that had no grounding in reality. She learned to delay becoming upset until she knew all the facts.

Some people don't realize that they see the world through mental filters. Like filters placed on camera lenses, mental filters change our view or interpretation of events. Some people apply rose-colored mental filters to their thoughts, imagining best-case scenarios, as did the always cheerful optimist of the fictional *Pollyanna*. But most people use dark filters, turning incidents into something worse than they really are. By using a negative mental filter, you can become blind to the positive experiences around you.

Look at what you've written in your journal, and identify how many types of negative cognitive patterns you use.

- Do you overgeneralize? Below the journal entries where you have done this, write entries that more accurately reflect the circumstances you are discussing.
- Do you catastrophize? What are the worst-case scenarios you imagine? Write down some examples of how you negatively exaggerate future events, and then write some possibilities that are neutral or positive.
- Do you tend to see the world in absolute terms? Do you engage in black-and-white thinking? Can you modify such statements to include more shades of gray?

- How often do you use the word *should* in sentences? Write down some examples and then replace them with sentences containing the word *could*.
- Do you jump to conclusions before knowing all the facts? Write down some alternate possibilities.
- Do you assume you can mind-read or predict the future? Write down some assumptions you make about other people and future events, and see if you can come up with other possibilities.

Continue this exercise by writing down the negative thoughts you have every day, and then think of positive ones to replace them. Keep the positive statements specific and brief. The act of writing them down helps make change more effective. By reading these statements out loud several times a day, the positive effects will be increased. If you complete all the above steps consistently, you should begin to see that your negative thoughts will decrease in strength and frequency.

In addition to keeping a daily journal, there are several other effective ways to derail negative thoughts and replace them with more positive ones. Here are a few examples.

Interrupt Your Cognitive Patterns

When you catch yourself having a negative thought, disrupt it by doing something else, such as calling a friend, singing a song or looking at a magazine. Any activity outside the parameters of the negative thought can distract you, and help you to change your focus to a more positive one.

This method was quite effective for Jade. As you may remember, she was angry that her husband took her for granted. If he did not say "thank you" after she made dinner for the family, she would stew with resentment while doing the dishes. She would start to remember all the other times he had not acknowledged her hard work. Before she knew it, she had a lengthy list of his past transgressions, and was much angrier than before she had started to clean the kitchen. I suggested that she interrupt this chain of thoughts to prevent anger from building up, and asked her what she could do when she recognized she was starting to build a case against her husband. She told me she loved to whistle, and would whistle a song when she realized that she was preparing a resentment list. What can you do to keep negative thoughts from growing?

A warning: Changing your focus is not a good idea if it prevents you from handling an urgent problem or carrying out a necessary task. Then it merely becomes a form of procrastination. Learn to distinguish between times when you need to deal with negative thoughts in order to solve an important problem and times when dwelling on negative thoughts is just a way to perpetuate your unhappiness.

Small Actions Make a Big Difference

When we are feeling bad about ourselves, it can be hard to change our feelings. Do you find yourself paralyzed by your problems, overwhelmed and unable to act? In such situations, think about doing one small activity to help you feel better. In this way, you can begin to outsmart your negative patterns. As you know, self-esteem isn't an innate characteristic that only some people have. All of us need to develop it, by performing actions that build self-esteem.

At the end of each meal she'd prepared, Jade began to ask her husband and stepchildren if they had enjoyed it. This usually elicited a "thank you" from them, so she did not start to feel resentment. What are some small actions you can take to feel better about your life? Will a phone call to a friend help? Do you need a few minutes of privacy to restore your sanity? It often doesn't take much to shift your mood and boost your self-esteem.

Small Acts of Kindness Lead to
Big Personal Rewards

It may sound like a message on a bumper sticker, but the fact is that helping others is a very effective way to improve our moods. Small gestures, such as holding a door open for the person following you or giving up your seat on the bus to an elderly person, go a long way toward connecting with people and feeling appreciated. If you get into the habit of making such gestures regularly, you will begin to feel better about yourself.

In your journal, list:

- Ten "treats" or rewards you enjoy (ones that don't include food and don't cost anything), such as walking, watching children at play or gazing at beautiful flowers.
- Ten things that make you laugh.
- Ten acts of kindness you can perform to help a family member or friend.
- Ten things you have always wanted to try that take you out of your comfort zone.

On days when you are feeling bad, go to your journal, examine the lists you have recorded and choose at least one action to take (more, if possible) to improve your mood.

Affirmations

An affirmation is a phrase (said either silently or out loud) that can guide you to release negative energy and move in a positive direction. For instance, you might say, "I release my negative energy, and I will focus my attention on positive feelings today and every day," or "I choose to live today and every day to the fullest." Affirmations can state your positive characteristics, recognize your past achievements or focus on your future goals. To remind yourself of your positive attributes, make a list of them and repeat them several times a day.

In your journal, list:

- At least five of your strengths. This may include characteristics such as persistence, courage, friendliness or creativity.
- At least five things you admire about yourself. Among the many possibilities may be the compassionate way you treat your stepchildren, your excellent work ethic or your commitment to leading a balanced life.
- At least five of the greatest achievements of your life so far. Again, there are probably numerous choices, among which may be recovering from a serious illness, graduating from high school or learning to use a computer.
- At least twenty accomplishments, which can range from simple ones, such as learning to play a computer game, to complex ones, such as earning a graduate degree.

You can modify a negative self-concept by using affirmations on a daily basis. This can improve your attitude, boost your self-esteem, and motivate you toward emotional growth and progress. Beginning with the words *I am,* state your positive attributes. These may include:

I am a good person.

I am a caring person.

I am a generous person.

I am a smart person.

I am a creative person.

To reinforce the positive emotions you experience from this exercise, select a different one of your strengths every day, and apply it in your life in some way. For instance, if you pick *creative* as your personal strength, do something creative that day. This will reinforce that strength and improve how you feel.

**In your journal, write down five affirmations beginning with
I am that highlight your positive qualities.**

Affirmations can also bolster your belief in your ability to
grow, change and improve your life. Begin with the words *I can.*
Examples of such affirmations include:

> *I can laugh and have fun.*
>
> *I can be assertive.*
>
> *I can heal.*
>
> *I can succeed.*
>
> *I can overcome obstacles placed in my path.*

Repeating a positive phrase, such as *I can do this,* encourages
you to tackle difficult tasks and be your own coach, rather than your
own detractor.

**In your journal, write down five affirmations that begin with
*I can.***

Affirmations can help you move toward any success you want
to achieve. Once you decide on some short-term goals, you can use
affirmations with sentences that begin with *I will.* Examples
include:

> *I will control my temper today.*
>
> *I will grow emotionally stronger each day.*
>
> *I will feel less guilt each day.*
>
> *I will face my fears courageously today.*
>
> *I will take on only what I can handle today.*

**In your journal, write down five affirmations that begin with
*I will.***

Affirmation of the day exercise: Each day write one positive
affirmation (from your journal list) on a small index card. Carry

it with you, and repeat it several times a day to reinforce its message. Write a different one each day.

Visualization

Visualization is another way to help you change negative thought patterns. By visualizing a positive outcome, you help to install positive rather than negative thoughts in your mind.

You need to be in a relaxed state to do this exercise, so sit in a place that is away from noise and other distractions. Close your eyes and focus on your breathing. Now visualize your desired outcome: For instance, if you are worried that an upcoming weekend with your stepchildren may be unpleasant, visualize the weekend going well, and think about activities that you could participate in during this time to make you happy.

Each time you find yourself dwelling on an unrealistic expectation that bothers you, imagine releasing it by seeing it float away from you. Replace it with an image that soothes you, such as a beach or lake, a rainbow, a sunset or puppies or kittens at play.

Visualization can also help you achieve your goals. Sit in a comfortable chair, close your eyes and imagine a future time when you have achieved your goal. Enjoy this image. It is important to believe that your goal is possible to achieve. This is the most important step to take toward succeeding.

Work with Your Thoughts

You have more influence on your thoughts than you may realize. I am not suggesting that you should manipulate them by rationalization or overintellectualization, or suppress them because they are too painful. What I am suggesting is that it is possible to *work with* your thoughts in order to shift them. The brain, like other parts of the body, is dynamic, not fixed and rigid. Just as you can exercise your body to become more physically fit, you can also exercise your brain to change the way you think and feel. The ability to overcome negative energy gets easier with practice, so that in time, it will become second nature to you, and you will be better able to invest your energy in living in the present.

Although these cognitive techniques work well for life's daily ups and downs, they will probably not be sufficient when you are seriously angry, depressed or anxious. So how can you tell the difference? People who are seriously depressed can have trouble with simple activities like taking a shower, brushing their teeth or getting out of bed. Intense anxiety can lead to obsessive negative thoughts that are extremely difficult to escape. In these cases, trying to shift your thoughts will not serve as a substitute for psychotherapy or prescribed medication, and in this case, cognitive strategies should be used only as a supplement to professional help.

If you believe you are suffering from chronic depression or anxiety, consult with a qualified mental health practitioner. Do not let pride or shame stand in the way of seeking treatment. Cost should not be a factor, either. Many health insurance plans cover such services, and if this does not apply in your case, look for a clinic or practitioner whose fees are set on a sliding scale according to the client's income. You don't have to suffer with either mild or severe negative thoughts. Make the commitment to help yourself, or to get professional assistance, if necessary, so you can begin to feel better.

Chapter Five

Step 3: Your First Priority: Self-Care

In trying to fulfill all the obligations we *believe* we have, we stepmothers often shortchange ourselves. Only after we have taken care of everyone else (including the family pets) do we feel free to focus on our own needs. But by that time, we may be too exhausted or depressed to do much for ourselves. This is a shame, for as Buddha said, "You, yourself, as much as anybody in the entire universe, deserve your love and affection."

In the early years of my marriage, I tried so hard to be a caring wife and stepmother that I spent most of my leisure time on activities that my husband and stepdaughter wanted to do. I expended so much energy making sure they were having a good time that I actually lost my zest for living. I stopped pursuing activities that nurtured my soul, such as traveling to exotic destinations, going to foreign movies and taking interesting classes. Instead, I constantly arranged and participated in family activities, whether or not I enjoyed them. It wasn't long before I became bored with my life, and in fact, I probably became boring to be with.

I learned an important lesson from this experience. The truth is that unless we place our own emotional needs first on our list of priorities, we will be of limited use to anyone, including ourselves. Emotional needs are as important for our survival as the basic needs for food, water and shelter. These include the needs to love and be loved, to socialize and to belong to a group, along with the needs for esteem, approval and recognition for our achievements. Emotional self-care allows us to grow and develop to our full potential, to have warm, close relationships with others and to be productive members of our communities.

You cannot truly be considerate of others if you don't put your own emotional needs upfront. Taking good care of yourself is never selfish or self-centered. When you take care of yourself, you are not abdicating your concern for others—you are merely shifting your priorities. This is not about being greedy, materialistic or callous about other people's feelings. Rather, it is about living your life to its fullest, and making sure that you are the architect of the kind of life you want to lead.

If you are placing your own emotional needs last, after everyone else's, you'd do well to remember the instructions given on every airplane flight. In an emergency, you should put your own oxygen mask on before assisting others. Just as you cannot take care of a child on an airplane without enough air to breathe yourself, you need emotional "oxygen" every day to take care of your loved ones.

Finding Happiness

It's not always so easy for us to know what satisfies our emotional needs. Some days we may not even be sure of what we want to eat for lunch, let alone what we want or need emotionally! Yet, the quest to fulfill these needs requires us to continually reevaluate what is important to us.

It is important to look for happiness in the right places. Happiness is far more than eating a good meal, watching an exciting movie or spending the day at the beach. You may "have fun" while doing these activities, but "having fun" is a state of being that only lasts for a short time. Contrast this with the "overall experience of pleasure and meaning," which is how Harvard psychologist Dr. Tal Ben-Shahar defines happiness in his book, *Happier.* This experience of happiness, he says, can be achieved only by being fully engrossed in work, and by being actively engaged with the people we love and the leisure activities we enjoy.

People who are genuinely happy are not joyful at every

moment of their lives. They endure hardship and pain at times, just like everybody else. They get annoyed and frustrated when things go wrong. However, they maintain an overall positive mood and attitude toward life. They are generally satisfied and content with their lives, and have an optimistic view of the future.

Dr. Martin Seligman, a cognitive psychologist and founder of the positive psychology movement, has identified three components of happiness: pleasure (or positive emotion), engagement and meaning. He says that happy people are those who have satisfying relationships, experience pleasure in what they do and choose activities that are meaningful to them. In one study, Dr. Seligman and Dr. Ed Diener compared very happy people to those who were less happy and found only one difference between the two groups: very happy people had rich and satisfying relationships while less happy people didn't. Spending meaningful time with family and friends is an important ingredient for happiness.

In your journal, take note of the current relationships in your life, and answer these questions:

- Are your relationships satisfying?
- With whom do you enjoy spending your time? How often do you see these family members and friends during a given week?
- How often are you spending time with people whom you don't enjoy?

Another important component of happiness is having a sense of purpose, a reason to be alive. To lead a purposeful life, each of us must think carefully about what we want to accomplish and what experiences we wish to have. This knowledge is easier to discover for some of us than for others. Certain people, from an early age, have a "calling," a specific vocation, whether it is the ministry, politics or firefighting. Those with special creative or physical talents, too, usually know what paths to follow. But most of us have to dig deep into our psyches to find our true purpose in life. We may know we want a family, a career or to travel, but we may not know what specific skills and pursuits will truly nourish our souls.

One way to recognize our level of interest in an activity is to notice how we perceive the passage of time. Have you noticed that time can go by slowly, where each minute seems like a lifetime, or it can pass by so quickly that you can hardly believe it? Ideally, when your attention is fully absorbed in the present moment, time seems to race along with lightning speed. This happens when we are engaged in good conversation or immersed in interesting work that requires our full concentration.

Are you leading the life you want? If not, you may need to think about what would give you the greatest satisfaction. "Energy flows where attention goes" is an expression that succinctly lays out one of the realities of life. Remember that to be happy, you need to be aware of where you are focusing your energy. If we focus on negative feelings, we build on these feelings. Likewise, if we aim our feelings and thoughts in a positive direction, we are likely to increase the positive energy in our lives.

In your journal, write down:

- The activities that you find most pleasurable and meaningful.
- The amount of time you devote to each of those activities every week.
- Activities during the day that you feel you *have* to do rather than those you *want* to do.
- The amount of time you devote to each of those mandatory activities every week.

Your responses to these questions will give you a clearer picture of how you spend your time. You may need to revise your schedule to include activities and interests that you really value so that you better enjoy each day. Ideally, you want to devote the majority of your time to accomplishing your life goals, rather than spending it doing odious chores or other unpleasant activities.

To figure out what your life goals are, imagine that you only have one year to live. Think about what you want to accomplish before you die and what you would like people to say about you, and remember you for, after you die.

In your journal, write down your life goals in these different areas:

- *Creative pursuits:* Are there any artistic goals you hope to achieve?
- *New experiences or activities:* Is there any activity you want to try that you have not yet experienced? Are there any places you want to visit?
- *Education:* Are there any areas of knowledge you want to explore or new skills that you want to learn?
- *Career:* Do you have any career objectives that you would like to realize?
- *Interpersonal:* Are you the relative or friend you want to be? Do you need to do anything differently to be that person?
- *Physical:* Are there any athletic goals you want to achieve? For instance, do you want to run a marathon or learn how to play tennis?
- *Community service:* Is there anything you want to do to make the world a better place?

Look at your list and consider how you can accomplish each one of your goals. You have already completed the first step by writing them down, which will crystallize them and give them greater force. Next, develop an action plan by writing the specific steps that will lead you to accomplish each of your goals. Remember to be reasonable;

don't set yourself up for failure. For instance, if you want to run a marathon, and you expect to train for just one month, more likely than not, you would get injured and fail to reach your goal. Give yourself sufficient time for each goal and reward yourself each time you reach a milestone toward its completion.

Are there any obstacles that prevent you from achieving your life goals? List them, along with strategies you can take to prevent them from interfering with your progress. Don't forget to celebrate when you reach your goals!

Our goals change throughout our lives. What is important to us when we are thirty may no longer seem relevant when we are fifty. It is helpful to reevaluate our goals every few years to make sure our daily behaviors are in line with what is most important to us. Remember that the process of implementing our goals is as important as attaining them. To make sure the process is an enjoyable and rewarding experience, we need to be kind to ourselves along the way.

The Importance of Self-Care

Too many stepmothers cannot achieve our purpose in life because our time is consumed trying to fix the problems in our stepfamilies. As a result, we feel overwhelmed, out of control, angry, depressed and resentful. You can reduce or even eliminate such destructive feelings if you take the time to fit self-care into your daily routine. As I've suggested previously, you may need to give up some activities to make room for those that provide you with the most meaning and pleasure.

Unfortunately, self-care cannot solve all our problems. Certain situations are so grave that no amount of self-care will eliminate them. For instance, when a stepfamily member has a serious physical or mental illness, self-care can reduce stress, but will not provide lasting peace and contentment. That won't happen until the problem is resolved. Also, self-care should never be substituted for taking stronger actions when a situation is intolerable. For instance, if you are experiencing physical abuse from a partner or stepchild, you need to tell others about your predicament and get away from anyone who is threatening you.

In most situations, however, self-care can be highly effective. It can restore emotional vitality for stepmothers who habitually place their own needs last. The forms of emotional self-care I suggest below will help you to feel more content and satisfied. The first few suggestions will also help you relax and eliminate negative energy, while the next few will give you more positive energy. All these techniques are highly effective for everyday situations.

Get Rid of Unnecessary Emotional Baggage

Daily life is filled with annoyances and frustrations that can darken our moods. My moods used to swing from happy to sad, from depressed to optimistic, due to external events, even those as minor as rainy weather. Sometimes, after trying to resolve a minor problem by phone, I could spend hours stewing with frustration about the difficulty of trying to reach a human being instead of an automated recording. When I was upset by more important problems—for instance, a conflict in my stepfamily—this would really darken my day. I was an emotional yo-yo.

I believed my moods were determined by influences beyond my control. I didn't realize then that I had a choice about the way I reacted. Now, when I get sad, angry or frustrated, I use some of the cognitive tools suggested in the last chapter. I may ask myself, "How important is this one event in the scheme of my life?" Sometimes, I apply internal speech to help overcome negative feelings, saying to myself, "Shake it off, shake it off." At other times, I actually shake my body or wash my face to symbolically get rid of toxic energy. I remind myself that I can choose to let a bad experience ruin my day, or I can choose to let it go. Knowing that I select my own emotions, rather than being led by them, is empowering. Always keep in mind that *you are responsible for the way you feel*. Don't let yourself become a victim of your emotions.

How much negativity do you experience in a given day? Try monitoring your feelings for a week to evaluate how frequently you experience anger, sadness, depression or any other negative emotion. Record the frequency, duration and intensity of your moods in your journal. Each day, rank your overall mood on a scale of zero to ten, imagining that zero is the worst you have ever felt and 10 is the best. After a week, add the days' scores together and divide by seven to find your average score. If it is lower than seven, consider adding some pleasurable activities to your life that will raise your overall level of satisfaction.

While it is normal to experience unpleasant feelings from time to time, no one should tolerate misery on a daily basis. Tolerating negative feelings isn't healthy, and the longer you wait to rid yourself of such emotions, the harder they may be to overcome. If you recognize that you are chronically unhappy or frustrated with your situation, there is no reason for you to tolerate it. Consider using one or all of the following techniques to help you achieve serenity.

"STEPMOTHERS SPEAK"

I realize I am more than just a mom, stepmom, sister, aunt, cousin, wife or daughter. My soul—my inner core—makes me unique, and I need to nurture it by taking some time to do things for myself. I also avoid sweating the small stuff.

—4 GRACE

The Value of Meditation, Self-Hypnosis, Yoga and Exercise

Meditation

By suspending the stream of thoughts that normally occupy our minds, we can achieve mental calmness and physical relaxation. Meditation has been shown to reduce stress, alter hormone levels and elevate mood. People who meditate report feeling more spiritual and tranquil, and have an increased sense of emotional well-being. Generally practiced once or twice a day for approximately ten to twenty minutes, meditation is simple, free and can be done anywhere.

Recent studies by Dr. Paul Ekman and his colleagues have shown that Buddhists are generally happier than other people, and he attributes this to their practice of daily meditation. Regular meditation tames the amygdala area of the brain, where fear memory resides. It's no surprise, then, that Dr. Ekman found that meditators are less likely to be shocked, flustered or angry. In another study, he found that two advanced Buddhist monks were able, with almost perfect accuracy, to identify the emotions of others by watching subtle, rapid changes in facial expressions. So Dr. Ekman concluded that meditation also increases sensitivity to the feelings of others.

As a result of advances in medical technology, scientists can see how regular meditation actually changes brain activity. Dr. Richard Davidson and his colleagues found that Buddhists show activity in their left prefrontal lobes—the area linked to positive emotions, self-control and calm that is activated during meditation—all the time, not only when they are meditating. Dr. Davidson's study suggests that meditation is an excellent way to achieve contentment and peace of mind.

To begin meditating, sit in a quiet place where you will not be disturbed. The room should be silent, without any music or other sounds to distract you. Sit on a cushion on the floor in a cross-legged position, or in a chair. Your eyes may remain open or closed, whichever is most comfortable for you. Depending on your personal preference, the room can be either brightly lit to prevent you from falling asleep, or dimly lit to turn your focus inward.

Begin by following your breath. Inhale through your nostrils and exhale through your mouth. Concentrate on observing your breathing. If any thoughts intervene, do not banish them. Rather, imagine them floating through your mind, and let them dissipate naturally, like smoke. The goal of meditation is to allow the chatter in your mind to gradually fade away. To accomplish this goal, some people repeat a word or phrase, while others simply prefer to observe their breath.

As you continue to focus on your breathing, begin to relax every muscle in your body. You can start at the top of your head and work your way down to your toes, or move in the reverse direction. Take your time while doing this, remembering that this moment is only for your benefit, and that you don't have any other responsibilities to be concerned about.

66STEPMOTHERS SPEAK99

It has taken me a long time to follow the basic healthy principles of life: Get enough sleep, eat nutritiously and exercise. Now I have added daily meditation to my regimen. At first I could only do it for three minutes before getting antsy, but I've stuck to it, practicing it every day, and I'm up to fifteen minutes. It's so simple, it's time just for me, and I love how balanced I feel.

—Rejuvenated

Like anything worthwhile, meditation takes time to learn. It may sound easy, but it takes effort to quiet one's mind. Some people grow frustrated after a few minutes, while their minds are still struggling to settle down. If you experience this, be patient. As you meditate, you will gradually become mindful of what is happening in the present moment, without judging or interpreting the experience. Your alertness will increase, and you will feel more centered and calm.

If you believe that meditation may help you, you may want to read one of the many books about it (see Appendix C: Resources for Stepmothers) for suggestions or find a place in your community that holds meditation sessions.

Self-Hypnosis

In some ways similar to meditation, self-hypnosis is a practice that relaxes and conditions the mind. Although we are generally unaware of its power, the unconscious mind can be very helpful in solving problems, making plans and even locating missing objects. When a new idea comes to us seemingly "out of the blue," it's usually because our unconscious minds have already processed the information.

You can access your unconscious mind by entering a trance state. While in a trance, your conscious mind can work hand in hand with your unconscious to help you achieve your goals. Trance states are natural, and we all go into them several times a day without knowing it. For instance, have you ever been so immersed in a book on a train or bus that you almost missed your stop? Have you ever been surprised by the sound of a bell announcing the end of a class? These are examples of trance states.

When used by trained professionals, hypnosis (also referred to as hypnotherapy) is a highly effective tool. True hypnosis has nothing to do with the hocus-pocus entertainment of stage hypnotists. It is often utilized for pain management; some doctors even use hypnotherapy instead of anesthesia when performing surgery. Hypnosis has also been shown to reduce the frequency and intensity of migraines, control nausea and vomiting during chemotherapy, and treat the symptoms of asthma. Many gynecologists teach pregnant women self-hypnosis techniques to reduce the pain they will experience during labor. Hypnotherapy is commonly used to lower anxiety, as well as for weight loss, smoking cessation and boosting self-esteem. However, you don't necessarily need a professional hypnotist, since the benefits of hypnosis are available to everyone without a fee.

Self-hypnosis is simple and safe—nothing harmful can occur. To begin, sit in a comfortable chair with your eyes open or closed. It helps to have an idea about what issues you want to work on beforehand. Begin focusing on your breathing and relax each muscle in your body. Then, as you exhale through your mouth, imagine that all tension and stress are leaving you. When you inhale through your nostrils, imagine comfort and relaxation entering your body. You can visualize each part of your anatomy becoming lighter and lighter as the tension leaves it. Take as much time as you need.

To deepen your state of relaxation, imagine that you are descending a flight of ten steps. From the top step, silently count from ten backward to zero until you reach the last step. Imagine feeling each step under your feet, as you go deeper and deeper into relaxation. While you are doing this, if you are distracted by images and thoughts that intrude themselves into your consciousness, just gently brush them aside and continue.

Once you reach the bottom step, imagine that you are happy and relaxed. Your unconscious mind is now more open to receiving suggestions, and you can begin to address whatever issues you want help with. Speak to yourself in the present tense, and keep your suggestions short and simple. Frame your statements in a positive manner. Rather than saying, "I don't want to be tired anymore," say something like "I am feeling more and more energized and healthy." Or you might say, "I am getting stronger and stronger, and can deal with everything that comes my way."

"I am going to take care of myself in a healthy and loving way" or "I am letting light and love into my life" are other examples of suggestions you can make to yourself. Language, by the way, is not necessary. Your suggestions can simply be images of yourself as stronger and happier.

When you are finished with the suggestions, begin climbing back up the stairs, counting from zero to ten, knowing that when you reach ten you will return to normal consciousness, feeling calm and relaxed. To help you end the self-hypnosis session, you may say to yourself when you reach the third step, "Three, I'm moving toward a waking state. Two, I'm becoming more alert, feeling refreshed. One, I'm completely awake." Open your eyes, if they were closed.

After completing this exercise, you may notice that you feel more energized, as though you've taken a restorative nap. Although people sometimes get results immediately, it's likely that a little time will pass before positive effects kick in, so don't be impatient. If you don't feel any change within a couple of weeks, consider changing the suggestions that you use.

Yoga

Yoga, an Eastern practice that has become popular in the West, focuses on exercises that achieve flexibility, calmness and "centeredness." There are many forms of yoga, all of which share a spiritual component. Yoga combines a series of stationary and moving poses, called asanas, and a form of breath control, known as pranayama, with concentration techniques. The various yoga postures are designed to balance the different systems of the body, including the central nervous system and the endocrine and digestive systems. By slowing down mental activity, taking your mind off the causes of your stress, and gently stretching your body in ways that massage your internal organs, yoga helps you create dynamic peacefulness within yourself.

Laughter yoga is a variation invented more than a decade ago by Dr. Madan Kataria, an Indian doctor. Convinced of the benefits of both laughter and yogic exercises, he combined the two. People simply gather in parks in the early morning and laugh together. This may seem silly at first glance, but laughter is contagious and has many positive benefits for our bodies. It releases hormones and chemicals that help reduce stress, lower blood pressure, lift depression and boost the immune system. Laughter yoga is a great way to start the day. See Appendix C: Resources for Stepmothers for more information on this.

Yoga improves flexibility, strengthens and tones muscles, increases stamina, improves digestion and circulation and boosts the immune response. It also sharpens concentration, relieves chronic stress, increases a sense of well-being and promotes spiritual growth. Yoga classes are now taught across the United States, and videotapes and DVDs are also available so you can practice at home. (See suggestions in Appendix C.) Try it. You may be delighted with the results.

Exercise

Daily exercise is highly beneficial, and does not have to take a lot of time. Even just walking for fifteen minutes can help remove toxic energy from your body. It can also be fun! Or how about taking a bicycle ride through a park or on a country road? If being part of a group will motivate you, look into a walking club or exercise classes near your home. Did you enjoy softball, swimming or tennis when you were younger? Chances are, you can find a community team to join. Make the effort to find them and you will have new friends, as well as helping yourself physically and emotionally.

For a home workout, investigate the many books and videos

available for purchase or at your local library. There are also regular workout programs on television. Don't let an hourlong exercise tape intimidate you. If you are short of time or not in good shape yet, try working out to a short segment, then lying quietly for a few moments before resuming your day. You might also consider buying a stationary bicycle, rebounder or other home-exercise equipment.

Even though your time may be limited, finding a few moments for physical activity once a day can make a significant difference in your mood by raising the level of endorphins, the chemicals that ward off depression. Exercise also releases tension and pent-up frustration, helps you to sleep better and boosts self-esteem.

Other Methods

You can also reduce your stress level by listening to soothing music; taking long, hot baths; using aromatherapy; or looking at beautiful images. Don't reject these techniques because they seem too simplistic, and do remember that the more you practice them, the more they will become an integral part of your everyday life, like brushing your teeth and taking a shower. When activities become habitual, you derive consistent benefits from them.

You can obtain great results from meditation, yoga, self-hypnosis and exercise. To make one of these a part of your life, commit to practicing it at least once a day. Just make sure that you do not use these techniques instead of seeking treatment for problems that require professional care. Although self-care alone cannot heal a serious condition, it can facilitate the healing process for both medical and emotional problems.

Releasing Negative Energy

Many stepmothers are filled with rage, resentment and bitterness from their stepfamily situation. Too often, I have heard women wish that a stepfamily member would suffer horrible pain, sometimes even die, for causing trouble and chaos. While I am sympathetic to the suffering these stepmothers have experienced, this kind of un-resolved anger doesn't serve any useful purpose. Even worse, it often becomes toxic, corroding our health and ruining our relationships.

For some women, anger is a way to maintain the status quo. For years, they may have been disappointed by people or events, and anger has become a way of life. They are used to being negative. For others, this situation perpetuates the belief that they don't deserve any happiness, and are fated to struggle throughout life. Can you relate to any of this? Consider whether you are stuck in a rut, surrounded by negative feelings.

When I tell stepmothers that, although their anger may be jus-tified, they are the only ones who are damaged by holding on to it, they often counter with, "But this is how I feel." I agree with them, and then I ask if they are willing to let go of this negativity and experience positive energy in their lives and relationships. Would they like to get to the point where the bad behavior of others seems like water rolling off a duck's back? In most cases, the behavior of others doesn't have to affect you. You, too, can let it roll off.

Increasing Positive Emotions

The positive psychology of Dr. Martin Seligman postulates that when we dwell on disappointments and unsatisfied desires, we are more prone to unhappiness. By contrast, when we focus our attention on positive aspects of our lives, we have a higher probability of attaining a sense of well-being.

According to Dr. Seligman, "Positive emotions are increased and the pleasant life is promoted by exercises that increase gratitude, that increase savoring, that build optimism and that challenge discouraging beliefs about the past." One of the exercises he rec-ommends is the "three good things exercise." The instructions are simple: Every day write down three good things that happened to you and why they happened. In a study of people who took this simple step, Dr. Seligman and Dr. Tracy Steen found that participants were happier and less depressed at three-month and six-month follow-ups than were those in a control group. This is something you can easily practice.

In your journal:
- Every day, write down three good things that happened to you.
- Review your list every few days, and notice if your state of mind improves.

Count Your Blessings, Literally

When most of our time is filled with chores and hard work, expressing gratitude for the good things in our lives can be a challenge. Even when things are going well, we may take our good fortune for granted and be complacent about expressing thanks. This is an easy mistake to fix. Keeping a gratitude list is an effective way to release stress and improve physical and emotional well-being.

Research conducted by Dr. Robert Emmons and Dr. Michael McCullough found that people who kept gratitude journals exercised more regularly, felt physically healthier, had more energy and experienced more positive emotions and life satisfaction than people who recorded negative or neutral sentiments in a journal. They also experienced more optimism about upcoming events than those who did not keep journals, and were closer to achieving their goals after a two-month period. The results of this study have been corroborated by Dr. Tal Ben-Shahar. In his book, *Happier,* he reports that feelings of gratitude, a sense of well-being and sensitivity to others increased for those who kept gratitude journals. He suggests that we keep gratitude lists as a daily ritual so that expressing gratitude becomes second nature to us.

Keeping a daily gratitude list can even help people cope with illness. Dr. Emmons studied people with neuromuscular disease and split them into two groups; half participated in a "twenty-one-day gratitude intervention," in which they were asked to write in a journal each day for three weeks those things they were grateful for; the others were not asked to keep a journal. Those in the gratitude group felt more energetic and connected to others and slept longer and better, compared to the control group.

Dr. Emmons emphasizes that expressing gratitude is not intended to fool us into believing that everything is perfect or blind us to the negative aspects of our lives. However, by noticing and appreciating the positive things, we reinforce them. By acknowledging our gratitude to others, we become better friends and community members. Our friends and families appreciate us more, which strengthens our relationships with them; in turn, we have more to be grateful for. Gratitude lists are a win-win situation.

In your journal:
- Keep a daily gratitude list. Begin and end each day by thinking of five things you're grateful for in your life. A written reminder reinforces your awareness.
- Write a gratitude thank-you letter when your partner, stepchild, parent, friend, mentor or anyone else has helped you and deserves recognition. This is more than an offhand note of a few sentences. Before writing, take some time to reflect on the meaning and pleasure you derive from the relationship. Saying "thank you" will be meaningful for the person you thank and to you, as well.
- Tell your partner how much you appreciate him on a regular basis. He will be grateful that you are conscious of his thoughtfulness.
- When things go your way, remember to smile and be thankful.

You will be happier and healthier if you learn to savor life's daily pleasures. Live in the moment, become more aware of everything you do, and enjoy the little things in your life. For instance, take pleasure in savoring the spray of hot water on your body when you shower, relishing your first sip of coffee in the morning and snuggling with your pet. Your senses can be fully alert to everything surrounding you by practicing mindfulness of the moment, and this will help you to better appreciate your daily experiences.

Of course, there are situations, such as when a stepchild steals or is thrown out of school, or when an ex-wife falsely accuses you and your partner of hurting your stepchild, that require stronger interventions than reframing your perceptions and doing self-esteem-building exercises. By all means, take strong action when it is called for. But remember that the methods described above can still be used to support you throughout any difficult time.

The Art of Forgiveness

People who keep a running list of the ways they have been wounded by others might be called "injustice collectors." Do you dwell on past transgressions that others have committed against you? If you can recall many times and places when you have been hurt by others, you may be an injustice collector. While you may be justified in being hurt, who really suffers from the feelings of anger and revenge you are experiencing? You do—no one else.

Another way to rid yourself of negative feelings is to forgive the frailties of others. As I've said previously, holding in anger, bitterness and resentment is emotionally and physically unhealthy. In his book, *Forgive for Good,* Dr. Frederic Luskin discusses the emotional benefits of forgiveness, which he defines as the process of healing personal grievances to restore a feeling of peace. When you forgive others, you can live your life in the present, instead of dwelling in the past. Why allow remnants of feelings from long ago to prevent you from experiencing the joys of the moment?

Dr. Robert Enright, who pioneered research on forgiveness, has found that "a willed change of heart" is necessary to forgive. He defines forgiveness as "a willingness to abandon one's right to resentment, negative judgment and indifferent behavior toward one who unjustly injured us, while fostering compassion, generosity and even love toward him or her." Dr. Luskin's definition of forgiveness is similar: "The feelings of peace that emerge as you take your hurt less personally, take responsibility for how you feel, and become a hero instead of a victim in the story you tell."

Numerous studies have found that forgiveness has many

psychological benefits. At the University of Wisconsin, Madison, participants in several studies who had experienced parental neglect, incest and spousal emotional abuse showed significant improvements in levels of depression, anxiety, post-traumatic stress, self-esteem and coping skills when they forgave. Participants who had alcohol and substance abuse addictions were less vulnerable to relapses when they forgave.

Let's be very clear: When you forgive someone for hurting you, you aren't condoning his behavior, nor are you willing to let him do the same thing to you in the future. Some people confuse forgiveness with opening one's arms unconditionally to a person who has hurt you. Forgiveness is not the equivalent of "letting bygones be bygones." Rather, it is an acceptance of the personality flaws of the person who hurt you, so you can move on in your life without the

"STEPMOTHERS SPEAK"

I need to live life to the fullest and enjoy every day, no matter what comes my way. I was sitting outside yesterday and took a good look around me, noticing the birds singing, the dogs playing in the yard, kids laughing and the fragrance of the flowers each time the wind blew. I had been taking the simple things in life for granted and focusing on all the havoc caused by one family member. I let her take over my life. It stops here. I am putting her to the back of my mind and enjoying the wonderful life I have.

—No Longer Stepped On

burden the offense has caused you. Forgiveness must also be distinguished from reconciliation. Forgiveness is the moral choice of the offended people themselves, whereas reconciliation is a decision that involves both the offended and the offender. It is possible to forgive those who have hurt you without reconciling with them. This allows you to pursue your own personal growth without needing the wrongdoer to be ready, willing or able to share your goals.

You can learn how to forgive. Dr. Luskin has developed a program for forgiveness that combines cognitive therapy with Buddhist principles of loving-kindness. He utilizes techniques, ranging from meditation to biofeedback, to demonstrate what it is like to be in a loving, peaceful state. Feelings of betrayal and suffering, he explains, develop from overidentifying with the personal aspect of events. When we retell our stories of how we were hurt, we trigger sympathetic nervous system arousal that imprints the trauma in our brains all over again. To diminish the impact of their wounds, he teaches people to talk about the betrayal and pain while maintaining an open, peaceful state. This helps reprogram their psyches to dispel the hurt by connecting it to kindness.

There are several steps to finding forgiveness. First, you need to acknowledge that you are still experiencing pain from the transgression, and that this is weighing you down. You also need to recognize that you have a choice in the way you live your life now. Forgiving others is for you and you alone. Once you realize that you are burdened by negative feelings from the past, you can begin the process of releasing these feelings. Dr. Luskin suggests that you practice how you would forgive someone even before you are actually ready to do so. By imagining how you would go about it, you are prepared to forgive when the time is right for you.

ONE STEPMOTHER'S STORY: SOPHIA

You can benefit from forgiving those who have caused you pain. Sophia introduced herself to me by saying, "I would be the poster woman of stepmothers if it weren't for my mother-in-law." Sophia was handpicked for her husband by her stepchildren and their mother. She had been working as a speech therapist at a school, and was assigned to help her future stepson. She connected so well with the boy and his mother that they both suggested introducing her to the child's father. And here she was now, happily married to him. Everyone got along well and all the adults cooperated on parenting decisions, with the exception of her mother-in-law, who insisted on dropping in unexpectedly, talking about Sophia behind her back, criticizing her parenting skills and even calling her "a childless woman."

Sophia was having hateful thoughts about her mother-in-law that were taking up too much space in her mind. Her partner had suggested that she simply ignore his mother, as he did, but she wasn't able to do this.

I asked Sophia to list what her mother-in-law had done that was painful to her. Sophia wrote:

She criticizes me in front of my stepchildren and husband, she has bought items for my stepchildren that I told her I would buy, she insists we eat the food she has cooked rather than mine, and she gives me her opinion without my asking for it.

What motivated her mother-in-law to behave this way?

My stepchildren are my mother-in-law's full-time job now that she is retired and widowed. She doesn't want to lose her place in the family. She is threatened by me.

What was Sophia's part in this situation?

I did not speak up for myself at first. I was scared of her authority and wanted her to like me. I let her buy the clothes without telling her I was upset about her going against my wishes. I have been too passive.

What were the positive aspects of the relationship?

She truly loves my stepchildren, and wants the best for them. My husband depends on her.

I asked Sophia to write a letter to her mother-in-law that included all her feelings. The letter would be for herself only, and was not intended to be sent. This is what she wrote:

Dear Sue,

I'm sorry you speak without thinking about what you are saying. You have hurt me and many others. I know this has prevented you from having more friends and has created lots of conflicts for you. I have tried to ignore your jabs, but my self-esteem is being affected. I don't expect you to change in any way; I know I must be the one to modify my behavior. From now on, I am going to speak up for myself when you criticize me unfairly. I hope you understand that this is my way of taking care of myself, and is not meant to hurt you. I appreciate all the love and time you have given to my stepchildren. You have a lot to offer others; I hope we can develop a better relationship as I express my feelings more directly and honestly with you. I am going to pray that the remaining years of your life will be filled with love.

Sophia felt empowered after writing the letter. She no longer felt weak, and became aware that she was a force to be reckoned with. She felt she could talk to her mother-in-law directly, and also use humor to make her point when she needed to defend herself. She understood that this exercise gave her the ability to change both her actions and her feelings, though she didn't expect her mother-in-law to be any different as a result of these changes.

I encouraged Sophia to have a special ceremony with the letter she wrote, to reinforce that the pain was no longer a part of her life. Sophia decided to bury it under a favorite hydrangea bush in her garden. She hoped that the beautiful blooms of the hydrangea would absorb her past pain.

Are you carrying around unnecessary burdens from past grievances? Could you benefit from performing a forgiveness exercise? Remember that no one is perfect. We all make mistakes, even you, and the sooner you can accept human frailty and forgive those mistakes, the easier your life will be.

In your journal, do the following exercise:

- Make a list of the people and the actions you need to forgive. What was done to you that caused your pain? Be specific.
- Put yourself in the shoes of the person who hurt you. What was her underlying motivation? Did she hurt you because her needs were greater than yours? Does she even realize that she hurt you? Understanding why the person hurt you is not a prerequisite for forgiveness; if you don't know why she acted as she did, that's perfectly all right. But if you can develop an understanding of her motives, it's an additional way to help you see things from her point of view and protect yourself from further harm.

- Acknowledge your part in this painful episode. Did you tell the person you were hurt or did you hide your pain? Did you stay in a bad situation when you could or should have left? Is it possible that you, too, bear some responsibility? Taking ownership of your role in causing this event will help you stop feeling like a victim.

- Make a list of the positive aspects of the relationship. While you may be dwelling on the transgression, there may be some ways that you benefit from your connection with this person. What are they?

- Write a letter to the one who hurt you, acknowledging what you gained from the relationship and expressing your forgiveness for the hurt he has caused you. Allow yourself to express all your feelings fully; do not focus only on the hurts. There is no need to mail the letter—this exercise is only for you. Writing down your feelings helps to clarify them, and eventually to release them, so they no longer cause you pain.

- Create a ceremony in which you dispose of your list and letter. This act will symbolize the end of the association between you and the pain you have experienced. You can bury or burn your writings, or come up with another ritual to separate these painful feelings from your current life.

- Visualize the person you are forgiving being blessed by your forgiveness. You can imagine and hope that, as a result, she will be freed from continuing the behavior that hurt you; but remember, your forgiveness does not require any action on her part.

- Once you have freed yourself from these connections and released the pain, feel yourself growing lighter and more joyous. Now you are able to move on with your life, without being burdened by feelings of bitterness from your past.

Remember, forgiveness is for you. Do you have to tell those who hurt you that you have forgiven them? No, not necessarily. While you may want to repair the relationship, it isn't imperative for you to communicate with the other person in order to feel better. Reconciliation may not be possible if the person who hurt you has not apologized or even acknowledged the transgression.

Take Charge of Your Happiness

It is of paramount importance that you take care of your own emotional needs first and foremost, before everything else in your life. When you make your emotional welfare your number one priority, you are actively making an effort to be happy. Happiness isn't a state of being that just happens for some and not for others; everyone must work hard to achieve and maintain it. While it is true that life is not fair and that some of us must work harder to achieve our goals, everyone needs to expend energy to create a meaningful life. We do this by focusing on what we want and then taking action to get it. Take charge!

Chapter Six

Step 4: Make Your Relationship Your Second Priority

To be content as a stepmother, your relationship must be the number two priority in your life and the life of your partner—right after your own well-being, which should always come first. This may sound like a selfish statement, but it is essential to the success of your relationship. A strong, effective partnership is an absolute necessity if you are to survive the stresses of stepfamily life with your dignity and self-respect intact. A strong relationship will help you cope with any problems that arise with your stepchildren and your partner's ex-wife.

Ask yourself this: What does it really mean to be happy together? This is not about how much money you have, the type of car you own, the size of your house or the exotic vacations you take. I'm talking about the kind of happiness that comes from within: the serenity, the inner feeling of well-being, the "we-ness" that can be experienced by a couple.

Defining good relationships is difficult; what works for one couple may not work for another. There are certain factors, however, that all happy couples have in common. Dr. Judith Wallerstein, the psychologist who conducted the twenty-five-year study on the effects of divorce on children, and her colleague Sandra Blakeslee, interviewed fifty happily married couples in the San Francisco Bay area. They chose couples who had at least one child and had been married for more than nine years. Both members of each couple in the study said that they were happily married.

In their book, *The Good Marriage*, Wallerstein and Blakeslee explain that first and foremost, the happily married couples in their survey respected and cherished each other. Their bonds showed high levels of both closeness and autonomy, as well as these other characteristics:

- The partners liked each other as friends and enjoyed spending time together.
- They were comfortable with each other, and viewed their relationships as safe havens in which they could be their authentic selves.
- Each partner felt that they were a central part of the other's life, and that their partner truly understood who they were.
- They were interested in each other's thoughts and feelings, and each had a genuine interest in the other's welfare.
- They shared similar values and goals, and strived to reach them together. They each supported the other's dreams.
- They each encouraged the other to develop in new ways, as their interests grew and changed over time.
- They each satisfied the other's needs for physical and emotional intimacy.
- They were each able to express both positive and negative emotions to the other.

Happy couples are committed to their relationships, and are willing to work to maintain them. They are realistic about the ups and downs of life, and believe that together they can work through difficult times. The inevitable conflicts that come up do not escalate to become unmanageable arguments or lead to despair, because these couples have well-developed problem-solving skills and the ability to deal with both change and stress.

Dr. John Gottman, who has studied the interactions of couples for more than twenty-five years, also observes that a positive climate exists in happy marriages, where both partners believe that the marriage enriches their lives. They admire each other's strengths and feel that they are lucky to be married to unique and special people. They each notice and acknowledge the thoughtful gestures made by the other. Happy marriages are filled with kindness, compassion and respect, characteristics that promote emotional health for each partner.

How healthy and happy is your relationship?
Consider these questions:

- What needs do you expect your relationship to fulfill for you?
- What is your partner willing to do to meet your needs?
- Has he let you down often by not meeting them? How?
- What are your partner's needs for your relationship?
- What you are willing to do to meet his needs?
- Have you let him down by not meeting those needs? How?
- Have you have sacrificed your own needs to meet those of your partner? How?
- Can you list three enjoyable and rewarding ways that could help you to satisfy each other's needs?

"STEPMOTHERS SPEAK"

I'm scared that my marriage is going to be wrecked because of the fights we're having over my husband's children. He doesn't understand what I'm upset about.

—SAD STEPMOM

Characteristics of Healthy Relationships

Good marriages are not free of bad times, crises and stress. In his research, Dr. Gottman has found that conflict is an integral part of marriage. It isn't the degree of conflict itself that distinguishes good marriages from ones that will probably end in divorce, but how conflict is handled.

Dr. Gottman and his colleagues have shown that, on the average, only 31 percent of conflicts between couples are ever resolved. In healthy marriages, he says, couples learn to manage or ignore the approximately 69 percent of issues that cannot be settled. He advises couples not to waste time trying to fix unresolvable problems, but instead, to strengthen their relationships by focusing on what they have in common.

It's the small, daily, positive actions that keep relationships strong. Often, Dr. Gottman notes, when couples are struggling, it is not necessarily because there is more negative behavior than in the past, but because couples have often forgotten the many kind and thoughtful gestures they exchanged in the early period of their relationship. To avoid getting into this rut, it's a good idea for both partners to express appreciation frequently for the things that they do for each other. As you learned in the previous chapter, expressing gratitude benefits you in two ways. When you thank your partner for his good deeds, you make him feel good and remind yourself of his positive contributions. So thank your partner often. You may need to model this behavior before your partner understands that it's equally important for him to acknowledge you for all that you do.

Some people resist giving thanks to their partners for doing chores around the house. After all, they reason, why give thanks every time someone merely does what he's supposed to do? It is a choice, however, whether or not to follow through with our assigned tasks. If we don't receive acknowledgment for our efforts, we tend to grow resentful, and a negative atmosphere begins to permeate

the home. By thanking our partner each time he walks the dog,
takes out the garbage or mows the lawn, we are creating a positive
emotional climate in our households.

Dr. Gottman also found that happily married people notice
and respond to their partners' small bids for attention. He recommends that partners "turn toward each other," by observing and
acknowledging each other's verbal and nonverbal cues. Responding
to a glance, being receptive to a pat on the arm or chuckling at a
partner's joke all demonstrate that you are paying attention to
your partner and care about him. If you ignore your partner,
you communicate a lack of interest, and he may look elsewhere
for attention.

People in healthy relationships tend to focus on the positive,
and give each other the benefit of the doubt. These couples act as a
team by "turning toward each other," having fun together, sharing
values and goals, and also by compromising and overlooking any
irresolvable issues or personality differences. They have the tools
to defuse tense, angry exchanges and return to a calm state rather
quickly after a disagreement. Dr. Gottman and his colleagues have
determined that in such couples, positive interactions outweigh
negative ones by a ratio of at least five to one. Couples who have more

negative interactions than positive ones, or even an equal number of negative and positive interactions, can be headed for trouble.

Dr. Gottman observes that couples in unhealthy relationships use four types of negative, highly destructive means of communication: being critical, contemptuous and defensive, and stonewalling (giving a partner the "silent treatment"). All couples resort to these behaviors once in a while, but if used often, they begin to erode a relationship.

Unfortunately, there are ample opportunities for negative communication in stepfamilies. See if you can relate to this common scenario. You see a problem in your stepfamily and bring it up with your partner, hoping to resolve it. Your partner interprets your observation as criticism and becomes defensive. You feel that he is not dealing with the problem, so you get angry, say something unkind and your partner then withdraws and ends up stonewalling you. In the end, the problem does not get resolved, and is simply swept under the carpet. Over time, this cycle repeats itself.

Negative vs. Positive Communication Techniques

How frequently do you and your partner resort to being defensive, critical, contemptuous, or to giving each other the silent treatment? Be honest with yourself.

"STEPMOTHERS SPEAK"

I have found that when I thank my husband for doing chores around the house, his eyes light up, he really feels good, and then he thanks me more for all the stuff I do at home. Saying thanks begets thanks.

—FILL-IN MOMMY

In your journal:

- Think about the last few disagreements you had with your partner. How did you handle these conflicts?

- How do you deal with conflict in general? Do you try to avoid it as much as possible? Do you tend to hold things in until you can't stand it any longer and then explode in frustration? Or are you the type of person who openly expresses how you feel and shares negative thoughts as freely as positive ones?

- Do you try to smooth things over when disagreements arise? Do you become afraid that your relationship is going to deteriorate or end if you experience conflict with your partner? Or are you the type of person who can tolerate conflict and can deal with a problem, whatever it may be?

Too often, relying on the four negative elements of communication begins to weaken a relationship, and eventually leads to its demise. Learning a few tools for positive communication can help you address conflict in a more constructive way.

Have you noticed that sometimes it can take just one sentence from your partner to trigger a big blow-up? "You remind me of your mother" is an example of one phrase that can set off a major fight. After it's over, you may not even be sure what happened and what the argument was about. Frequently, too, fights are triggered when one partner misinterprets the underlying meaning of a word or phrase. Don't assume that you understand what your partner is saying. Ask him for clarification so you can be sure you are responding to what he actually means.

Keeping silent and then finally exploding can be another problem, hurting both your relationship and your own emotional health. Many stepmothers bottle up our feelings until one incident too many finally makes us erupt with rage. I'm guilty of this myself.

My husband is a caring and committed father who, like many other divorced parents, felt guilty for any trauma his daughter experienced because of his divorce. To give her the security and stability she needed, he made a vow to uphold his visitation schedule by being punctual and consistent. For more than five years, he faithfully followed the schedule without exception, until an occasion arose when he had agreed to go away for a long weekend with me, which meant that he had to take his daughter back to her mother's home an hour early.

Before our trip, my husband told me how much he was sacrificing to go on vacation with me because he had to take his daughter back early. I suddenly found myself screaming with rage, "You're sacrificing one hour of your time with your daughter. Well, I've sacrificed every other weekend for the past several years, spending time with you and your daughter rather than doing what I wanted to do. Tell me, how big is your sacrifice compared to what I've done for you?" My husband was shocked by my outburst. He had no idea that I felt I was giving up so much to be with him and his daughter. Of course, I felt terrible that I had lost my temper. In retrospect, I wish I had told him early on that something was bothering me, rather than letting my resentment build until I blew up, shocking us both.

When we hold in negative emotions, long-term frustration and depression, as well as many physical problems will often develop. For your sanity and welfare, as well as for the harmony of your relationship, it is important to deal with these issues as they occur.

Remember that there is a difference between exercising self-restraint and suppressing feelings. When you exercise verbal self-restraint, you decide when, where and how you raise sensitive topics. You understand that there is an appropriate time and place to discuss certain issues, and you do your best to communicate calmly, without a negative attitude or anger, to avoid hurting your partner. This is important for the success of any relationship, whereas suppressing your feelings, also called self-silencing, can be harmful to your well-being.

Self-Silencing Can Harm Your Health

When women resort to self-silencing during disagreements with their partners, they suffer more heart disease, even death, than do those wives who feel free to express themselves. According to Dr. Elaine Eaker, the lead researcher of the Framingham Offspring Study, which examined the relationship between marital communication and physical health, women who didn't speak their minds during marital fights were four times more likely to die than women who told their husbands how they felt. Interestingly, men who self-silenced during marital disagreements did not experience any health risk. Other studies have also linked self-silencing to physical ailments, such as irritable bowel syndrome, as well as depression and eating disorders. While there are times during an argument when it's important to keep quiet, women who hold in their feelings to an extreme degree run a greater risk of developing serious health problems.

In your journal, consider these questions:
- Are you afraid to express your opinions and feelings during a disagreement with your partner?
- Do you keep your opinions to yourself because you are concerned that your partner will be hurt if you tell him how you feel?
- Are you afraid you will be hurt if you tell your partner how you feel during a fight?
- Do you believe your "voice" is equally as important as your partner's in your relationship?

If you realize that you have a tendency toward self-silencing during arguments with your partner—and especially, if you feel that your health may be harmed—then becoming more open in your relationship may be extremely important for you.

Expressing our feelings is important, but *how* we express them also matters. When we share negative feelings with our partners, we need to be aware of the nuances in our communication. Hashing out differences in destructive ways can have serious physical as well as emotional effects. The remainder of this chapter will be devoted to how to create a safe, health-supportive and open atmosphere in which to express conflicts with your partner.

"STEPMOTHERS SPEAK"

I learned an important lesson the hard way. My husband would focus exclusively on his children when they spent weekends with us. I bottled up my feelings of rejection until I came down with a terrible case of hives. My doctor told me they were caused by stress, and that I needed to talk to my husband about how I felt. It was never as clear to me how interrelated mind and body are. Take my experience so you don't end up suffering from migraines and other ailments, and talk to your husband, even if you are uncomfortable doing it.

—Serene Stepmom

The Right Way to Share Feelings

Partners don't always have to agree with each other. It is important, however, that they understand each other. Feeling understood is a very important need for us, almost as essential to our survival as food, water and shelter, and it is a vital ingredient in a healthy relationship. When you are discussing important issues with your partner, don't assume that he already understands how you feel. He probably doesn't, since his experiences are most likely different from yours. Focus first on becoming more open with him.

Your feelings and beliefs often stem from childhood experiences, which you should share with your partner. It will be much easier for your partner to understand how you think if he is privy to your past. The reverse is also true—you will understand his feelings with more sensitivity if he tells you about the experiences that have most shaped him.

Using the "I" Point of View

Using "I" statements and speaking from the "I" point of view can help defuse tension. It is helpful to address these issues from the "I" perspective. Rather than saying, "Your daughter is whiny and manipulative," it is better to say, "I have difficulty being with children who are irritable. It gets on my nerves. Is there anything you can do to help me?" Or, as another example, it is preferable to say, "I have trouble concentrating when your children make noise," rather than, "Your kids are so noisy." The distinction may seem minor, but there's a greater chance of avoiding a defensive reaction from your partner when you speak from the "I" perspective.

Every relationship has "hot button" issues that cause particular stress, and these need to be dealt with head-on, rather than "swept under the carpet." When you are talking about difficult topics with your partner, Dr. Gottman asserts, using kind words and a gentle tone of voice can go a long way. Instead of holding in your negative feelings, express yourself fully, but in a calm and constructive way. This is an opportunity to develop a closer bond. Isn't it amazing how we can be respectful to strangers, yet lack the same decency when we communicate with our partners? Intimacy is not an excuse to forgo good manners. When we learn to communicate with our partners with acceptance, love and respect, we can avoid "pushing each other's buttons."

We are more likely to resolve difficult conversations successfully as couples when we begin them gently. When a conversation is initiated harshly or critically, there is a high probability that it will end in bitterness and anger, with both parties feeling hurt, and with little resolved. When you begin a conversation with an attack—such as, "Why didn't you tell me about the change in plans? You obviously don't respect me, or you would have let me know about this"—chances are that you will provoke a defensive reaction, and the conversation will escalate into a fight.

Dr. Gottman recommends that instead, you launch a conversation with a "softened start-up." Opening a discussion gently increases the chances that understanding and consensus can emerge. For example, if you are upset that your partner did not tell you about a schedule change for your stepchild, it is better to begin by asking an open-ended question such as, "How was your day?" This way, you are providing your partner with the opportunity to share his feelings in a nonthreatening atmosphere. It is possible that he had wanted to communicate this information to you, but was too busy, forgot or was not sure how to express himself. After he tells you what he has experienced, you can gently point out what is upsetting you. You might say, "I know you were busy and forgot to tell me about the change in plans. But I feel disrespected when I'm not included in these schedule changes. Could you make sure you tell me about them in the future?"

How to initiate a conversation with a "softened start-up"

1. *Begin the conversation with a positive comment. For example, you might say, "You know how much I love and respect you." Or you also may begin with "I don't want to hurt you. I just want you to understand how I feel, so will you try to listen without becoming defensive?"*

2. *Don't make assumptions about your partner's perspective. He may not even be aware that there's a problem, and he may be happy to help solve it if you approach him gently.*

3. *Use "I" statements to express your viewpoint and your feelings. Don't assume that your perspective is the only possible truth.*

4. *State your requests clearly, firmly and politely.*

5. *Acknowledge any concessions that your partner makes.*

These steps are just the beginning of the discussion, not the conclusion, and you'll also need to have a number of other communication skills in your repertoire in order to succeed.

There's No Need to Hurt Someone You Love

For your family to truly be a loving unit, each partner should refrain from engaging in behavior that demeans the other. The University of Utah study found that 93 percent of couples who "fought dirty" by unreasonably yelling at and criticizing their partners were divorced within ten years. The way you communicate really does matter. It's best to avoid anger, name-calling, put-downs and sarcasm because these are very damaging to relationships. While you should be honest, it is also important to be diplomatic and compassionate. After all, you are talking to a person you love.

Before you initiate a conversation with your partner, always think first about what you would like to accomplish, then bear that intention in mind. If you are expressing your emotions just for the sake of releasing negative energy, talk to someone else. When you address your partner about problems with his children, for instance, try to discuss the ways he can help them improve their behavior—areas in which he has some influence—rather than complaining about their personality problems, which he cannot control. If you want your partner to know how frustrated you are with a family situation, and just need him to provide you with reassurance and support, be clear with him that this is what you are seeking.

Men tend to want to solve a problem or improve a situation. When a man feels incapable of resolving an issue, he often views himself as ineffectual, weak or a failure, and he is likely to become defensive. In fact, many stepmothers find that their partners get defensive when they attempt to discuss problems with them. Generally speaking, men like to avoid conflict, and this is one way they do that. This male strategy may be unconscious, but over time it can aggravate a problem, rather than resolving it, and their defensive behavior can put a stop to your attempts to have productive discussions.

One of my clients, Sydney, complained that she could not have a peaceful conversation with her partner about her stepson's manners without having it degenerate into a fight. Sydney was hurt that her stepson would not acknowledge her by saying hello when she came home from work. Instead, he would ignore her and continue playing a video game. Her partner did not correct his son's oversight. When Sydney would raise this issue with him, he would reply, "He's just a kid. It's no big deal. Let it go." This infuriated Sydney because she knew that her husband maintained a double standard; he would be upset if he were ignored in his own home. She also wondered how her stepson would learn to be polite to others if no one taught him the basics of good manners.

Within a few minutes of raising the issue of her stepson's lack of manners with her husband, Sydney would begin to cry from the sheer frustration of being unable to make him understand what was troubling her. Her tears would trigger an angry response from her husband; he would accuse her of manipulating the conversation. Sydney was desperate to change the way they spoke to each other, both for their own welfare and for the sake of their relationship. I suggested that she leave her emotions out of the conversation, and in a calm, neutral manner say, "I know you can do this. Tell your son to say hello to me when I come home. This is all I want." She followed this suggestion, her partner agreed to her request and the tension between them was greatly reduced.

Don't expect that your partner will be immediately receptive to all your comments. He may be defensive, no matter how you present your thoughts. The important point, from your perspective, is to remember to communicate respectfully. Be patient. It may take a while before his emotional walls come down, and he becomes capable of really listening to you.

Criticisms vs. Complaints

Dr. Gottman draws a crucial distinction: Criticisms are attacks on the other person, while complaints focus on specific behaviors. Don't belittle your partner when discussing a problem; rather, explain how a particular behavior of his (or of his children) adversely affects you. Rather than saying, "You're a slob," a statement assailing his character, you might share a complaint about his behavior: "I find it hard to be comfortable in our bedroom when clothes are strewn all around. Will you pick them up and put them away to help me feel more comfortable?" If you use criticism, you are eroding your partner's self-esteem, whether you intend to or not. Your relationship will be weakened, and rather than becoming stronger through teamwork, the two of you will end up as adversaries. When you address the problem rather than attacking the person, you are communicating with respect and helping to preserve your partner's sense of self-worth.

If you have to choose just one way to improve your relationship, Dr. Gottman recommends that you avoid being contemptuous of your partner. Contempt can take many forms, from rolling your eyes in exasperation to insulting your partner by calling him names. Expressing contempt is the most toxic and unhealthy kind of communication, and you should avoid it as much as possible. As much as you may want to call your partner a bad name—and no matter how aptly that name may seem to describe his behavior at the moment—refrain. It won't help him see the error of his ways, nor will it help him to correct his behavior. It is equally important that you don't tolerate contempt from your partner, either. It's just as inappropriate for him to call you insulting names.

66STEPMOTHERS SPEAK99

My partner tells me to mind my own business when I comment about the way he takes care of my stepdaughter. For instance, he will let her go to bed without taking a shower even though I have noticed—and pointed out to him—that she needs to bathe. He gets mad at me, makes an excuse for his laziness and tells me to stop interfering.

—CAN'T TAKE IT

Emotional Safety

Being in a committed relationship is an opportunity for each partner to heal from past emotional traumas, and to feel emotionally safe and secure after experiencing harsh judgments or having endured silent disapproval from parents, teachers or friends. Too many of us grow up believing that we must be perfect to avoid the anger or disappointment of those we love. Perfection is an impossible task for anyone to achieve; as human beings, it is only natural for us to make occasional mistakes. Ideally, a relationship can be a haven from damaging criticism. One goal of a healthy relationship is for it to be a place of acceptance and love rather than ridicule.

A Better Way to Fight

All couples argue at times. However, the happiest couples know how to defuse tension when it arises. Feeling understood is as important to us in the midst of an argument as at any other time. Successful couples de-escalate fights by showing that they understand the other's perspective. You may not agree with your partner's point of view, but you can still put yourself in his shoes and accurately repeat back to him what he is saying.

In his research, Dr. Gottman has found that happily married couples make more "repair attempts" than unhappily married couples. One partner may use conciliatory gestures, such as lightly touching their partner's arm, or may make a caring remark to soften the impact of a fight. Statements such as "I know this is hard for you" or "We'll work this out somehow" can balance the negativity of a bad moment. These are soothing reminders that you still care about each other. Even injecting a bit of humor can prevent tensions from boiling over. Such small gestures can trigger good memories of a shared past and are reminders of a promising future together.

Communication is hard work and requires the full use of all of your sensibilities and senses. Too often, we hold important conversations while we are doing other things, like driving, watching television or preparing a meal. Not only must you pay attention by actively listening to your partner, you must also notice the nonverbal cues he is sending you. Multitasking may be fine for some activities, but when you talk to your partner about a serious topic, everything else should be set aside.

When a discussion becomes too heated, successful couples often take a time-out. Since it's almost impossible to discuss any topic reasonably once you are upset, it's a good idea to take a fifteen- to twenty-minute break from an argument to calm down before you continue. Before the next argument, work together to come up with a signal, such as the one used for time-out in sporting events, to indicate that this is a good moment to take a break. During the time-out, be patient and focus on your breathing. Imagine that you have all the time you need to discuss this issue in a fair and loving manner. Besides releasing stress, time-outs also allow you to think about how to continue the discussion. Then, it's important to return to the conversation or nothing will be resolved. Rather than attempting to win an argument, try to find common ground so both of you walk away feeling satisfied.

During a heated discussion with your partner, follow these rules of fair fighting:

- Do not engage in physical violence or emotional abuse.
- Focus on the present.
- Deal with one issue at a time.
- Do not bring up past transgressions.
- Avoid critical or contemptuous remarks. Steer clear of sarcasm when making a point. Do not belittle each other's accomplishments.
- Do not engage in name-calling or cursing.
- Avoid accusations.

- Avoid modifiers like *always* or *never,* as in, "You always do this." Statements like this keep us stuck on a negative track, and do little to promote resolution.
- Do not give ultimatums or threats. If you get your way because your partner feels threatened, this will only lead to future problems.
- Remain calm. Speak softly.
- Make repair attempts.
- Seek compromise.

In your journal:
- Write down ten things you really like about your partner.
- Memorize them.
- Next time you find yourself frustrated with him, remember these positive traits to balance the negatives.

Clarify Your Role

For any relationship to succeed, both partners must be willing to compromise and show self-restraint. However, when one partner compromises to excess—usually the woman—that person can become miserable. Why does this happen more often to women? In many cases, little girls are still brought up to be cooperative and to please others, while little boys are raised to take care of their own needs first. These cultural beliefs become embedded in our adult relationships, and often cause trouble for stepmothers. Once we live with our partners, we tend to focus on trying to please them and their children, and put our own needs last. But that doesn't have to be if you make it very clear to the man you love just what you are and are not willing to do.

Your partner may be so preoccupied with his own emotions while "blending" the family that he may be entirely unaware of yours. He may think that if you are not complaining, everything is fine, and so remains oblivious to your mounting frustrations and resentments. In making your relationship with your partner a top priority, it is important to ask him to be clear about his expectations of you. Be sure to express how you feel about his expectations firmly and clearly. What many men don't understand is that the duties their ex-wives took on may not be acceptable to their new partners. Just because an ex-wife cooked and cleaned for him and his children does not mean you have to. Conversely, just because an ex-wife had certain limitations doesn't mean that you have to make up for them.

"STEPMOTHERS SPEAK"

When my stepdaughter was eight, I told my husband quite sincerely (and without an argument) that I just didn't have it in me to offer her much more than I was giving. I would be kind and helpful, but I was at the limit of my involvement. He got defensive at first, but things shifted after that, since I think for the first time he understood that she wasn't my daughter, and that I had the option of opting out altogether. He "got" it that he was lucky that I was doing as much as I was. I have to admit that, at the time, I was fed up enough that I was think- ing of leaving if I didn't start feeling better. I suppose this gave me the strength to speak up, and although I didn't make any threats, he picked up on that strength.

—NOT A "BRADY BUNCH" MOM

It is important for stepmothers to value our needs as much as those of others, but it is also important for our partners to consider our welfare and happiness as much as their own. For their new relationships to survive, the men in our lives may have to learn to compromise, something that may be difficult for them to do. They also may have to be willing to pitch in more around the house than they did before. This may go against traditional gender roles, but once you agree to more equal parenting and domestic responsibilities, it will lead to a closer bond.

Remember, you have a choice about what you do for your stepchildren. It is your responsibility to be kind, compassionate and respectful to them, but you don't have to cook, clean or chauffeur for them. Your partner, as the biological parent, is responsible for their day-to-day needs. Communicating with your partner about these issues with your stepchildren is an opportunity to get to know each other better, and build on the positive aspects of your relationship.

What Should We Discuss Before My Partner and I Get Married or Live Together?

Before marriage or cohabitation, it is important for all couples to discuss their expectations, goals and dreams for their future, in order to be aware of their similarities and differences, as well as any potential conflicts. If you haven't yet had this discussion with your partner, it's never too late to discover what is and is not negotiable, and to gain a better understanding of each other's needs and preferences. The following are some suggested topics for discussion:

1. *What are your expectations for maintaining your household? Do you agree about who will manage the different chores?*

2. *Who will be responsible for taking care of your partner's children? What does he expect you to do for them? What are you willing to do for them? Is compromise possible?*

3) *If you have children, what do you expect your partner to do for them? What does he expect to do for them? Is compromise possible?*

4) *What are your attitudes about disciplining children? What do you and your partner think are appropriate consequences when children misbehave? Work out your differences before problems occur, and make sure you both agree to the plan.*

5) *Do you and your partner have similar views about gender? Should boys be treated the same as girls? Should they share the same rules regarding their behavior? Do you expect their sexual behavior to be similar?*

6) *Disclose your health histories, both physical and mental, as well as those of all children and ex-partners. It's particularly important to know if any family member suffers from a chronic illness that requires long-term care. Will you be expected to shoulder additional responsibilities if one of your partner's children or his ex-wife has special needs?*

7) *Discuss your personal styles of communication. Do either of you need to work on being less defensive, critical or contemptuous? Do either of you tend to give the other the "silent treatment" when you're upset? Do you truly listen to each other and consider one another's ideas and complaints fairly?*

8) *Are you comfortable with openly discussing your sexual needs, preferences and fears? Many couples shy away from talking about sex. It is far preferable to work out any differences prior to marriage. Consider sharing books on the topic, if necessary, to get the conversation going.*

(9) Discuss how you will handle money as a couple. What are each of your financial obligations and goals? Do your ideas about spending and saving mesh? Who will be expected to support the stepchildren and cover the household expenses? Would lack of financial resources hinder your ability to have a child of your own?

(10) How much time do both of you devote to work or other commitments? How much time do you expect to spend together? If your expectations do not match the reality of your current circumstances, what compromises can you work out?

(11) Are you supportive of each other's careers, hobbies and other interests? Do you encourage each other to pursue your dreams? If one of you were to be offered a career opportunity in a distant location, would you both be prepared to move even if it required greater physical distance from your stepchildren?

(12) Have you reached a clear understanding of each other's spiritual beliefs and needs, and have you discussed when and how the children will be exposed to religious or moral education?

(13) Discuss your respective definitions of appropriate boundaries. You are less likely to commit boundary violations when you understand where your partner's boundaries lie.

(14) How much conflict does your partner experience with his ex-wife? How much contact does he anticipate having with her? Will conversations be restricted to their children, or will they include chats about their lives? Discuss how the two of you could work as a team during any possible times of stress with her.

(15) *Do you like and respect each other's family and friends? Do you think they may interfere in any way with your relationship? Are they supportive of your relationship? If they aren't, how will the two of you deal with their disapproval?*

(16) *Are there some things that you and your partner are not prepared to give up in your relationship? Make a list of nonnegotiable items and discuss them with each other. My husband and I did this before we married, and he was surprised by the items on my list. I only had two: monogamy and travel. He easily agreed to be monogamous, but he had to think about travel. He wasn't accustomed to visiting exotic destinations, and was worried about feeling uncomfortable or unsafe in strange places. After some thought, he agreed that as long as I considered his needs, he would travel with me. Travel is my passion. Although this might seem like a small thing to others, if he hadn't agreed to travel with me, I would not have married him. You may have other, similar potential conflicts to resolve before marriage.*

(17) *Do you feel confident that you and your partner are fully able to commit to your relationship? Do you believe that your bond can survive whatever challenges you may face?*

Don't shy away from these questions because you think you may not like your partner's responses. It is better to work out differences sooner rather than later.

For any relationship to endure, the positives must outweigh the negatives. If you and your partner have difficulty resolving the negative aspects of your relationship, consider seeking help from a couples counselor. Sometimes, professional intervention comes too late, because couples have waited so long that, after years of conflict, they are each entrenched in their respective points of view and are unwilling to listen or to compromise with each other. Learn a valuable lesson, and look for help before irreparable damage has been done.

Chapter Seven

Step 5: Balance Love and Money

Ever heard the saying, "Two can live as cheaply as one"? Some people assume that it is more of a financial strain for a woman to be single than to be married. And while single women may struggle to make a living, since they still earn considerably less when performing the same jobs as men, some women may not fare better financially when they marry a man with children from a prior relationship. If his child support and/or alimony are high, he may have little income left over for his new family. If you think you'll be better off financially if you marry, you could be in for a rude awakening. Some men may expect stepmothers to contribute money toward the care of their children, or pay for most of the household expenses.

Therefore, it is quite important for you to have specific information about your partner's financial commitments, as well as to understand his attitudes toward money. Equally important, he needs to understand your financial position, your commitments and your attitudes toward money. As with everything else in a good relationship, communication is essential.

Do you understand the financial side of your relationship? Is most of your partner's money going toward supporting his children and ex-wife? Will you have to work to help him support his children? Will you be able to afford a child of your own? These are questions that can significantly affect your life, and it is important for you to understand in advance what you will be getting into.

Money can be a big problem for stepmothers, as it is for other
women, for a myriad of reasons. For some women, problems stem
from a deep-seated, unconscious desire to be taken care of. As
young girls, we all heard the fairy tale stories about the prince on
the white horse who falls desperately in love with the heroine and
whisks her away to a wonderful new life. Growing up, many of our
fantasies were fueled by these romantic stories. Such fantasies can
persist into adulthood.

There are others who want to rescue a partner, tend to his
emotional wounds and help him achieve the success they think
he deserves. It's a wonderful feeling to contribute to a partner's
success, but fantasies of being taken care of and rescuing can
both cause us problems, if our reality does not match our
fantasy.

Our society as a whole frowns on frank discussions of finances. Money can actually be more uncomfortable for some couples to discuss than sex. So it is not surprising that a large number of stepmothers do not speak to their partners about financial arrangements before moving in together or getting married. They hope that things will just work out. It can take a long time—months or even years—before they gather the courage to have such an important discussion. This is a mistake. As a mature adult, you need to be aware of and take care of your own financial needs. Your future security and well-being are at stake. Even though you feel that your partner has your best interests at heart, it's vital for you to be knowledgeable about family finances and have a voice in financial decision-making. This is true even if you've never been interested in money matters—or feel intimidated by their complexity.

Understanding Your Feelings About Finances

Before initiating a conversation about finances with your partner, you may want to think about your own financial situation, and examine your attitudes and values toward money.

In your journal, answer the following questions:

- How would you evaluate your spending pattern? Do you save money regularly? Do you spend most of the money you earn?
- What is most important to you? Rank these in order, from most important to least important:
  - Owning a home
  - Education for yourself and your children
  - Travel
  - Clothes
  - Cultural activities
  - Sporting activities

- Material objects, such as a computer, camera, television, stereo, or other items
- A car
- Jewelry
- Art
- Pets
- Other activities

- Are you in debt? What are your personal financial obligations? Do you have outstanding student loans? What are your overall liabilities?
- What is your perspective about debt (including student loans, car loans and mortgages)? How do you feel about owing money to a credit card company or a mortgage company?
- What are your assets? Do you own a home? Do you have a savings account? Do you have a retirement account?
- How did your family of origin handle money? Were they comfortable with it? Did they struggle financially? Who paid the bills? Who held the power with regard to financial decisions? (Your father? Your mother? Was it shared equally?)
- How did your family spend most of their money? On the children? On the parents? On the house? On luxury items? On savings?
- How do you expect money to be spent in a family—primarily by the wife? By the husband? For the children? For the home? For savings?
- How did you handle money when you were in former relationships? Did you pay for almost everything in the relationship? Did your former boyfriend or husband pay most of the expenses? Did you split costs equally? Were conflicts about money partly responsible for ending your relationship?

- What role do you believe each partner should play in earning money? Making financial decisions? Managing financial resources?
- Are you secretive or open about what you earn and how you spend your money?
- What mistakes have you made with your money? What have you learned from those mistakes so you won't repeat these mistakes in the future?

As you can see from these questions, financial issues are complex even when they involve one person. When there are two of you, they become even more complicated.

Our feelings about money usually come from the way we were raised. If you have a partner whose parents had a similar style to yours, you may not experience any conflict when it comes to managing your finances. But if you grew up with significant differences in attitudes toward handling money, the two of you are likely to have different approaches about how money should be saved and spent. There may be other reasons, too, why you and your partner have different styles of dealing with money, and you need to be aware of what they are in order to be able to discuss and resolve them.

If you feel awkward talking about financial issues with your partner, consider why that is. Some of us are afraid to bring up the subject because we believe our partners will be uncomfortable talking about their finances. Are you trying to protect your partner from feeling hurt and embarrassed about the state of his financial affairs? Some of us are afraid to bring up a discussion about money because we don't want to disclose our own financial situation—we may have outstanding debts, or conversely, a lot of money that we don't want others to know about. Some women were taught that it is rude to discuss money, and that this topic is taboo, even with close partners. Others are afraid that they won't like what they'll find out when discussing this with their partner. Can you identify with any of these issues?

Whatever has prevented you from discussing finances in the past, both of you should lay your cards on the table now, since this is an important issue that can have a major impact on your relationship. As you and your partner deal with your finances, realize that there are both practical and emotional aspects to consider.

The Importance of an Open Discussion

Studies show that couples fight about money more than about any other topic. When couples have children from prior relationships, this can be an even more sensitive issue. Your partner may have had unpleasant financial experiences in his previous marriage, and may have continuing financial obligations from that relationship. His experience may color his current attitudes and further compli- cate his relationship with you. If you want to avoid fights with him about money in the future, share your beliefs about family finances with him now, clearly and calmly.

ONE STEPMOTHER'S STORY: LYDIA

Lydia came to work with me because she was upset about her finances. She was fighting with her new husband, who didn't share her perspective on saving for the future. She believed that a good portion of a person's salary should be put aside for retirement, while her partner liked to live well in the present. Consequently, he had accumulated more than $25,000 of debt. When they married, she had paid off his debt, and made the entire down payment on the home they purchased. She was upset that her husband was continuing to purchase expensive items for their home and his children, and beginning to run up credit card debt once again. They hadn't discussed finances before marrying, and had established joint savings and checking

---

accounts. Lydia regretted this decision and wanted to separate her money from her husband's, fearing that he was going to jeopardize their future. She refused to bail him out of debt again.

I asked her to write down what was bothering her, and to rank the items in order of priority. Then I asked her what she wanted to communicate to her partner. Lydia said that she really wanted him to respect her need to save money. She wished that he would share her goal, but she felt that wish was secondary to having him acknowledge and respect her needs. She said, "Saving for the future is part of my DNA. If he can't understand this about me, he doesn't get who I really am." I suggested that Lydia write down her specific complaints. That way, when they talked, she could stay on the subject without straying, and they could refer to her notes afterward, if necessary.

This exercise helped Lydia remain calm when she talked to her partner, and she felt he finally understood what she had been trying to communicate to him for months.

Unless you are a wealthy couple, financial considerations may play a big part in your childbearing decisions, as well. All couples must decide if they want to have children, and this decision is greatly affected when one of the partners already has them. Some stepmothers have to let go of the dream of having a child when finances are limited in their new relationship. Not all women want to have children, and, for some, maternal instincts may be fulfilled by stepchildren. But if that is not true for you, you must deal with the issue. If you give up the idea of having a child, will you regret your decision for the rest of your life? Although breaking up is difficult, staying in a relationship where such a fundamental need will not be met may be a far more painful choice in the long run.

How to Speak About Finances Without Fighting

It's easy to get upset when discussing finances, but don't allow your emotions to overrun reason. Try to remain calm and relaxed, and stick to one issue at a time. As long as you maintain your composure, your blood pressure will remain at a normal level. But once your body becomes physiologically aroused, you will tend to focus only on your emotions. If your partner also becomes upset, it is likely that the two of you will react to each other's emotional states, rather than staying centered on the topic.

You can begin a conversation about finances by saying something like "I'm a bit uncomfortable talking about this, but I feel that it's important for us to discuss it. Let's try to be as open and honest as possible so we can really understand our financial situation as well as our feelings about money. These are some very basic questions that affect most couples, including us, and we need to address them."

Here are some questions that you and your partner should consider discussing:

(1) *How are you going to handle your earned money? Will you have joint or separate checking and savings accounts, or some combination of the two?*

(2) *If separate accounts are established, which expenses will be paid from each account?*

(3) *How are you going to handle money that you each earned or inherited prior to this relationship? Will you keep it separate or pool your resources?*

(4) *How will your prior debts be handled?*

(5) *Will assets acquired during the remarriage be held in joint or separate ownership? (Be sure to know the specific laws regarding these issues in the state where you live, since*

state laws vary. Even if assets are held separately, they may be considered joint property in certain states.)

(6) *Who will be responsible for paying bills and keeping financial records organized?*

(7) *How will unexpected expenses be dealt with?*

(8) *What financial obligations do each of you have to your families?*

(9) *Make separate wish lists of the things you want to do and the purchases you would like to make in the future. Then compare lists, discuss similarities and differences and the compromises, if any, you are willing to make.*

Developing a Financial Strategy

There are basically three strategies that remarried families use to deal with finances: (1) You can decide to pool all of your financial resources, and allocate funds according to the family's specific needs as they occur; (2) you can keep your finances separate, with each partner retaining control over his or her own income and expenses; or (3) you can combine the two options, with each of you maintaining a separate account, plus a joint account for combined household expenses.

Depending on your particular situation, it may take a while to develop a joint financial strategy that works for both of you. If your circumstances change over time, you may want to switch from one approach to another. Talking about your feelings, as well as the different options available to you, is the only way to arrive at a financial arrangement that supports a warm and loving relationship.

One of the stepmothers in the online chat room asked the others for financial advice:

My husband and I argue about bills and his child support
all the time. I don't feel that any of my paycheck should be
spent on his daughter, including his child support payments.
I wasn't there when she was born; we didn't even know one
another. Therefore, his daughter is his responsibility, not
mine. I think his paycheck should have to pay for her care. He
says that we should split the bills. He believes that is only fair.
I am happy to split household bills, but not child support.
What do you think?

—Resentful

The responses to her question were unanimous: Every couple must decide for themselves how to split expenses. As with so many other stepfamily issues, there is no one correct way of doing things; there are merely different options. It's not how you share expenses that determines the health of your relationship; it's how you communicate about your decisions.

Child support payments can present problems for many stepfamilies. The amount of support a child receives, which is determined at the time of divorce, may not be sufficient to cover the child's expenses in the future. After a certain period, your partner may feel obligated to provide more support for his children, or the biological mother may go back to court to request more support. Modifying child support payments is a time-consuming and expensive process that can create stress, and result in greater support payments or large legal fees. On the other hand, your partner may have difficulty paying the predetermined amount of child support if he loses his job or becomes ill, and this, too, may create hardship for your stepfamily.

Even though you may not be legally obligated to contribute to child support for your stepchildren, you may feel pressured by your partner to help, or you may feel morally obligated to provide money for your stepchildren when they need extra assistance. Also, child support may not cover unforeseen expenses, like braces or other health issues or tutoring. Such expenses may cause financial stress for the family, particularly if they come at the same time that you need home repairs or were planning a long-deserved vacation. It's important that you participate in all such financial decisions.

What about additional expenses for your stepchildren that you may feel are nonessential, such as school trips, piano lessons or a car? Some people believe in providing their children with as many material advantages as possible, while others believe that less is better. What will you do if you and your partner have different attitudes about these add-on expenses?

"STEPMOTHERS SPEAK"

I'm the one who suffers. I get broken promises, extra bills and no consideration from my husband. This isn't about my stepchildren. It's about how my husband bows down to his ex and gives in to every financial demand she makes, in addition to the child support he pays monthly. I believe that as long as he is comfy and cozy at my expense, he doesn't care that she is breaking me financially and emotionally.

—ALMOST NUTS

Do you believe that the way expenses for your stepchildren will be handled are fair to you? These are some basic questions that you need to address:

- Who will be responsible for your stepchildren's everyday expenses? Will expenses for biological children be dealt with separately from those for stepchildren?
- Is the child support your partner is paying or receiving adequate for his children's needs?
- If you are receiving child support, how will that money be used?
- Who is responsible for your stepchildren's health care decisions and expenses (including health insurance)?
- How will you handle college tuition for your stepchildren?
- Who receives the tax deductions for your stepchildren?

Preparing for Unexpected Life Events

If you are like most stepmothers, you hope that your relationship will last for many years, and you don't want to even consider what would happen if your partner is suddenly no longer alive. Have you discussed drawing up wills in the event that a tragedy occurs? Many couples, especially young ones, do not see the necessity of having wills when they marry. What to do if one of you dies prematurely can certainly be uncomfortable to discuss, particularly when you are young or in the throes of a new relationship. But it can be even more devastating if you don't deal with these issues. Your financial security depends on your willingness to face these possibilities and take responsibility for your financial future.

Dividing a deceased partner's assets becomes more complicated when children and an ex-wife are involved, and you have more potential to be hurt. For instance, if you moved into your husband's home after marriage, where will you live if he dies? While some states protect a surviving spouse when a will does not exist, other states do not. If a husband has a prior will that leaves his assets, including his home, to his ex-wife and children, a second wife could be forced to move out of the home they shared. Would you feel comfortable if your husband left all his money to his children? If you have children from a prior relationship, you, too, may need to discuss distribution of your assets in the event of your death. Preparing wills for each of you and reviewing them annually are of paramount importance to stepfamilies.

Questions to think about:
- Do you have life insurance? Who is the beneficiary? Will the children be protected?
- Do you each have a will? Who are your beneficiaries? Will you have enough to live on if your partner dies?
- If your partner has a pension or retirement plan, who will receive the benefits upon his death?

If you are considering marriage, do you need a prenuptial agreement? Do you have assets that you want to protect in case of divorce? For many young couples marrying for the first time, it is acceptable to risk waiting to discuss wills until the relationship reaches a deep enough level of trust. But for stepmothers, it is important to discuss wills in the beginning of the marriage, or even at an appropriate point in a serious relationship before marriage. It could take some time before your partner is comfortable providing for you in his will. Is this acceptable to you? Depending on your financial situation and your beliefs about marriage, you may or may not want to go along with this. You can't force someone to give you something just because you want him to, or believe it is fair, so the best way to accomplish your goals is through clear and sensitive communication.

Here are some basic guidelines about financial planning for you to consider:
- It is important to discuss finances with your partner, no matter how uncomfortable that may be.

- As an integral member of your stepfamily, you are entitled to participate in family financial decisions, and have a say in how money is spent. If you don't have a full voice in this area, then more than likely you will develop resentments, which will cause future problems for both you and your relationship.

- It is crucial for you to develop mutual trust and respect for each other about finances. One way to build trust is by discussing, agreeing to and then implementing a plan of action together. Teamwork doesn't develop by magic—you and your partner will become a team by working though difficult issues together.

- It is important to avoid power struggles when dealing with money. Money represents power and control for many people. Ideally, you and your partner will strive for equality in every aspect of your relationship, including decisions about how money is spent. Too often, I have worked with stepmothers who earn most of the income in their stepfamilies, but have little say in spending decisions, which eats away at their self-esteem. How ironic! You need to be in a relationship that enhances your self-esteem and nurtures the positive feelings you and your partner have for each other.

- Remember that you don't have to be an expert in every area of finance. Consider using the services of a financial planner if you don't know how to plan to pay for a home, college or retirement.

- You can also seek legal advice if you are uncertain about how to proceed with wills and estate planning. Laws vary from state to state, so be sure to find out about the specific laws in your state, rather than making assumptions that may hurt you in the future.

Rather than dampening romance, discussing these practical concerns in your relationship can give you the sense of security and common goals that allow love and romance to flourish. So, don't hesitate to be proactive in protecting your financial life!

Chapter Eight

Step 6: Set Clear Boundaries

M any of the problems that stepmothers experience with partners, ex-wives and stepchildren are boundary violations. You may be unfamiliar with the term, but I'm sure you can relate to the actions it describes. Consider the frustration you would feel if your privacy were invaded by an ex-wife calling ten times a day to speak to your stepchildren. That is an example of a boundary violation, which is, unfortunately, all too common. These types of boundary violations can hurt feelings and damage self-esteem.

To maintain your emotional well-being, it's important to establish clear boundaries that protect your privacy and personal space. Oftentimes, stepmothers tolerate these transgressions because they don't believe they have a choice if they want to stay with their partners. Many stepmothers don't know how to define our personal space to prevent others from emotionally stepping on our toes.

Boundaries are important in all areas of life—at work, in friendships—but they are especially important in stepfamilies, since there are so many members involved, each with a different set of potential issues. It's crucial that you develop and maintain healthy boundaries, along with respectful and compassionate ways to enforce them.

Defining Boundaries

Boundaries are personal rules that distinguish our beliefs and values from those of others, and define what behaviors we consider appropriate in our relationships. We need to state these differences to define where one person ends and the other begins.

There is no emotional equivalent of a physical layer of skin. Unlike the way our skins protect us physically from the outer world, there is no built-in safeguard for preventing other people's emotions, attitudes and beliefs from influencing us emotionally. So, to ensure that we are not overpowered or overburdened by demands or interference from others, we construct boundaries composed of rules and behaviors expected of others to:

- Protect our privacy, possessions and sense of autonomy.
- Help us to recognize our uniqueness, value our own opinions and trust our own judgment.
- Make it possible for us to ask for help when we need it, and to handle rejection when others deny our wishes.
- Show us when to say yes or no to requests from others.
- Allow us to find personal happiness and fulfillment and give us the wisdom to let others live their lives without our interference.
- Regulate the pace at which we get to know others, allowing us to share personal information gradually as trust develops.
- Most important, they protect us from physical, emotional or sexual abuse.

Each of us develops a unique set of boundaries, influenced by our culture, our families and the experiences we had growing up. For example, some of us grow up in cultures that encourage members to hug and kiss when greeting each other, while other cultures endorse a handshake, a less physical form of social contact. Our greeting ritual shapes our level of comfort with physical contact when meeting others. As another example, some of us grew up in homes where bedroom doors were closed to maintain privacy, while others had families with an open-door policy. Something as simple and basic as whether bedroom doors are kept opened or closed can affect what we consider appropriate physical and emotional contact.

Ideally, boundaries should be clear, yet flexible enough to accommodate unusual circumstances. While some of us have developed healthy boundaries from childhood, others have only weak or overly rigid ones. Women with weak boundaries tend to have low self-esteem and troubled relationships. They may feel incomplete without a partner, and may give in to unreasonable requests, simply to avoid rejection or abandonment. They may ignore their inner voices and compromise their values and beliefs to please others and head off conflict. Women with weak boundaries often think their own needs are secondary to others', and believe their first responsibility is to keep others happy and fulfilled.

In the Steps for Stepmothers online chat room, "Mrs. Nice Guy" complained that her work as a paralegal was suffering because of the excessive requests made by her teenage stepdaughters. Mrs. Nice Guy worked most days at home and was paid at an hourly rate, while her husband and his ex-wife worked long hours in the city. The stepdaughters lived only a couple of miles away with their mother, and constantly rode their bicycles to her house, asking her to drive them to the mall or to soccer practice. At first, she gladly chauffeured them to their various activities because she wanted them to like her, but when their requests grew and her salary began to decline, she began to feel like a free taxi service. She was afraid to say no to them for fear that they might reject her. She was also concerned that her husband would not understand that her need to work was more of a priority to her than being constantly available to her stepdaughters.

Can you identify with her fears? Have you ever sacrificed your own work or needs to take care of others? Have you ever been afraid that your partner would resent you for taking care of yourself? If so, your boundaries may be too weak. While it is nice to help out family members and friends at times, it is also important to be able to say no when a request is too inconvenient or difficult for you to undertake. It isn't emotionally healthy to do a favor just because you fear you will suffer negative consequences if you don't comply.

On the other hand, people whose boundaries are too rigid are likely to avoid close interaction with others. They may fear abandonment or rejection, and handle this by withholding personal information or by refusing to ask others for help. They avoid intimacy by picking fights with others, or working long hours to avoid being at home with family members.

Another stepmother in the Steps for Stepmothers online chat room, "Craves Privacy," talked about her difficulties adjusting to being a stepmother. She complained that her two young stepdaughters were too needy, and that all they wanted to do was to play with her. She said she enjoyed playing with them for a few minutes at a time, and then she wanted to be alone to read, think or clean. She was surprised by the reactions to her post. Most of the other stepmothers said they were jealous of her and wished that their stepchildren wanted to spend time playing with them. They recommended that she appreciate the feeling of being wanted, because she wouldn't necessarily experience it in the future.

Can you identify with the desire of Craves Privacy to pick and choose the times she was involved with her stepdaughters? While everyone needs privacy, it is important to prioritize. Playing with young stepchildren is a good way to form an intimate relationship with them, and can be more important for your future emotional contentment than reading a book or folding the laundry. Of course, moderation is essential in all things. Playing with stepchildren to the exclusion of other activities does not provide balance and health in your life. However, if you resist getting close to others who benefit (rather than harm) your life, your boundaries may be too rigid.

How healthy are your boundaries?

In your journal, answer these questions:

- Are you sometimes unable to say no to a request from a family member or friend, even if it will be very inconvenient for you to comply?

- Do you find yourself disclosing a great deal of personal information to people you have just met?

- Do you trust the opinions of others more than your own?

- Do you often go along with your partner's wishes just to avoid conflict?

- Do you find it difficult to ask others for help?

- Do you find yourself compromising your values or integrity in order to avoid rejection?

- Do you often have sex because your partner wants to, rather than because you want to?

- Do you give to others excessively, or are you too demanding of them?

- Do you sometimes adopt the thoughts and feelings of your partner or a close friend?

- Have you ever spent time thinking obsessively about another person, to the detriment of your own work or studies?

- Do you frequently expect others to anticipate and fulfill your needs?

- Do you frequently avoid getting together with family and friends because socializing makes you uncomfortable?

- Do you frequently screen your phone calls to avoid talking to certain people?

- Do you try to keep certain people at arm's length so you won't be hurt by them?

- Do you avoid talking about anything personal with family, friends and coworkers because you don't want them to know anything about your life?

- Do you compartmentalize your relationships? Do you try to prevent your friends from getting to know each other because you are afraid you will be hurt or rejected if they become close?

Answering yes to more than three of these questions may indicate unhealthy boundaries. If you need to strengthen your boundaries or make them more flexible, don't despair. I will share several ways to help you do this. Understand that (as with any life change) this is a process rather than a one-time fix, and one that will take you practice and patience to master.

How do we establish healthy boundaries? First, we need to know who we are—what we like, need, want and don't want in our lives. Knowing who you are and what you stand for will help you resist pressure from others. It's vital to be honest with yourself about your true feelings and opinions. Once you develop stronger self-awareness, you must be willing to share who you are with the people in your life so that they can respect your personal space.

In your journal, answer the question, "Who am I?"
To help answer this question, consider:
- What are your political beliefs?
- What are your religious or spiritual beliefs and practices?
- What social policies do you believe are important? (If you were a philanthropist, what charitable causes would you fund?)
- What kinds of music, movies and art do you like?
- What are your favorite foods?
- What countries do you want to visit?
- What animals do you like?
- What are your passions?
- What are your pet peeves?

- What other characteristics and interests best
  describe who you are?

One way to tell if your boundaries are healthy is to examine
your feelings after you grant a request from someone close to you,
such as your partner, an in-law or a friend. If you feel good afterward, then you know your willingness to help stems from love and
compassion. If you feel bitter and resentful, then you need to evaluate
your motives. Perhaps you didn't feel you had a choice, and that to
remain part of that relationship, you had to fulfill all her requests.

Perhaps you are uncomfortable saying no to others because you
are a "people pleaser," someone who believes she must honor
everyone's wishes in order to maintain her relationships. If this
describes you, then you probably don't have much experience
turning down requests for help, regardless of how inappropriate
or inconvenient they may be, and you are afraid to let others know
what you will and will not do for them. People pleasers need to
learn the art of saying no, because the more they do for others,
the more others will demand of them.

Instead of being annoyed or frustrated when people make unreasonable requests, realize that you are better off communicating
honestly with them. Remember that it's your own responsibility
to protect your boundaries. No one else can do this for you.

What If You Feel Guilty?

You may be worried that if you say no to requests from your
partner or stepchildren, you will feel intensely guilty later. Such
feelings are a form of "afterburn," an emotional pain—comparable
to the sting one can feel after shaving—commonly felt after you
change your customary behavior. Remember that it is better to
experience afterburn as a result of establishing healthy boundaries
than it is to suffer the pain of letting others take advantage of you.

We can feel guilt when we cause (or think we have caused)

others pain or hardship, or when we make (or think we have made) a mistake. Guilt has an important role to play in preserving relationships, by motivating us to take other people's feelings into account and helping us to recognize and correct our mistakes. However, it can become a problem when it becomes excessive.

Many stepmothers suffer from too much guilt. Stepmothers set impossibly high standards for themselves, and their inner voices tell them that nothing they do is ever good enough. Excessive guilt can make it difficult to set boundaries, and lead to unhealthy actions. It can also interfere with your ability to make decisions, and can even be emotionally paralyzing.

Do you suffer from excessive guilt?
In your journal, answer the following questions:

- Do you torment yourself over every small transgression?
- Do you say you're sorry repeatedly when you have hurt someone's feelings or broken something that belongs to someone else?
- Do others tell you that you're too hard on yourself, and that you expect too much of yourself?
- Do you tend to be over-responsible? Do you work too hard in an attempt to make everyone in your life happy?
- Do you tend to believe that everything that goes wrong is your fault?
- Do you overanalyze your own behavior?
- Do you frequently worry that an action you take may have negative consequences for others?
- Do you believe that your relationships are so fragile that any mistakes you make could result in their destruction?
- When you feel you have made a mistake or hurt somebody, do you engage in negative inner dialogue such as:

    "If I feel guilty, I must have done something wrong."

"I can't do anything right."

"I am a bad person. I don't deserve to be happy."

"I am going to be punished for not taking care of others."

"I am being selfish if I take care of my own needs."

"I must have done something wrong if others fail at work, school or in a relationship."

"There is only one 'right' way to do things."

If you answered yes to two or more of these questions, you probably suffer from excessive guilt. Guilt is probably your biggest obstacle to taking better care of yourself. To define and better protect your boundaries, you will first need to confront these feelings.

Overcoming Guilt

Sometimes you have to make tough choices. Accept that once you decide to protect your boundaries, you *will* feel guilty for a certain period—see the guilt as a sign that you are on the right track. Making any kind of change is challenging, and it takes courage to persevere until the change becomes a natural part of your life. Rather than striving for perfection, try to understand that developing these new skills will take time and practice. At first, when you say no to an inappropriate request, you may sound strident to yourself. With practice you will be able to say no with greater ease. A simple "I'm sorry, I can't help you with that" or "Please don't do that. I'm uncomfortable with it" may be all that is necessary to stand up for yourself.

Before agreeing to do a favor, tell the person who requested the favor that you need a little time to think it over to make sure it fits your schedule. By giving yourself a few minutes, an hour or even a day to consider whether or not you can do something, you eliminate the pressure to say yes immediately.

In your journal, respond to the following questions:

- Think about various times when you went against your own interests: What, if anything, caused you to put others' needs ahead of your own?
- List your closest family members and friends, and think about whether each of them has healthy or unhealthy boundaries. Do they ever violate your boundaries? How?
- What requests do you consider appropriate to ask of family and friends? What are inappropriate requests?
- Do you often overlook boundary violations by others because you don't want to hurt their feelings?
- What, if any, negative consequences have you experienced due to weak boundaries?
- Have you missed out on closeness with anyone because your boundaries were too rigid?

Setting personal boundaries is not meant to threaten others. Nor is it a way to control a situation. It is simply a way to take care of your own needs and have a greater influence over your own life. It is one step toward taking responsibility for yourself, and living your life to maximize your own satisfaction and contentment.

Boundaries with Your Partner

Mature love requires healthy boundaries. Without them, people may settle for mediocre relationships that prevent them from reaching their full potential. Boundaries need to be strong, yet flexible, for partners to treat each other with dignity and respect.

When two people with healthy boundaries enter into a relationship, they can establish trust and security, communicate clearly without ambiguity, express their wants and needs openly. Each partner feels comfortable knowing that he or she will be listened to with care and compassion. Both partners are committed to their own personal growth as well as to building and strengthening the relationship.

Healthy boundaries allow partners to:
- Retain separate identities.
- Pursue their personal preferences and interests.
- Have the freedom to grow and develop.

What can you do if your partner does not have clear boundaries? First, consider what types of boundaries you want in your relationship. There are no right or wrong answers to the following questions. These are merely guidelines to help you define what is appropriate to you.

In your journal, respond to the following questions:
- Are you comfortable if your partner shares personal details of your marriage with his ex-wife, parents or friends? Is it acceptable if you divulge such details to your former husband or boyfriend, parents or friends?
- Do you feel it is appropriate to open your partner's mail or e-mail? Does your partner have your permission to open your mail or e-mail?
- Is it acceptable to you if your partner listens to your voice-mail messages? Is it acceptable if you listen to his?
- Would you object if your partner lent his children one of your possessions (such as a scarf, camera, coat or belt) without asking your permission?
- Do you share everything with your partner, or do you avoid disclosing certain information, such as what you have paid for certain items? Is your partner willing to share such information with you?
- How comfortable are you with nudity? Do you feel it is ever

acceptable for family members to walk around the house nude or partially clothed?

- Are you comfortable with family and friends dropping by unexpectedly? Do you want people to call before they come over?

After you answer these questions, you can discuss them with your partner. These questions may suggest other boundary issues and stimulate an important discussion with your partner. By stating your preferences to your partner clearly, you will make it easier for him to understand and respect you. Ask him to define his own preferences as well so you can appreciate and respect his point of view. Where your views differ, discuss how you might compromise so you both feel respected.

Poor Boundary Choices

Sometimes very intelligent people make poor choices "for the sake of the children" or to keep the peace with exes. One of my clients, Ivan, who had been recently divorced, told me that he was taking his two teenage daughters and his ex-wife to dinner to celebrate her fiftieth birthday. When I asked what had led to his decision, he said he was doing it for both his daughters and his ex-wife. He wanted his daughters to see that he and his ex could be friends.

I thought that his daughters might question why their parents had divorced if they still celebrated special occasions together and were acting like an intact family. They might wonder if their parents would eventually reconcile, and might resist getting to know anyone he or his ex-wife might date. While this decision had no immediate negative consequences for his daughters, I thought that it might send them confusing messages. For instance, the girls knew that their mother had initiated the divorce proceedings, and that she had been abusive to their father until the divorce was finalized.

Would they now believe it was acceptable to mistreat partners or be mistreated by them, and still remain friends? It seemed to me that this father was giving his daughters a poor role model for their future relationships.

Ivan said that he wanted to do something special for his ex-wife, since a fiftieth birthday is one of the "big ones." While the thought was admirable, I wondered whether this gesture would set a precedent for her. She might expect them to continue celebrating birthdays together, something that his future girlfriends would have difficulty accepting. Finally, I wondered if celebrating his ex-wife's birthday was a way for him to blur his own boundaries, delaying his acceptance that he was, in fact, divorced.

Sometimes, remarried fathers are so concerned about making sure that their children love them that they undermine our boundaries as stepmothers in order to look like the "good guy." Rather than reinforce our standards of conduct in the household, they ignore them, or undermine them. By doing so, they create a division in the parental unit, and they show disrespect for the boundaries that we, their partners, are attempting to create.

Children easily learn how to maneuver a situation to their advantage. In this example, the father taught his son that he didn't

"STEPMOTHERS SPEAK"

Why is it that my husband always makes me out to be the bad guy? Last night, my stepson decided he wanted to go home to his mom at 11:30 p.m. I told him it was too late for a thirteen-year-old boy to go home, but my husband brought him home.

—Wicked Stepmommy

have to respect his stepmother's wishes. The wife learned that she could not trust her husband to be sensitive to her boundaries. She felt that he was using her to make himself look good to his son, and she resented him for making her out to be the "bad guy." Not only did this man lose his wife's respect, but he may have also lost her support in future situations. This marital breach could easily have been avoided if the father had discussed his son's request with his wife behind closed doors, before making the decision that the boy could go home to his mother's. If he had honored her boundaries by telling the child, "Let me discuss this with your stepmother first," he could have avoided many problems.

What Possessions Are Appropriate to Keep?

Boundary issues can play out over long periods. What to keep from past relationships and what to throw away can be very sensitive issues for remarried couples. Some people are far more sentimental than others, and may want to keep photographs and other memorabilia from their former marriages. Some stepmothers feel that their boundaries are violated if their partners hold on to anything from their former life. One of the women in the online chat room asked:

> During a recent cleanup, my husband stumbled across the
> wedding video from his first marriage. He feels that he should
> save this for his kids, along with a note saying how "in love"
> they were. I am resentful and jealous that he wants to do this.
> I see no purpose in keeping a video that his ex-wife didn't want
> when she cleaned out the house. I don't want our biological
> child upset by watching his father make vows to another
> woman. Is it bad form to ask that this video be destroyed?
> —Confused Stepmom

In this example, the husband places the needs of his children first, by believing that they would appreciate having this wedding video and a note declaring the love that he and his ex-wife had for each other. He is not considering his present wife's feelings. She needs to tell him that she sees keeping this video as a form of disrespect to their union. However, she would be committing a comparable boundary violation if she destroyed a video that did not belong to her.

"STEPMOTHERS SPEAK"

We keep boxes of old photos in the basement for each family member. When the kids move out, they can decide whether or not to take these boxes with them. Destroying memories is permanent. Leave it up to your stepchildren to decide what to save and remember. You should not be the one to control that.

—JUST CHILL

Here is another example of the dilemma:

My stepson has wedding photographs of his mother and father in his bedroom. Both my husband and I want to show him that we care about his feelings for his mom and dad, yet we are concerned that, inadvertently, we are sending him a mixed message by having these photographs in our house. My stepson makes comments like "I wish you and Mommy could get married again." What do you think?

—NEED NO DRAMA

Most children of divorce want their parents to reunite, regardless of how bad their relationship was. Younger children, in particular, may be confused by seeing photographs of their parents together, and this can reinforce their fantasy of their parents reconnecting. As one stepmother said in the online chat room:

> I think this sends a mixed message. We went through a similar situation with my stepdaughter, who is now five years old. She expressed a desire that her mother go on vacation with us. We had a little discussion, saying that her mommy and daddy would never be together again. She mentioned a framed photograph of her mother and father that she'd seen in her room since she was a couple of months old. Now, we allow her to have pictures of her mother, but they are kept in a photo album that includes pictures of all of us.
>
> —Does It All

When boundaries are clear and consistent, stepchildren (and biological children) understand the structures of their new families, and their fantasies of reconciliation don't get out of hand. When you serve as a healthy role model for your stepchildren, you also set the tone for respect and cooperation in your household.

Safeguarding Stepchildren's Boundaries

Just as you want family members to respect your boundaries, you should be considerate of theirs. Some stepmothers, particularly those with full-time custody of their stepchildren, perceive themselves as the "true" mothers, even though they didn't give birth to the kids. This can happen when a biological mother abdicates her maternal responsibilities, leaving the stepmother to provide for all the children's needs. Yet, even if a stepmother feels like the sole

or primary mother, it violates her stepchildren's boundaries if she
pressures them to forsake their love for their biological mother.

A mother's neglect does not necessarily diminish the feelings a
child has for her. Even when a stepchild has a limited relationship
with his mother, or she is an inadequate caregiver, chances are the
child still maintains a strong sense of loyalty, along with a hope of
developing a better relationship with her in the future. You should
not tamper with that. It is not fair to expect your stepchildren to
criticize or betray their mother on your behalf.

You can respect the boundaries of your stepchildren by never
saying anything unkind about their mother in front of them. Be very
careful, also, when expressing negative sentiments about your husband's ex-wife to others—even when you think your stepchildren

are out of earshot. Most children have excellent hearing and like to listen in on adult conversations, particularly when they know they shouldn't. Even if your criticism is valid and justified, it will only hurt your stepchildren to know how you feel. The resentment this might produce could last for years, regardless of all the wonderful things you do for them.

Some biological mothers explicitly instruct their children to love them, and only them, and this is equally harmful to children. Biological mothers may say terrible things to their children about their stepmothers, without realizing the emotional damage this causes. If you experience this type of boundary violation, you are trapped between the proverbial "rock and a hard place." Refuting the nasty comments will only make you seem more like the stereotypical "wicked stepmother." On the other hand, if you remain silent, it may seem like an admission that the statements are true, and may create more inner conflict for the child.

While there are times that it is better to say nothing, there are other times when it is best for you to clarify and correct misinformation. If you are in this situation, focus on communicating with your partner in order to solve this problem. Do not, under any circumstances, act out on any resentment you may feel with your stepchildren. Any conflicts you have with your husband's ex-wife must stay between the adults—you, your husband and his ex-wife—and even if she does not honor this principle, make sure that you do.

It's also a good idea to extend this same restraint to all other close family members. Don't risk damaging your relationship with anyone in the family by criticizing or judging them. Remember that expressing your feelings in an offensive manner can cause long-term repercussions.

Needless to say, it's completely inappropriate to belittle, patronize or demean your partner in front of his children or anyone else, no matter how angry you are. If you criticize him in front of your stepchildren, you send them a message that it's all right to disrespect others, which is a very poor life lesson. Since their loyalties will most likely lie with their father, they will also resent your criticisms of him, even if he deserves them.

Boundaries with Ex-Wives

Some ex-wives do not demonstrate a good sense of boundaries. The appropriate level of contact between ex-partners depends on the ages of the children, the type of custody arrangement, the amount of interdependency between your partner and his ex-wife and the personal preferences of family members. For some custodial stepmothers, a once-a-day phone call to her children from the ex-wife may seem reasonable, but others may find it excessive. However, some actions are unacceptable under any circumstances.

Have you experienced any of these situations?

- Your husband's ex-wife asks for more money than the court stipulated for child support payments.
- She calls your home intrusively, at inappropriate times.
- She says negative things about you and your partner to your stepchildren.
- She undermines your attempts to build a positive relationship with your stepchildren.
- She asks you to help take care of your stepchildren during her scheduled times of visitation.
- She enters your home without permission.
- She changes the times she drops off or picks up the children without sufficient notice.

These are all examples of inappropriate behavior by ex-wives. How you handle them depends on your own sense of boundaries and those of your partner. One of my clients, Haley, complained that her live-in boyfriend jumped to respond to every request made by his ex-wife, regardless of the time of day or night. Even though he had been divorced for more than three years, he claimed that the sooner he responded to a request, the less interaction and aggravation he would have with his ex-wife. As an example, her boyfriend's ex lived in an apartment with large, heavy windows that were difficult for her to open and close. She would call him at midnight, asking him to come over to close the windows, so their son would not be in a draft and catch a cold. He would get out of bed and immediately leave to attend to the task.

At first, Haley didn't say anything to her partner about how she felt. After a while she became so annoyed by these untimely intrusions that she told him she didn't think he had to do every favor asked for by his ex-wife; some, she said, were inappropriate and interfered with their privacy. Haley's partner was defensive about his behavior, and said he didn't think he had to consult with her. Eventually, Haley broke up with him because she had lost respect for his inability to set boundaries. "I don't think he has a backbone," she said.

In an attempt to maintain peace at all costs, many partners are too accommodating to their ex-wives. They may justify their behavior by saying it helps their children, but in reality, it causes confusion for their children and ex-wives, and creates insecurity and discomfort for their new wives. Before you can discuss your view of appropriate boundaries between your partner and his ex, you first need to focus on developing healthy communication with your partner. Then the two of you can establish a set of rules that will keep her from encroaching on your time and space.

Understand that your partner may be resistant to change, even if you feel hurt by a boundary violation. He may be overly sensitive about the way he relates to his ex-wife (or children and parents). Knowing that other women have feelings like yours may give your partner more perspective. You may be able to prevent a negative reaction from your partner by describing someone else's experience. Sharing a story you've heard about someone whose partner insisted on maintaining too close a relationship with his ex and describing the problems this caused may help to you make your point in a way that your partner can understand and accept.

One stepmother complained in the online chat room that her partner was planning to stay at his ex-wife's home with his children while the ex was on a business trip. He failed to understand why his present wife was upset with this arrangement. After he read the responses of others in the chat room (which supported his wife's view), he grasped what was upsetting her and changed his plans.

If you believe that your partner will react defensively to a conversation about boundaries, or any other sensitive topic, consider writing him a letter. This will allow you the time you need to put your thoughts on paper in a calm, organized manner. Your partner can read the letter in private, when he is calm and receptive, and can reread the letter as many times as he needs to in order to understand what you mean. In addition to your complaints, remember to include suggestions for improving the situation, and the goals you are trying to achieve for your relationship.

Boundaries with In-Laws

Extended family members may inadvertently cause us emotional pain. For instance, you may be hurt if your in-laws invite your husband's ex-wife to a family function without consulting you first.

ONE STEPMOTHER'S STORY: KEISHA

One of my clients, Keisha, told me that while her mother-in-law was babysitting for her stepson and her biological daughter at Keisha's apartment, her partner's ex unexpectedly dropped by to give her son a sweater he had forgotten. Her mother-in-law invited the ex in for coffee;

Keisha arrived home to see the two women chatting at her kitchen counter. She was so angry that she walked out of the room without speaking to either one of them. Keisha was furious that her mother-in-law did not realize that she was violating Keisha's space by being hospitable to her partner's ex in her home.

To start, I asked Keisha to list the boundaries that were important to her. She had never defined her personal boundaries, and enjoyed this exercise. Her list was short and simple:

- I won't tolerate abuse of any kind.
- I want my family and friends to respect me.
- I want others to take good care of my home and possessions.
- I cherish my privacy.
- I want to communicate honestly and directly with others, and expect they will treat me similarly. I don't want others to talk about me behind my back.
- I want others to listen to me and value my opinions and feelings.
- As I mature, my boundaries can change. I am free to implement new boundaries as my needs develop.

Keisha realized that she had never told family or friends about her boundary preferences. How could she expect others to abide by them if they didn't know about them?

After Keisha created her boundary list, I asked her to outline what she wanted to communicate to her mother-in-law, and to rehearse it beforehand so she would be calm and comfortable during the conversation. She prepared this to say:

> *I'm not sure you know my house rules, so I want to*
> *explain them so you can abide by them in the future.*
> *My space is sacred to me, and I only allow friends into*
> *my home. Julia [her partner's ex-wife] isn't a friend,*
> *and I consider her presence in my home a boundary*
> *violation. I don't want to control what you do. You are*
> *welcome to have a friendship with her, but please do it*
> *outside my home. Can you promise me that you won't*
> *invite her into my home anymore? If you can't, I am*
> *sorry, but I will have to find another babysitter.*

Most people don't discuss their relationship preferences with others until a conflict occurs. We just assume that all of us share and agree to similar boundary rules. While this assumption may be perfectly natural, for your own mental health and peace of mind, it's best to clarify these issues before a problem arises.

In your journal:

- Make a list of the personal boundaries that you want to maintain in your relationships with others. Ask yourself these questions:

  - Is each of these a healthy boundary? Will it help you, and enhance your serenity?

  - Are you setting any of these boundaries as an attempt to control someone else's behavior or antagonize him? It's important to set boundaries for positive reasons, rather than to retaliate against those who bother you.

  - Are all the boundaries necessary? Do you need to let go of any of them?

- Look at your list every day to remind yourself of your boundaries, and be sure to abide by them.

- Whom do you consider to have healthy boundaries? Keep these people in mind. When confronting a challenging boundary violation, ask yourself: "How would that person handle this?" If your role model is a part of your life, ask her for suggestions.
- If you have difficulty saying no to others, look for opportunities to do so in an assertive, respectful manner. If you have difficulty saying yes, look for opportunities to practice doing so graciously.

Handling Boundary Violations

If you have stepfamily members who repeatedly violate your sense of appropriate behavior, you do not have to passively accept this. Let's discuss specific ways in which you can delineate your boundaries more clearly.

Before you initiate a conversation with a stepfamily member who has offended you, think about what you hope to accomplish. It may take you some time to figure out exactly what you are experiencing, and to define to yourself how the transgression affects you. Humans are complicated. Don't shortchange yourself by skipping over the process of examining how you truly feel. Consider clarifying your feelings using this simple outline:

- Feelings: What are you feeling?
- Goals: What do you want to accomplish?
- Behaviors: Which behaviors will you tolerate from family members, and which ones are intolerable?
- Consequences: What actions will you take if the disrespectful behavior persists?

Once you are ready to face the family member directly, first, try to learn what motives underlie her actions. You might say something like "I want to better understand your point of view. Can you explain to me why you invited my partner's ex into my home?

Did you realize that this might be an awkward situation for me?" An honest dialogue may clear the air.

Sometimes, merely expressing your feelings to the other person is sufficient, and may be all that you wish to accomplish. Communication is an important way to take care of yourself and to build your self-esteem. But there are other times when you have a specific outcome in mind, and you may need to take action to protect your space. For instance, since Keisha's objective was to keep her mother-in-law from inviting the ex into her home again, she might have had to replace her mother-in-law with another babysitter.

I recommended that Keisha let her partner know about her upcoming conversation with her mother-in-law, and be clear about what she expected from him, too. If she wanted him to speak to his mother to reinforce her boundaries, she could ask for this. If she simply desired his support and acknowledgment, she needed to say so. Many men tend to be solution-oriented, and unless you explain your needs, your partner is likely to focus on resolving the problem, rather than simply listening to you and supporting your feelings.

When stepmothers experience boundary difficulties with stepfamily members, our partners sometimes straddle the family fence, trying to maintain a neutral stance. Generally, we resent this tactic, because we want our partners to defend and protect us. Is your partner active or passive when conflicts arise in your stepfamily? If he is passive, you may need to let him know that you want him to take an active part in family situations, and support you by letting family members know which behaviors are appropriate and which are not.

Even when our partners do stand up to their families, this doesn't guarantee positive results. Men can have discussions with their parents, siblings or children about treating their wives with more respect and consideration, yet these conversations may fall on deaf ears. Still, it's important for you and your partner to work on such issues as a team. Working as a partnership will increase your chance of success and lead to greater mutual respect.

Holiday Celebrations

Holidays can be a particularly painful time for stepmothers, a time when boundary issues are most likely to resurface. Weeks before Renee, a client of mine, was to marry Daniel, he told her that he, his four children and his parents always spent holidays at his ex-wife's home. His ex-wife wanted to continue this tradition "for the sake of the children" after he remarried. Renee, a gifted chef, wanted to prepare a special dinner for her new family, and felt awkward about spending the holidays with Daniel's ex. Daniel wondered if his children would be hurt by this change. Renee responded that change was part of life, and boundaries were an important lesson to teach children.

Some stepmothers are excluded from happy occasions. This happened to me personally. My husband and I were not invited to my stepdaughter's Bat Mitzvah. My stepdaughter was so uncomfortable with the idea of her mother and father being together in the same room that she arranged to perform the religious ceremony in Israel and held a party "just for friends" in New York. Of course, I felt hurt by the exclusion and embarrassed to tell others that we weren't part of a special milestone in her life, even though I understood her discomfort, and felt bad for her.

This experience prepared me to expect similar painful feelings when my stepdaughter told us she was anxious about having us attend her college graduation. In deference to her feelings, we told her we would not attend. Why didn't we force the issue and insist on going? My husband regrets his decision to put his daughter's feelings of discomfort ahead of our desire to celebrate an important occasion with her. I, on the other hand, am uncomfortable attending an event where my presence is not welcome.

No matter how many years we are stepmothers, we may face experiences that hurt us to our cores and remind us of how much we remain outsiders in our own family. We are never immune from hurts, and must accept them as one aspect of life. Anticipating the pain and acknowledging it, as I was able to do when my husband and I didn't go to my stepdaughter's graduation, can make these painful experiences easier to handle.

Ideally, everyone should be invited to celebrations of major milestones like weddings or religious ceremonies. For other occasions, such as birthday and anniversary parties, Thanksgiving, Hanukkah and Christmas, new traditions will need to be established. All members of your extended family need to understand the importance of adjusting to the new family configuration.

How do you celebrate holidays? Think about:

- What aspects of the holidays are most meaningful and essential to you?
- What are some special ways you can celebrate the holidays, regardless of the actions of stepfamily members?
- Which family members are an essential part of your holiday celebrations? Whom would you prefer not to have present?

To avoid an unpleasant holiday experience, be sure that you arrange a celebration that is meaningful to you. Advance planning will lessen the impact of possible rejection or neglect by stepfamily members. Only you can determine your comfort level, and this will take you time and thought to establish. For example, you might decide not to attend gatherings at your in-laws' home when your partner's ex-wife is there. But what if staying away makes you feel even worse? You may decide that you prefer to attend, rather than sit at home wondering what is going on in your absence. If you do go, be sure to set your boundaries for the gathering in advance, and follow through with how you expect to be treated.

If you're like many people, you may fear that voicing your preferences will bring further rejection and isolation. While this is possible, in reality, it is far more likely that others will respect you even more if you set clear boundaries. Just be sure that you are willing to follow through on what you decide. If you lack consistency, your family (and others as well) are not as likely to respect your boundaries—or you.

Chapter Nine

Step 7: Provide and Receive Respect and Compassion

Experiencing respect, honor and a sense of self-worth are basic human needs that are essential to our well-being. To receive respect and compassion from stepfamily members, we must be willing to offer the same to them. In fact, we may have to be the role models for our families and demonstrate respectful and compassionate behavior, so they follow suit. Before we examine how you can get your needs met by other stepfamily members, let's first consider whether you are setting an example by providing them with the respect they deserve.

Think about your behavior and attitudes toward your stepfamily:

- Are you consistently kind and thoughtful to your stepchildren and in-laws?
- Are you open to developing a relationship with them?
- Do you engage in conversations with your stepchildren and in-laws about their interests and activities? Do you actively listen to their responses?
- If you haven't seen your stepchildren and in-laws recently, do you call them to ask how they are, and make arrangements to get together?
- Do you ever lose control of your feelings and "make a scene," or scream at your partner and/or his children?
- Do you ever engage in passive-aggressive behavior, retaliating indirectly if a stepfamily member treats you poorly?
- Do you undermine your stepfamily's attempts to get close to you?
- Do you ever withdraw into a shell when you are with them?

- Do you need to resolve any prior or ongoing conflicts with your stepchildren and in-laws?
- Do you need to explain clearly to them how you want to be treated?

Model Good Behavior

Our first challenge as stepmothers is to accept and welcome our stepchildren by being warm, kind and respectful. The integration of a stepfamily begins with you and your partner. As mature, responsible adults, you have the job of laying the groundwork for the new family.

One way you can help your stepchildren feel less anxious and more welcome is by introducing change to their lives as slowly as possible. One of my clients, Joseph, told me that, as a child, he had lived with his dad for several years before his father remarried. He still lamented the changes that he'd experienced when his stepmother entered his life. He bitterly recounted that the day after the wedding, his stepmother completely restocked the kitchen cabinets. His favorite cereals were gone, replaced by those that she and her biological son preferred. Fifteen years later, Joseph clearly remembered this abrupt change as a lack of concern for his needs. He still resents his stepmother's presence in his father's life.

Consider your stepchildren's needs as much as you can, without, of course, becoming overindulgent. See that they have privacy and space of their own in your home. You may not be able to give them separate bedrooms (especially if they do not live with you full-time), but make sure they have their own drawers for their clothes and shelves for their toys and books. Do everything you can to ensure that they feel as comfortable as possible when they're staying with you.

Another way to make your stepchildren feel welcome in your home is to include them in the family photographs you display. While it's understandable that decorating with photographs of your stepchildren may not feel completely genuine for you at first, think about how they might feel if they were left out. Remember, too, that it's your partner's home as well as yours. Consider how he might feel if photographs of his children were excluded from his home. They deserve a place of honor there.

When their parent remarries, many stepchildren initially see stepmothers as competition for their father's affection. To reassure them of his continuing love, devotion and commitment to them, and to prove that you are not a threat to his relationship with them, he may want to spend time with them apart from you. If this happens, be understanding, and encourage your partner to have whatever time he needs alone with his children.

Quality relationships are built from one-on-one interactions, so you, too, should try to spend private time with each of your stepchildren. Accompany them to activities they enjoy—shopping, baseball games, the movies. Try to find common interests; become knowledgeable about their favorite hobbies, sports or television shows, so you can discuss those with them. Go beyond superficial chitchat. For instance, without being too intrusive, you can ask questions about their experiences in school, at camp and with friends, so that you get to know them. It's also important for you to share your own personal interests and feelings with them.

While such efforts are worthwhile, remember not to go overboard. Don't try to develop relationships with your stepchildren too quickly, since that may be counterproductive. Above all, be patient. Bonds take time to develop.

Some of us embrace our new roles with gusto, fervently hoping that our efforts will be reciprocated with love from our stepchildren. Unfortunately, this doesn't always happen. Some stepchildren have such strong loyalties to their biological mothers that they can't—or won't—bond with a stepmother. Loving someone else may feel like a betrayal, so these stepchildren may dampen any feelings of affection they have toward their fathers' new wives.

If your stepchildren have trouble getting close to you, understand that this may be their way of honoring and respecting their mother. They may feel less conflicted if you explain to them that you do not want to replace their parent, that you respect their love for her and that you are just one of several adults who care about them.

Ex-Wives' Etiquette

Most stepmothers desire close, warm relationships with our stepchildren, yet want as limited contact as possible with their mothers. However, when we do interact with ex-wives, we want our conversations to be civil and polite. It can be baffling when ex-wives refuse to have anything to do with us, or are outright rude to us.

Even if you had nothing to do with the divorce, there may be several reasons why an ex-wife doesn't like you. Even ex-wives who initiated the separations may harbor fantasies of getting back together with their ex-spouses, and sometimes, they may come to feel that their marriages weren't so bad compared to life as a single parent. Once their ex-partners become romantically involved with someone else, their fantasies of reconciliation are dashed. Keep in mind that the reasons why your partner's ex-wife is angry with you may not be rational.

Your partner's ex may also harbor negative feelings toward him from the divorce. Some ex-wives project these negative emotions onto his current wife—you. If she sees her ex as a wrongdoer, she may assume that you must be a bad person to be involved with him. This assumption may have nothing to do with you personally, and may occur even if the ex-wife has not met you and knows nothing about you.

How far must you extend your good behavior toward the ex? Relationships between stepmothers and ex-wives vary tremendously. Several stepmothers in the online chat room mentioned that they try to get along with their partner's ex-wives to keep their stepchildren from experiencing additional trauma. Some stepmothers are willing to make concessions, such as celebrating holidays with ex-wives in attendance, and others will not speak to exes at all. It sometimes even happens that two such women become friends—after all, they may have quite a bit in common! Each stepfamily is unique and must work things out in a way that is satisfactory to all, depending on the particular circumstances.

What is the appropriate way to respond if you just don't like your partner's ex-wife? In addition to not saying anything negative about her to your stepchildren, it's a given that you will treat her with courtesy and respect. But you don't have to fake emotions about her that you do not feel. Deception is unhealthy for stepchildren to witness, and they will probably see through any disingenuous actions on your part.

Showing Respect to Your Stepchildren

Remember that it is inappropriate to criticize, put down, raise your voice or be cruel in any way to your stepchildren—no matter how much they may misbehave or aggravate you. Remember that all children know how to push parental "buttons," and it is important to show respect by responding calmly. *You* are the adult here. If you let yourself lose control, you will pay for it dearly, because your stepchildren will grow to dislike and resent you. (While it's equally inappropriate to yell at your biological children, a stronger foundation of love generally exists there, which may enable them to tolerate and

"STEPMOTHERS SPEAK"

Sometimes you may have a reason to be upset, frustrated or irritated toward your stepchildren, but that does not give you the right to scream, mistreat, insult, fight or abuse them or your partner. We must learn to work through our conflicts in a smart, patient way. Always remember, they are children, little ones who are going through a rough time themselves. Never descend to their childish level and become a player in their game.

—In Stepmom

overlook an occasional angry outburst on your part. Stepchildren, however, will not give you as much leeway.)

If you do find yourself lashing out at your stepchildren, make amends by apologizing immediately. By doing so, you are not condoning any misbehavior on their part, but you are taking responsibility for your own behavior. An apology is a sign of respect and an indication that you care about your stepchildren and your relationship with them.

Disciplining Stepchildren: Whose Job Is It?

The stepmothers in the online chat room, and those who responded to the stepmother questionnaire, agreed that most fights with their partners stemmed from a single issue: discipline of their stepchildren. Few people enjoy disciplining a child because the conflict that follows it is most unpleasant. Many parents can identify with the statement "This is hurting me more than it's hurting you." But discipline is even more problematic for stepmothers, because it is often met with resistance and resentment, not only from our stepchildren, but from our partner and his ex-wife, as well. Do you have a right to respectfully discipline your stepchildren when they misbehave in your care? In which situations have your partner and his ex-wife resisted imposing discipline? These are difficult questions that many stepmothers must grapple with.

Most mental health experts agree that, at least in the first few years of remarriage, disciplining stepchildren should be left to the biological parents. They believe that stepchildren need time to bond with stepparents, to learn to trust and accept them, before they can view them as authority figures. Accordingly, experts recommend that stepmothers maintain a background role initially, in order to avoid arousing stepchildren's resentment. If you don't, it may be difficult for you to overcome children's negative emotions once they have developed.

Under ideal circumstances our partners will discipline their children when necessary. However, some of us—particularly those who have full-time custody of stepchildren—may need to discipline them when partners are away from home for extended periods. To prevent stepchildren from resenting you, you should have a family conversation before your partner goes away to explain that you will be in charge while your husband is away. This way, your stepchildren will fully understand the consequences if they misbehave, and that the guidelines have been set by both of you.

In most cases, however, stepmothers should operate more as babysitters or aunts than as parents. In the event that you are alone with your stepchildren, you are the adult in charge, but you are not usurping the parental role. To enforce rules, for example, you can say, "This is the rule of the house. Homework is done before television." If your stepchild counters, "You're not my parent!" you can respond by saying, "Yes, you're right. You have a mom and a dad, and I'm not going to replace either one of them. Meanwhile, I'm the adult in charge here tonight, and the rule is no television until homework is done." If you meet with resistance, you and your stepchildren can discuss this with your partner when he returns home, and jointly decide how to handle future problems.

Maintaining Self-Control

Exercising verbal self-restraint is not always easy, especially if your partner ignores his children's transgressions, does not set appropriate limits and does not specify the consequences for violating them. If you devise a strategy, in advance, for whenever your buttons are pushed, you won't be caught off guard. Be aware of your own limits: For instance, if your stepchild doesn't heed a request, how long does it usually take before you lose your temper?

"STEPMOTHERS SPEAK"

This rule worked for all the kids in my house: If it is on the floor for more than seven days, the object belongs to me. I don't care whose it was. My kids tested me until they had nothing to wear and no music to listen to. Then they started picking up after themselves. Try this technique and see if it works for you. Tell your stepdaughter the new seven-day rule. Don't remind her to clean up after that. If she doesn't pick up after herself, leave the object on the floor for seven days [of her visits]. After the seventh day, you keep the object. She will learn to pick it up and put it away.

—OK AS A STEPMOM

If you think about this in advance, you will know when it's time to put your plan into action. You won't have to waste time analyzing each situation, wondering how to respond or asking yourself if you are overreacting. If you become involved in such an internal debate when you are under pressure, you may wait too long to react, and then explode in frustration.

Knowing what you will say ahead of time allows you to act immediately, with calm conviction, whenever you are reaching the boiling point. For instance, you might say, "I've asked you several times to get ready for bed. You know what the rule is, and if you aren't ready in five minutes, I am going to take away television privileges for one day." Then stand by your position; there should be consistency between what you say and what you do. Threatening without following through will only encourage children's disrespect and continuing misbehavior.

When Stepchildren Are Messy

Your home is your castle, and when standards of cleanliness are not maintained, it's natural to feel irritated and disrespected. Bear in mind, however, that stepchildren's messiness may not be laziness, but may reflect feelings about their parents' divorce. For example, stepchildren may consider any form of cooperation with you an act of disloyalty to their mother, and believe that they are betraying her if they do any housework for you. For some children, making a mess may be a way to "get even" for their mothers, who have had a difficult time adjusting to the divorce. Other children may believe they have already suffered enough pain from their parents' separation, and aren't willing to undergo any more hardship by helping keep your home clean. Quite possibly they believe that because of their struggles, they are entitled to be taken care of by you. More than likely, these beliefs are unconscious.

Messiness is not only a multifaceted issue for stepchildren, but it can be an equally complex one for stepmothers. Some of us view the messiness of our stepchildren as symbolic of the general lack of respect and acknowledgment we receive. As comedienne Wendy Liebman quipped on the *Tonight Show with Jay Leno*, "Before I got married at age forty, I believed I was an old maid. Now that I'm married [and the stepmother of two boys], I'm just a maid." Many stepmothers would agree, without necessarily sharing Liebman's sense of humor.

"STEPMOTHERS SPEAK"

Stop cleaning her room! *At age six, your stepdaughter should be able to pick up her toys after playing with them. If she isn't even going to attempt to clean her room, and if your husband isn't going to back you up, leave the room alone. Let her live in a dirty room, and let it get really bad until your husband notices. Then, all you have to say is that you asked her to clean her room; she never did. If he doesn't like it, make him clean the room.*

—HAD NO IDEA

ONE STEPMOTHER'S STORY: JOHANNA

Johanna first came for psychotherapy because she was frustrated that she constantly had to remind her stepchildren to put their backpacks in their rooms and their dirty dishes and glasses in the sink. These were the only chores required of them. She would remind them politely three or four times, then would lose patience, and finally she would become snippy and brusque. Things only got done, she told me, when she barked orders at them. She hated the person she was becoming, and asked me how to avoid becoming the "wicked stepmother."

Johanna was in a no-win situation. When she yelled at her stepchildren, she felt bad about herself, and she was still ineffective in accomplishing her goals. I asked her why her partner wasn't making sure that his children did their chores. She said that he did occasionally, but wasn't at home as much as she was, so it fell to her to remind them.

I asked her what bothered her when her stepchildren ignored her requests. She told me that she felt like an invisible member of the household, since her need for cleanliness was not considered important.

We came up with more satisfying ways for her to deal with her frustration, and I suggested that she share her plan with her partner, so that he could support her new position. Johanna spoke to her partner, and she was then able to be clear and direct with her stepchildren, saying, "When you don't put your backpacks away, I feel you don't respect my need for order." She then added reasonable consequences to her statement: "When you don't put your dirty glasses and dishes in the sink, I feel overwhelmed by cleaning up after everyone, and I've decided to charge for this service. If your dishes and glasses aren't in the sink by bedtime, I am charging you fifty cents each time I do it for you. Of course, it's only fair for you to be paid each time you clean up any dirty items that your father or I haven't put away." She kept a pad in the kitchen to list the number of times she cleaned up after her stepchildren and the amount of money they owed her, with separate columns for the times they deserved to be paid. Johanna transformed the tedium of doing chores into an activity that seemed like a game.

I reminded Johanna of the importance of following through with this plan; otherwise she would lose credibility with her stepchildren. As difficult as it might be for her, once she told them she was charging for her cleaning service, she had to abide by her decision, and collect the money owed to her by taking it out of their allowance, and pay any money she owed to them.

Johanna felt much better that she was no longer screaming at her stepchildren. Her stepchildren became much more conscientious about cleaning up after themselves, and were even eager to earn extra money by cleaning up dishes and glasses that their father left in the living room.

Getting Dads Involved

Fathers need to step up to the plate when it comes to teaching their children appropriate behavior. As discussed previously, many biological parents are too lax about providing structure and boundaries for their children after a divorce. They can be far too permissive, or inconsistent, when children misbehave, leaving stepmothers faced with unruly, out-of-control stepchildren. What should be done?

When stepchildren misbehave, first focus your attention on your partner, rather than the children. Let him know, gently and calmly, that you feel he needs to assert his authority in order to help his children grow and develop properly, and feel secure and protected, as well as to ensure that the family dynamic does not spiral

"STEPMOTHERS SPEAK"

When my husband and I first started dating, my stepson didn't hear the word no very often. I explained to my husband that if my stepson didn't start hearing no once in a while, we should just watch out when he is older. He would think he could do whatever he wanted, whenever he wanted. Needless to say, he started to hear no more often, and it has helped a lot.

—Seven More Years

out of control. If he isn't capable of being a strong parent, then your life, his life and your stepchildren's lives may become miserable.

It is best to discuss discipline with your partner before an incident occurs. Do you believe that spankings are ever appropriate? What privileges would you take away from children if they misbehaved, taking into consideration the age of the child and the severity of the transgression? If you wait to have this discussion until an incident comes up with your stepchild, you run the risk of damaging your relationship with your partner and hurting your stepchild as well, by demonstrating confusion, rather than unity, between the two of you.

66STEPMOTHERS SPEAK99

Make a "family plan" ahead of time that states how you would handle certain situations in the future. Discuss your view of discipline with your stepchildren. Spell it ALL out in writing so that there are no misunderstandings. My husband and I have talked about doing this and signing it on our upcoming anniversary. I am just trying to find a way for both of us to be on the same page without having a circumstance arise when one party says, "I don't remember saying that!"

—In for a Long Haul

House Rules

In order to ensure mutual respect in the stepfamily, it is essential for you and your partner to develop a set of rules that everyone in the family must abide by. If they are old enough, children can even participate in setting up these rules and consequences. Often, parents are amused to find that their children establish stricter punishments for breaking a rule than the adults would have!

Share the house rules with your stepchildren and any biological children you may have at home. When everyone in the family knows the house rules, you and your partner can back each other up when a transgression occurs. Working together as a team is important for you as a couple, and teaches children that they cannot "divide and conquer."

Gaining Respect from Stepfamily Members

Respect your stepfamily, and they are more likely to respect, rather than resent, you. Communicate calmly, and use these other ways to model and elicit respectful behavior:

- Sincerely value the opinions of your partner and stepchildren.
- Actively listen to what your stepchildren and partner have to say.
- Be considerate of the preferences of each family member.
- Never mock or tease family members—even if your intentions are to be humorous, you may offend them.
- Avoid gossiping about family members.
- Never pressure your stepchildren or partner to participate in activities they don't want to do.
- Plan ahead for any known problem times.

Now, think about how your stepfamily treats you:

- Which members of your stepfamily respect you and treat you well? Which members of your stepfamily tend to be disrespectful to you?
- Do you receive birthday and holiday gifts from stepfamily members?

- If you have biological children, do your in-laws treat them the same way they treat their grandchildren?
- Do your stepchildren and in-laws thank you for gifts that you and your partner give them, or do they only acknowledge your partner?

Many stepmothers are hurt by what they see as the disrespectful behavior of other stepfamily members. Not knowing how to handle these awkward situations, some stepmothers remain silent, keeping their pain within, while others explode at the offender. Neither method, ultimately, is effective in healing these kinds of emotional wounds. If there are any stepfamily members who disrespect you, what can you do to protect yourself? How could you stick up for yourself in an assertive manner?

Are Your Emotional Hurts Mountains or Molehills?

Stepmothers experience a variety of emotional injuries, from minor to major ones. Can you distinguish between small and large transgressions? Some people have been so hurt by past experiences that they immediately defend themselves as though every painful situation were potentially life-threatening. If this is you, you may need to develop a thicker skin to overcome the pain of minor incidents that are bruising rather than deeply damaging, such as when stepchildren sometimes ignore you or discuss their mother in your presence.

One stepmother complained in the online chat room that she felt hurt when she viewed a project at her stepdaughter's school titled, "All About Me." Her stepdaughter had drawn a page showing "My Family," that included everyone except her stepmother. "I know I'm not her 'real' family," the stepmother said, "but my feelings were hurt. My husband told me I was overreacting."

It was natural for this stepmother to be hurt, and she is entitled to her feelings, yet she could also ask herself how important
this incident really is in the overall context of her life. Certainly, it
would have been helpful if her partner had acknowledged her pain,
but she still is capable of self-healing this emotional injury. We
all know how to treat minor cuts and bruises. You can help heal
emotional wounds of this kind by telling yourself that the pain will
stop in a few minutes, and by using other self-soothing devices.
The stepmother in the example above could have reminded herself
that her stepdaughter is only a child, and may not understand the
definition of *family*. She might also talk with her stepdaughter,
gently telling her that she *is* part of her family. These steps would
help her heal the hurt from her stepdaughter's oversight.

ONE STEPMOTHER'S STORY: EMMA

Emma was upset that her in-laws rejected every attempt
she made to get close to them. Her stepchildren were
sweet and friendly, and they had fun together, but her in-
laws completely ignored her. She didn't understand why
she was treated so coldly, especially since she had met her
husband eight years after his divorce. Emma was unac-
customed to being treated this way, since she was popular
at work, had many friends and enjoyed socializing. She
said, "I'm a good person—why are they acting like this? I
don't deserve this." When I asked her if she considered
this injury a mountain or a molehill, she said she felt it
was somewhere in between. It wasn't the worst transgression, but it was difficult to overcome, because it was
so persistent.

Based on Emma's description of her in-laws, I sensed that
they were inflexible—set in their ways, and therefore not
likely to warm up to her. Even though this emotional wound

was painful, I asked Emma if she wanted to let go of her negative feelings. I explained that she could try to overcome them, or she could choose to remain bitter and hurt by the rejection. Emma hadn't realized that she could heal her own emotional injuries, even if her in-laws continued to ignore her. She had thought that their relationship needed to change before she could feel better. Remember that although improving a relationship is an admirable goal, it is not necessary to overcome hurt feelings.

Emma overcame her hurt feelings by realizing that they stemmed from her underlying belief that life should be fair and equal for everyone. Being treated poorly by her in-laws didn't accord with her sense of justice. I explained to Emma that while it would be nice if life were fair, this isn't always the case. Some people are born into wealthy families while others grow up in poor ones. Some people are blessed with loving in-laws; unfortunately, Emma was not. However, she was blessed to have many other loving friends and family in her life, and could appreciate their devotion and concern. Their love for her was more than enough to satisfy her need for close, loving relationships.

I suggested that Emma could replace her belief in the "fairness doctrine" with the "happiness doctrine." Rather than waste her time accounting for what is fair and unfair in life, the "happiness doctrine" could help her accept life as it is, and not how it *should* be. Emma asked me how she could do this. I explained that every time she became aware that she was thinking of the ways her in-laws were not considerate to her, she could interrupt these negative thoughts by replacing them with positive ones (as explained in more detail in step 2). For instance, she could divert her attention to the many thoughtful gestures she experienced from her friends and enjoy these memories. I also recommended that she keep a daily gratitude journal, do the "three good things a day" exercise, and count her blessings each day (described fully in step 3). These simple exercises focus on the positive aspects of life, and could enable Emma to feel happy again.

Healing the Wounds of Disrespect

The phrase *Time heals all wounds* is misleading. Time simply passes by; it's what we do while time passes that really matters. We can either stay stuck in our pain or help ourselves to heal. If you have been hurt by the disrespect of a stepfamily member, you can decide if you want to feel better. Healing happens more quickly when you consciously initiate the process.

In *Why People Don't Heal and How They Can,* Caroline Myss identifies several common reasons why wounded people may be reluctant to heal. Some people tend to identify themselves with their wounds. If they are rejected by a partner, for instance, they then see themselves as a spurned lover. Other people believe they deserve to suffer because of their perceived flaws. And some people believe that they have tried everything in their power to improve their situation, and that nothing will work for them.

Unwittingly, some people remain stuck in their misery by playing a sad scene over and over again in their minds—complaining about the unfairness or injustice of the experience to anyone who will listen and making it a central theme in their lives. They remain bitter and unforgiving about the transgression and make themselves into victims of the event.

You have to believe that you deserve to feel good in order to actually begin to feel good. If your identity is based on feeling like a victim, you may need an identity makeover for healing to truly occur. If your self-esteem is low, you may need to upgrade it in order to bounce back from emotional injuries. You can change your self-perception from that of a victim to that of a warrior, capable of healing yourself. You can use the same techniques discussed in step 1—self-soothing statements, modifying your inner speech, affirmations and visualization—to help you overcome any obstacles that are keeping you from emotional healing.

Defending Yourself Against Transgressions

Understand that stepfamily members who seem to be disrespectful may simply be acting without thinking things through. For example, suppose your partner changed his children's visitation schedule without telling you about it. Perhaps he was considering their needs, and did not realize that his actions would affect you. Naturally, you might be annoyed by this. However, by realizing that your partner wasn't intending to disrespect you, you can forgive him for this oversight, especially if he promises to discuss any future changes of plans with you. Give him the benefit of the doubt, if his oversight is a one-time occurrence. However, if this seems to represent an overall lack of consideration for your feelings, then use the communication skills discussed in step 3 to tell him how you feel and what you want to change.

To help overcome the pain of small emotional injuries, ask yourself:

(1) *What does this incident remind me of? Is it similar to other slights that I've experienced? By recognizing that an emotional injury is similar to earlier ones, you may be able to identify an underlying, recurring pattern in the events that hurt you. For instance, I don't like to be ignored. If a mutual friend or family member leaves a message such as "Happy New Year" on the answering machine for my husband, I feel hurt that I wasn't included in the greeting. I realize that this incident is similar to other times when I*

have felt ignored, though this time it may not be as extreme. Rather than being negatively affected by such a minor oversight, I can choose to put my energies into making sure I am a significant presence in my community of family and friends. When we understand the reasons why we feel hurt, we have the insight to take positive steps toward healing.

(2) After identifying why an injury is hurtful to you, ask yourself what you need to do to feel better. If you can think of something constructive to do, go ahead and do it.

(3) If you can't think of anything to remedy the hurt, ask yourself how you will feel about this next year. Are you likely to remember it? If the answer is no, move on. To ease the transition from feeling hurt to feeling better, I sometimes wash my face and hands to symbolically get rid of toxic energy; at other times I shake my body the way a dog shakes water from its fur. Both gestures help me separate from negative energy and put myself in a more positive emotional state.

(4) Put the emotional injury in its rightful place. Realize that though you were hurt by what happened, it's now in the past. Just as with a past illness, remember that you have already been through it and don't have to repeat the experience again.

(5) Ask yourself if the person intended to hurt you. You don't have to take every insult or transgression personally. You may need to reframe a person's bad behavior by remembering that it's not about you.

(6) Don't be quick to point fingers at the wrongdoing of others. Remember, we all make mistakes.

(7) Learn to be patient. You can prevent others' behavior from getting to you by refusing to react until you know all

the facts. Tell yourself that you will postpone feeling upset, rather than let the experience ruin the moment. If your feelings are getting the better of you, meditate for a few minutes to help you get calm and centered.

(8) As I've said previously, when we focus our thoughts in a different direction, our moods can change. If you can, take a time-out from a painful situation by going for a walk, taking a hot bath, listening to uplifting music, reading a book or doing something else that relaxes you. Visiting a friend may give you some time and space to regroup and allow stepfamily members to ponder their own behavior.

(9) Remind yourself that everyone gets hurt or rejected sometimes. Pick yourself up, dust yourself off and move on.

Not all emotional injuries should be handled this way. More serious transgressions—such as when a stepchild tells lies about you or steals your belongings, or when a partner's ex-wife verbally or physically assaults you—will only escalate if you turn the other cheek. Here are some techniques that will help you take care of yourself when you are disrespected in ways that can seriously harm your self-esteem, security or peace of mind.

Assertiveness

Assertiveness means taking care of your own needs while being respectful of others. Assertive communication can help you handle difficult family, friends and coworkers more easily. Of course, it cannot guarantee successful outcomes, but it is an excellent tool to help you strengthen your relationships, reduce your stress, and enhance your self-esteem.

Verbal judo is a tactic taught to police officers, to help them communicate more effectively in difficult situations. Officers are trained to respond rather than to react and to be assertive rather than aggressive, when communicating with uncooperative or hostile civilians. They are taught to behave with empathy: to display an understanding of what the civilian is experiencing while maintaining control of the situation. Verbal judo can be helpful to stepmothers as well as to police officers. How can you employ this tactic?

Try to avoid your natural first reaction to lash out in anger when you feel disrespected. While anger is a natural feeling, staying angry generally isn't the best way to channel your feelings or to take care of yourself; giving in to it will only diminish your power. Rather than showing your anger at someone who is disrespectful to you, project a calm attitude. Make sure your body reflects confidence: Stand up straight, hold your head high and carry yourself with assurance and authority. Relax, breathe deeply and look people in the eye. When you communicate your displeasure, be neither aggressive (forcing the person to submit to your will), nor passive (allowing others to take advantage of you). Instead, try to achieve a middle ground. Tell the person who offends you, quietly and firmly, that you will not tolerate inappropriate behavior. With practice, assertive behavior will become second nature to you.

In your journal, ask yourself:

- Are you comfortable dealing with conflict? Think about experiences you have had in the past with conflict, and what the outcomes were.
- Do you find yourself being too passive out of a desire to keep peace in your stepfamily?
- Are you able to control your angry feelings? Are you aggressive when expressing your displeasure?
- Can you state what you need clearly? Are you able to say no calmly and without guilt?

Let's take a look at assertiveness in action. How can you respond assertively to a stepchild who refuses to listen to you? One stepmother said in the online chat room:

> *I'm having such a difficult time with my seven-year-old stepdaughter. She yells at me and tells me I'm not her mother and she doesn't have to listen to me. When she lived with us full-time, she was well-behaved. Now that she's living with her mother, she has been acting up and not listening to anything I say. Today I asked her to help me pick up leaves in the yard and clean the living room, and she said, "No, I don't have to. You're not my mama. Leave me alone."*
>
> —What Happened?

This is a common scenario, experienced by many of us stepmothers. An assertive response would be similar to ones we've already discussed: "You're right—I'm not your mother. But I *am* the adult in charge right now, so I expect you to do what I ask you to do." Assertive responses are a way of sidestepping someone's attempts to "push your buttons," by clearly stating your boundaries and expectations.

Another stepmother responded with a similar experience:

> *My stepson once tried to pull the line "You're just my stepmother," and I looked at him and said, "Okay, then. You are just my stepson." I think he really got the point I was making. He was trying to tell me that I wasn't his mom and therefore he didn't need to listen to me. I was telling him that he wasn't my son, and therefore I didn't have to clean up after him,*

wash his clothes or feed him. He changed his tune as soon

as soon I said what I did.

    —Not Quite a Mom

This is also an assertive statement, and an indirect way of saying, "This is where I draw the line." Being assertive can prevent small conflicts from escalating into major battles.

If you find that one of your stepchildren or your partner's ex-wife is addressing you abusively, you can calmly say, "I don't allow anyone to talk to me this way. We can continue the conversation when you speak to me respectfully." Then, leave the room or hang up the phone. You don't have to tolerate anyone's disrespectful behavior.

Handling Criticism Assertively

Are you afraid of being criticized? Criticism does not have to hold negative power over you, as long as it is expressed respectfully. What should you do when a member of your stepfamily is upset with you and has a valid criticism, and you want to work things out with that person? Again, try your best to keep cool. There's no need to be provoked and become defensive, even when you are engrossed in a difficult conversation. In fact, you will feel more empowered if you remain calm, since the critic will not have the satisfaction of seeing you become rattled. You can respond to the criticism by saying, "You may be right. I need to think about that, and I will get back to you in a couple of hours [or tomorrow, or next week]." Or you might say, "That's a good point." By agreeing to some of the comments, or by promising to think about what is being said, you will defuse some of the heat from the conversation, and will also be giving yourself more time to think about it more clearly.

There are a number of techniques to help you keep your head when you're under fire. During a difficult conversation, visualize invisible armor protecting you. Or, imagine that your body is being held in place by strong roots embedded deeply in the ground. As the critical person is speaking, repeat to yourself, "No one can hurt me. I am strong." You can also tell yourself that you don't need everyone's approval, and that it's only natural for some people to disagree with you.

After the conversation is over, avoid internalizing blame. Calmly think about the criticism that was directed toward you. What have you learned? What behavior can you change? Promise yourself that you will act differently in the future, then forgive yourself and move on. Remember, none of us is perfect. We all make mistakes from time to time, and we can see these mistakes as opportunities to help us grow.

Techniques for assertive behavior:

1. *Use a firm, but pleasant, tone of voice.*

2. *Maintain good eye contact.*

3. *Be as specific as possible about what you want, think and feel. For example:*

   "I want to ..."
   "I don't want you to ..."
   "Would you ...?"
   "I liked it when you ..."
   "I have a different opinion. I think that ..."

4. *"Own" your message by expressing your feelings, beliefs and attitudes as your personal point of view. If you make statements like "You're wrong," you are likely to provoke resentment and resistance. Instead, use "I" statements, such as "I don't agree with you." You will further understanding and cooperation when you own your feelings.*

5. *Ask for feedback from others, to make sure they understand what you are trying to communicate. Questions such as "Am I being clear?" convey that you want to correct any misperceptions, and help others to realize that you are expressing your own opinions, feelings or desires, rather than making a demand on them. Encourage others also to be clear, direct and specific in their feedback to you.*

6. *Don't assume you know what the other person's motives are, especially if you think they are negative. Ask questions to elicit the information you need, such as "How do you see this situation?" or "What did you mean to communicate to me?"*

7. *Don't forget to listen. It's important to understand the other person's point of view, as well as communicating yours.*

8. *Aim for a win-win outcome. See if you can find a compromise or a way for everyone to be satisfied.*

ONE STEPMOTHER'S STORY: KENDRA

Assertive communication worked well for Kendra. The first time her teenage stepdaughter called her a bad name, Kendra was so shocked that she did not respond. Naturally, she was offended, and she decided that since she did not tolerate this kind of language from others, she was not going to allow her stepdaughter to speak to her this way, particularly since it might send a message to her young son that this was an acceptable way to treat others.

A few weeks went by before her stepdaughter was upset and used the same adjective again. Kendra took immediate action, sat her stepdaughter down and said, "Nobody calls me bad names. I do not have the authority to punish you, nor do I want to, but I will not have anything to do with you until you apologize, and can interact with me respectfully. I am happy to listen to your reasons for being unhappy with me when you discuss them calmly, but I won't allow anyone to express contempt for me."

Using Assertiveness in Your Family

Assertive communication techniques are an excellent means of self-protection. Let's use the issue of gifts as an example. Many of us feel hurt when we don't receive thanks for presents we've bought for stepchildren or in-laws. Others of us are upset when our birthdays are overlooked by stepfamily members. These kinds of oversights are embarrassing, and many of us remain silent because we don't want to draw any attention to ourselves. While it's natural to feel uncomfortable when you aren't treated respectfully, remember that you didn't do anything wrong. Your stepchildren, in-laws or partner are the ones who behaved thoughtlessly. You can remedy this type of situation by being assertive.

If your stepchildren or in-laws thank your partner alone for a present to which you contributed, simply ask them, "Do you like your gift?" When they respond with a yes, say something like "I'm so glad, because I wanted to get something special for you, and I looked all over to find this." If that does not elicit a thank-you, they may be too stubborn to acknowledge you or they may be ungrateful for your contribution. Remember that you aren't obligated to buy them future presents, and you can communicate this assertively to your partner. You have a choice about where you bestow your generosity and attention.

If you didn't receive a holiday gift from your in-laws or stepchildren and you feel upset by the oversight, don't overlook it, since silence will merely make the situation worse. Consider saying something like this: "My feelings are hurt. I want to be part of this family, and I feel so sad not to be included." This is a simple, direct and honest statement of your emotions.

If you are uncomfortable being assertive, ask your partner to speak up on your behalf, until you feel ready to stand up for yourself. Ask him to discuss with his children or parents why you (and/or your children) were excluded from receiving a gift or a thank-you and whether it's possible for you to be included in the future. If they agree, then your goal has been accomplished. If they refuse his request, have him ask them about their reasons; at least then you will know where you stand.

If disrespectful behavior persists, consider limiting your contact with the stepfamily member(s) involved. Discuss possible alternative holiday arrangements with your partner. Utilize some of the resources discussed in step 2, such as meditation and self-hypnosis, to help restore your emotional balance and facilitate healing.

As I've mentioned before, while you cannot always control what others do, you will feel better when you are able to take care of yourself. However, just as serious physical injuries need to be treated by a physician, significant emotional hurts will benefit from professional expertise. If your emotional pain is great, self-help techniques will probably not be sufficient. In that case, don't hesitate to consult a mental health professional. You may also want to contact the police if you feel physically threatened. You do not have to suffer in silence or tolerate the toxic behavior of others.

Chapter Ten

Step 8: Disengage, When Necessary

Disengaging can be quite effective for those of us who are burned out from excessive responsibilities, overinvolvement in stepfamily crises, or toxic relatives for too long. Disengagement is a process by which you pull back from some responsibilities or relationships. There are a variety of ways to do this, depending on your circumstances and needs, ranging from a gradual withdrawal from just one activity that causes you distress, to completely avoiding an abusive stepfamily member. In some circumstances, disengagement may be the most effective way to regain control of your life.

Disengaging will not be necessary for all stepmothers. It is a method of last resort, an option to use only after you have tried all the other ways to improve your circumstances without success. Disengaging protects you from further negative emotional encounters. When you limit your contact with difficult people, you are no longer in a position to be ignored, rejected or taken advantage of. Disengagement can also give you perspective on the unchangeable realities of your stepfamily, as well as the emotional space to heal from preoccupying thoughts, activities or people who have harmed you.

Disengaging is very different from giving an ultimatum. When you give your partner or other stepfamily member an ultimatum, you are asking the other person to change and threatening consequences if he doesn't. When you disengage from an activity, you aren't trying to teach anyone a lesson. You are taking action for your own emotional health.

Disengaging from Stressful Activities

Changes in your mood and health can be indicators of high levels of stress.

In your journal, consider these questions:

- Do you experience frustration or exhaustion when you engage in a particular activity with your stepfamily? How long has this been going on?
- What is it about the activity that makes it burdensome for you?
- How have you tried to improve the situation?
- How would you describe your overall state of mind:
  □ Are you tired and frazzled most of the time?

  □ How often during the day are you on the verge of tears?

  □ How close do you come to tearing into someone when he or she does something to you that you feel is rude or inconsiderate, such as cutting ahead of you in a line or playing the television with the volume on too loudly?

- How frequently do you suffer from headaches, stomachaches, colds and other stress-related physical complaints?

If you are stressed because of overfunctioning in your stepfamily, you may need to give up one or more responsibilities (such as doing everyone's laundry or cooking every meal) to improve your overall health. It will probably be less traumatic for you and your stepfamily if you disengage slowly, one step at a time, rather than withdrawing from several activities at once. Try to pinpoint the duty that is most problematic for you—and the one disengaging action that would most effectively alleviate your stress.

Before you take action, you may need to change the way you think about your role in the family and disengaging in general. Can you relate to any of the following statements?

"My stepfamily can't manage without me."

"Being disengaged seems cold and aloof. It's not possible to be involved with someone while being disengaged."

"I should never think about my own emotional concerns when one of my stepfamily members badly needs help. It's selfish to disengage."

"It doesn't matter if my efforts aren't acknowledged or appreciated. I must always help and support my stepfamily."

For disengaging to succeed, these kinds of thoughts need to be reframed into more self-caring statements, such as these:

"My stepfamily can function without my doing this one activity."

"I can still care about my stepfamily, even if I give up one responsibility."

"I need to look after my own physical and mental health. Taking care of my own needs is not selfish."

"As an adult, I have the right to choose those activities that are healthy and rewarding for me."

How to Disengage from an Activity

Once you have decided just what activity you intend to give up, explain your decision clearly to your partner (and to your stepchildren, if appropriate). In a respectful and calm manner, express your frustrations and be specific about your plans. Do not change your way of doing things without prior notice to your stepfamily. For instance, you may tell your partner that you are frustrated because he doesn't appreciate it when you do everyone's laundry, so, from now on, you will be responsible only for your own. Or, you might decide that since no one seems to appreciate what you cook for them, you will be preparing just your own meals in the future.

After you eliminate one task from your routine, give yourself a week or two to see if your emotional balance is restored. If you don't feel significantly better, you may need to give up still more responsibilities. Some of us are so overburdened that we may need to disengage *fully* at least for a while, in order to restore our emotional equilibrium. Disengaging fully from stepchildren, for example, means that you hand to your partner complete responsibility for his kids. He must now provide their meals, clean up after them,

"STEPMOTHERS SPEAK"

Basically, I have turned practically all requests or demands over to my stepdaughter's father, my husband. If a glass isn't properly washed, I tell him to point it out to her, or I give it to him to drink from. He's fast to correct her when I do that. We have been doing this for the past year and a half, and it works. I am no longer the bad guy. If she wants to do anything that requires parental permission, she has to ask him. I thought at first I'd lose my place in the hierarchy of my family, but I haven't. It really has helped.

—Been There, Done That, Finished with That

discipline them and be their chauffeur. If he can't do some of these things, he will have to arrange for others to do them.

When you are fully disengaged, and your stepchildren ask you for something you have provided in the past, you simply tell them, "Go ask your father." This can be your new mantra, a refrain that

"STEPMOTHERS SPEAK"

Disengaging is letting the chips fall where they may. If your stepchildren need a drink of water, they know where the sink is; let them get it for themselves. If they need new clothes or clean clothes, let them ask their biological parents for help or let them do it themselves. If your partner complains how terrible his ex is, you say, "Hey, you picked her. Did you see this or that on the news today?" Change the topic as quickly as possible.

If your partner complains that you aren't being supportive, you can say, "I am allowing you to make all the decisions regarding your children in your own way. I may not agree with them, but I will not be drawn into a debate about who is right. Since they are your children, you have the right to make these decisions. I support you."

If the school calls you about something for your stepchildren, give them your partner's or his ex's work numbers. Or give them their grandparents' or aunt's numbers. If your stepchildren get Ds and Fs on their report cards, don't comment. If your partner complains about their grades, again, say nothing. Do not say, "I told you so," even if that's what you think.

Just listen and nod with a sympathetic look on your face,
while planning to change the subject ASAP.

If your stepchildren need a ride, tell their father or
mother: Don't drive them. Your partner can ASK (not TELL)
you if you would be kind enough to help him out, and you can
decide on a case-by-case basis if this fits into your schedule.
If he tells you that you need to do this or that for your stepchil-
dren, set limits and say that you are busy doing something
else. He needs to be responsible for his children.

—LIFE IS GOOD

you must become comfortable repeating each time they approach you with any request.

For some stepmothers, the process of disengaging can be very simple. They just need, for example, to refrain from asking their stepchild one question, or stop overseeing one activity. For example, "A la Carte Stepmom," a full-time stepmother, wrote in the online chat room that she would no longer monitor her eight-year-old stepdaughter's homework. Her stepdaughter did not like school, routinely ignored assignments and lied about completing projects when, in fact, she hadn't even begun them. As a result, she was doing poorly in school. A la Carte Stepmom believed in the importance of education and wanted her stepdaughter to succeed academically, so during the school year she had constantly asked her questions like "Did you do your homework?" When her step-daughter was caught lying, she was reprimanded by her father, but never punished. The stepdaughter's poor study habits had continued, as had the tense and unpleasant atmosphere in the household.

Rather than blaming the conflict on the way his daughter handled the schoolwork, A la Carte Stepmom's partner blamed her for causing the strain in the stepfamily by overemphasizing the need for his daughter to complete homework assignments. While A la Carte Stepmom did not believe she deserved to be blamed for this situation, she did agree with her partner that the atmosphere in the family was unhealthy. She also realized that she should not be the only person in the stepfamily who cared how this child did in school. She decided that she no longer wanted the responsibility of supervising her stepdaughter's schoolwork, so she asked her partner to take it over—she disengaged. She continued to cook, clean and participate in all other stepfamily activities, but she just stopped asking about her stepdaughter's homework or checking on it. A la Carte Stepmom felt immediate relief and, in fact, the household became much calmer and more pleasant. She understood that the peace would be short-lived since, in all likelihood, her stepdaughter would have future problems in school, but she accepted that her partner and stepdaughter were making the choice to postpone dealing with her academic struggles.

Disengaging enabled this stepmother to preserve her relationships with her stepdaughter and partner. She was able to demonstrate love and concern without utilizing the rescuing, enabling or controlling behaviors she had used previously when tracking her stepdaughter's homework. By taking a step back, she removed herself from feeling guilty whenever her stepdaughter faltered academically. She stopped trying to protect the girl from academic failure, and her stepdaughter now had to accept responsibility for her own poor study habits. Disengaging also helped this stepmother realize that her educational values were different from those of her partner.

Be Prepared for Backlash

When stepmothers disengage, most of our partners will naturally object, because they must step in to fill the void. Your partner will very likely demand, beg and cajole you to take back your former responsibilities. Be calm and polite if your partner asks you to take on a task that you have given up. For instance, if he insists that you bring your stepchildren to soccer practice, you might consider saying something like "I'm sorry, I don't do that anymore. Remember, we discussed what I wasn't willing to handle now, and being a chauffeur is one of those tasks. You'll have to take care of it yourself, or ask someone else to do it."

Be aware that when your partner doesn't get what he wants, he may resort to manipulative tactics, like the following:

- Trying to convince you that he will suffer enormous hardship, illness or discomfort if you do not resume your duties.
- Attempting to arouse your sense of guilt.
- Trying to make you believe that *you* have a problem if you are unwilling to do as he wishes.
- Building a case that your former duties were the "right way" to do things.
- Trying to convince you that your plan to disengage won't work to your advantage, and that you should discontinue it.
- Threatening you with negative consequences, such as divorce, if you continue to disengage.

If you know about these tactics in advance, you won't be as likely to be intimidated by them. If your partner tries to pressure you into resuming certain duties, be firm and consistent about the changes you are making, and, eventually, he will understand that you mean business.

If your partner threatens you with divorce or some other serious consequence if you give up a certain household chore, you will need to have a serious discussion with him. What bothers him about your desire to change one customary task? Is he afraid that your proposed change will harm your stepfamily? Is he traditional, to the extent that the change goes against his view of gender roles? Listen until you comprehend his perspective, and then acknowledge that you understand. Calmly explain your feelings to him until he fully realizes your rationale for the change. Perhaps the two of you can find a compromise that you both find acceptable. If he remains unyielding, you will need to examine the reasons you are married to a man who is so set in his ways that he is unwilling to help you restore emotional balance to your life.

Many stepmothers are afraid to disengage for fear that they will be rejected, even if their partners have never hinted that they would do such a thing. Deep down, these women may believe that their partners are with them only because of the services they provide, rather than for who they are. Do not let yourself be trapped into doing anything that is unrewarding or unsatisfying because you feel that this is the only way to hold on to someone you love. Instead, test the validity of your beliefs, verifying whether they are based in reality or come from low self-esteem. Ask your partner what he loves about you, and what his reasons are for being with you. Most partners will automatically respond to this question with "Of course, I love you," and give you several reasons why they do. To assess your partner's sincerity, you will need to listen carefully to both the words and the underlying sentiments he expresses. Be open to hearing and accepting what he has to say. More than likely, your partner truly loves you, and your fear of rejection is ungrounded.

In the event that you still believe that your partner's motives for being involved with you are strictly selfish, then you should evaluate your relationship further. Take time to analyze and under- stand your partner's and your own motives and needs. Perhaps it is possible to resolve these unhealthy motives. Psychotherapy can help with this process, and you'll doubly benefit as it will help you to become stronger and more confident.

Disengaging from Toxic Relatives

Stepfamily relationships are rewarding when everyone involved respects each other and behaves appropriately. Unfortunately, some stepfamilies cannot maintain these standards, and instead of being civil, they interact in ways that are dysfunctional, even toxic. Communications are frequently laced with hostility, anger, blame, disapproval, criticism and threats, rather than kindness and acceptance. In these families members feel insecure and uncertain about when they may be facing ridicule or rejection. Stepmothers and other family members can suffer both emotionally and physically from these unhealthy relationships. If you have allowed members of your stepfamily to aggravate your emotional or

"STEPMOTHERS SPEAK"

Disengagement is not a form of punishment. It is often a survival tool and a means toward repairing a bad relationship. I am not punishing my stepchildren. I am simply making it clear to them that if they want a relationship with me, it will include respect, consideration and courtesy. If they call, I talk to them civilly, and if they visit, I say "Hello" and "Goodbye" to them. I am just not willing to have more involvement with them until they apologize for the years they took advantage of my kindness and generosity without ever once saying thank-you.

—No Longer a Doormat

physical health, you may need to disengage from them to restore a sense of balance to your life.

Disengaging from extremely negative stepfamily relatives can preserve your mental health. This is not a strategy to employ just because you dislike certain people or find them annoying or obnoxious. You should only disengage when a relationship is actually harmful to you. Being involved with a toxic person damages your self-esteem and drains your energy, while repeated contact can cause you to feel worn out, deflated, confused, belittled, undermined, insecure or controlled. Physical ailments, such as migraines, stomachaches or eye tics, may even result from such relationships.

Stepmothers can disengage from stepfamily members for various reasons, including:

- Constantly being criticized or put down by a stepfamily member.
- Being totally ignored by a stepfamily member.
- Being taken advantage of by a stepfamily member.
- Being maliciously gossiped about by a stepfamily member.
- Being falsely accused of abuse by a stepfamily member.
- Being unfairly blamed for problems in the stepfamily by a stepfamily member.
- Being consistently lied to by a stepfamily member.
- Having possessions or money stolen by a stepfamily member.
- Never receiving any form of gratitude or acknowledgment from a stepfamily member for your gifts and efforts.
- Being the target of a stepfamily member's anger, hostility or nastiness.
- Being excluded from events by a stepfamily member.
- Being physically or emotionally threatened by a stepfamily member.

Understanding Problem Relationships

Often, we stay in certain relationships because we do not understand that we have rights and options. We are under no obligation to take care of, or interact with, anyone who treats us poorly (aside from our biological children). Factors such as low self-esteem, fear of being alone, fear of upsetting the status quo or of hurting a partner, also may contribute to our tolerating negative people. Another reason we may continue to interact with them is because they mirror what we experienced as children, so we have no idea that our lives could be better without them.

Bear in mind that there are two people involved in any relationship. You are an active participant in a relationship with a toxic stepfamily member, and that means that you need to examine why you tolerate being with this person. Self-reflection is absolutely necessary to the disengagement process. Otherwise, down the road, you may unwittingly become involved with similar people again.

In your journal, consider these questions:

- Make a list of the toxic stepfamily members in your life. Analyze your relationship with each one. What are the particular qualities or characteristics of these relatives that make it difficult for you to spend time with them?
- What has kept you in these relationships?
- What benefits do you experience from these relationships?
- How have you coped with these relationships so far?
- What needs to change for these relationships to improve?
- What would have to happen for you to decide that you'd had enough?

To continue the self-examination process, take an inventory of your emotional state after spending time with particular relatives. This will be the first step in determining if and how you need to disengage from them.

Next, answer these questions in your journal:

- Can you be yourself with this person? Do you feel accepted by her? Is she critical or judgmental of you?
- Are you compromising your emotional or physical health when spending time with this person? Are you tired, angry or frightened, and do you experience migraines, skin rashes, eye tics or other physical reactions after being with him?
- Do you feel safe expressing your feelings around this person? Do you watch everything you say for fear that you will disturb or anger her? Do you tiptoe around this person or feel as if you are "walking on eggshells" when you're with her?
- Do you feel controlled or manipulated by this person?
- Do you feel punished or abused when you are with this person?
- Does the relationship involve an even give-and-take of energy?
- Does this person unfairly blame you for everything that goes wrong in your stepfamily?
- Is this person committed to having a good relationship with you?

If your answers suggest a pattern of negativity with a particular stepfamily member, it may be fruitless to spend your energy and emotions improving relations with him. A relationship may be beyond repair if you've exhausted all options to improve it, your emotional health is suffering and you feel a need to restore internal balance.

Disengagement Strategies for Relationships

When, why and how to disengage from a stepfamily member is a personal decision. There are a variety of ways to do this. Some of us need to pull back just a little, for instance, by refraining from giving this person our opinions unless solicited, while others of us need to completely avoid an abusive stepfamily member.

ONE STEPMOTHER'S STORY: BETHANY

Bethany decided to disengage from her adult stepdaughter, who had ignored her for the entire ten years of Bethany's marriage to her stepdaughter's dad. The last straw occurred for Bethany when she overheard her husband speaking on the telephone to his daughter. Based on his responses, Bethany knew that her stepdaughter was asking about their dog, but not about her. After her husband hung up the phone, he apologized for his daughter's insensitivity. Bethany told him that his daughter's lack of interest in her welfare was extremely hurtful, after all her efforts to be generous and kind. Bethany was grateful that her partner had acknowledged her hurt feelings, but she didn't ask him to try to change the situation. She knew that he had already talked to his daughter many times about her negative attitude, to no avail.

Bethany was determined to take responsibility for her relationship with her stepdaughter. She realized that she had two options: She could initiate a conversation and attempt to improve their relationship or she could disengage from her. Since there had already been many futile attempts at forging a relationship, Bethany felt it would be useless to have another talk with her stepdaughter. She decided that in the future, she would be civil and polite when they were together, but would not buy her presents, call her or extend herself in other ways. She didn't think her stepdaughter would even notice her change in behavior.

Bethany felt better after making her decision, but she was worried that her desire to be liked by others would prevent her from following through with disengaging. I asked her what was making her fearful and guilty. She told me that she had tried to be the model wife, doing everything possible for her marriage. By disengaging from her stepdaughter, she would no longer be giving 100 percent. She had never disengaged from a person before, and was worried that her husband would resent her behavior and ultimately reject her. As she talked about her feelings, Bethany realized that her anxiety stemmed from unfounded concerns. In fact, her husband had been encouraging her to disengage for some time.

I asked Bethany what she could do to relieve her anxiety. She said that she needed to accept that, as much as she might want everyone to like her, this was an unrealistic expectation. She could not do any more to develop a relationship with her stepdaughter, and had to stop trying, because she was investing too much effort in an impossible outcome. Every day she could remind herself that she had done her best, and that this was all she could expect from herself.

Bethany made a list of affirmations to help her keep her resolve:

"I need to stay strong to maintain my self-respect."

"I will not participate in any relationships unless I receive respect."

"I have feelings like everyone else in the stepfamily, and deserve to be treated equally."

Bethany found these affirmations very helpful during the time she disengaged from her stepdaughter. Within a month of starting this new way of relating to her stepdaughter, she felt much better.

The last straw occurred for "Stepped-on Stepmom," a member of the online chat room, when she discovered that her heirloom jewelry had been stolen from her bedroom. Her twenty-year-old stepson and his friends had been in her home when the theft occurred. When she and her partner confronted him, he vehemently denied that he or his friends were responsible, but no one else had been in the house at the time of the robbery.

Her stepson had been in trouble since he'd dropped out of high school. He had been arrested while driving under the influence of alcohol, and had had a number of other minor run-ins with the law. He earned money by occasionally working for her husband, but had little structure in his life and few goals to improve himself. He came and went as he pleased, choosing to live with his mother, or his father and stepmother, according to his whims.

Stepped-on Stepmom's partner was disgusted by his son's behavior, but he did not know what to do. Stepped-on Stepmom decided to safeguard her possessions by changing the locks to the house and banning her stepson from visiting or staying with them. She had a long conversation with her husband, explaining that she simply found it unacceptable that his son had stolen her jewelry. She refused to live with the feeling that her possessions were not safe in her own home. She was sorry, but she no longer could welcome her stepson into the house. She told her husband that if, in the future, her stepson got help for his problems and took responsibility for his actions, she would reconsider. Her husband agreed that this was a good decision.

Stepped-on Stepmom and her husband then had a conversation with her stepson. He was very angry, but she had anticipated his reaction and did not let it bother her. Her mind was made up, and she was relieved to have her private space back.

The best thing you can do when dealing with a toxic person is to walk away and not allow him to hurt you anymore. If you cannot do this physically, then mentally walk away, by focusing on something else, another person or an object in the room. You can daydream or listen to music with headphones. You can physically be in the presence of a person without interacting with him. Repeating a mantra, like "Sticks and stones will break my bones but names will never hurt me," will create a boundary that will shield you from harm.

Disengaging provides perspective. In the midst of a distressing situation, it is hard to tell whether the abusive treatment you are receiving is directed at you personally, or whether you are merely the target of someone's mishandled anger, frustration or narcissism. Whatever the reason for the behavior, you will find that disengaging allows you to breathe a big sigh of relief, and also to eventually see others' behavior more clearly.

Coping While Disengaging

How can you support yourself emotionally during the process of disengagement? Here are some suggestions:

- Know that when a person's behavior is toxic, it is because of her own issues. Accept that no matter what you say or do, you will not be able to control or change her.

- Focus on aspects of your own life that give you satisfaction. Rather than lingering over feelings of frustration and aggravation, concentrate on developing new interests, as well as better relationships with those who can bring you joy and compassion.

- Consider taking time for yourself by going out with friends, or on spiritual retreats, spa days or vacations by yourself, to find relief from stepfamily stress and to gain perspective during rough patches.

- Practice, practice, practice. Learning new behavior requires consistent effort. Be patient with yourself, and don't expect too much too soon. Remember that life's journey requires constant education and learning of new skills.

Most important, develop supportive relationships with your life partner, friends, family, workmates and associates. There is strength in numbers. Talking things over with those people in your life whose judgment you trust can help you overcome negativity. Just as animals and children can instinctively sense when someone is friendly or hostile, there are some people who are very good at recognizing when someone is hurting another person. If you are fortunate to have relationships with family members or friends who have good insights about others, seek their advice and support.

Disengaging is a skill that takes time to learn, and it also takes mental discipline. As discussed in step 2, we can change negative thoughts to positive ones by reminding ourselves that thoughts do not always reflect facts, and that they can be modified when they don't serve us. We can choose to ignore those thoughts that prevent us from leading fulfilling lives, and concentrate on ones that will help give us the experiences we want.

Affirmations can facilitate this process. When we repeat certain positive statements over and over again, our minds become accustomed to them and we become more open to accepting them as true. Here are some affirmations you can use, but also feel free to create ones that resonate just for you:

"From today onward, I am going to take good care of myself."

"Disengaging is absolutely necessary right now. I have already tried everything else."

"Disengaging from this activity will help me heal."

"I am strong. I can make healthy changes. Disengaging is one of them."

Building Self-Esteem While Disengaging

Disengaging is not easy, especially when self-sacrifice has become second nature. We are all creatures of habit, comfortable with the status quo. Any change, for better or worse, has the potential to cause distress, so it's natural to feel uncomfortable when we disengage. During this process, remember to focus on activities that will boost your self-esteem.

People develop healthy self-esteem by taking positive, self-enhancing actions. You can do this in many ways, some of which have been suggested in chapters 3 and 7 on taking good care of yourself, boundaries and self-respect. A few more examples follow:

- **Make a list of your accomplishments.** These can include anything that makes you feel good about yourself. Refer to the list whenever you need an emotional boost.

- **Use visualization techniques.** If you're anxious or doubtful about your ability to do something, visualize yourself handling it smoothly. This will lessen your fear and boost your self-confidence.

- **Stand up for yourself.** When we don't voice our needs, beliefs and emotions to others, we end up feeling bad about ourselves. Learn to express what you need, believe and feel, calmly and directly. The more you do this, the easier it will become.

- **Learn to say no.** When we can tell others that we can't or don't want to do something, we tend to experience relief. As the saying goes, "The truth shall set you free." Just remember to be polite and diplomatic when turning down a request for a favor.

- **Enhance your ability to cope with stress.** Develop a repertoire of strategies for calming your mind, such as meditating, reading a good book or taking a bubble bath, and incorporate them into your daily life.

- **Take care of yourself physically.** Eat well, get enough sleep, and exercise regularly. Treat your body the way it deserves to be treated!

Here are some additional ways to build self-esteem:

- **Try new activities.** Rather than avoiding certain activities because you doubt your abilities or feel insecure, take a deep breath, get out there and do the very things you're unsure about. Start small. You can conquer your fears by taking baby steps, while building your confidence. Even if things don't always work out as successfully as you'd hoped, you know that you tried!
- **Reject perfectionism.** Everyone makes mistakes from time to time—they are fundamental to the learning process. We would never have learned to walk as babies if we didn't stumble while practicing how to keep our balance. Striving for perfection leads to frustration. Keep this in mind as you venture out into the world, and be gentle with yourself.
- **Set personal goals.** There's no better time than the present to grow and develop in the ways you desire. Decide what goals—such as becoming proficient in a foreign language, taking an art class or getting into better physical shape—you would like to accomplish, and make a reasonable, yet challenging, plan to achieve them. Set deadlines and a system of rewards to keep you going.
- **Do things on your own.** If your friends or relatives aren't available to join you, do what you enjoy on your own. It's not healthy to depend on others in order to have fun. Go to the movies, to the museum, or even out to dinner alone. You will be doing what you like, and will feel courageous at the same time. Healthy relationships are important for our happiness, but it's more important to be comfortable with ourselves.

- **Associate with people who appreciate you.** When you decide who to spend time with, be sure to choose people who truly like and admire you. You'll feel more upbeat and energized after spending time with those who sincerely care about you.
- **Don't compare yourself to others.** Judge yourself by your own standards, since each of us is unique and special. Comparing ourselves to others can easily lead to unhappiness.
- **Practice truthfulness.** Be as authentic as possible by not telling white lies. When we use such fibs to avoid hurting others, we can end up feeling like phonies. Being honest (diplomatically, of course) builds courage and self-esteem.
- **Embrace life now.** The more time you spend dwelling on the past or worrying about the future, the more you are wasting the present moment. Life is happening right now, so get out there and enjoy it!

For too many people, struggling becomes so familiar that they forget there are other ways to live. Disengaging may actually be simpler than you realize. Is it possible that you are the only one in your stepfamily who cares if you keep up all the responsibilities or relationships you have set up for yourself? Bethany was right when she predicted that her stepdaughter would not notice the difference in her behavior. She didn't seem to care when Bethany no longer called her or bought her presents, and Bethany was soon relieved of her guilt.

Try disengagement when your stepfamily life is starting to overwhelm you. You may be surprised by how much better you feel.

Chapter Eleven

Step 9: Make It Fun!

The expression *Laughter is the best medicine* is absolutely true. Besides its many physiological benefits, such as reducing pain, laughter improves our performance, particularly in creative and problem-solving activities. Most important, laughter is the glue of intimacy—it cements our relationships.

I know from personal experience just how important it is to have fun and enjoy good times in life. For a couple of years after my marriage, I felt pressured to work long hours to pay our many bills. I was so busy taking care of my stepfamily the rest of the time, that I put fun on the back burner. I became overworked and overwrought, plodding through life on automatic pilot. I was unable to remember the last time I had cracked a joke or acted silly with a girlfriend. I had changed into someone I could not recognize: emotionally flat, dull and detached. I was experiencing very little joy in life, even though I had much to be grateful for.

One day, I realized that I was choosing to become emotionally bankrupt. No one but me was responsible for turning my life a dreary shade of gray. Something drastic needed to change, to bring color back into my life. That New Year's Eve I promised myself to make sure that I had fun each day, and I have honored that pledge ever since. Instead of thinking only about my husband and step-daughter's preferences, I began to choose activities for our family that I enjoyed: going to movies and plays, taking nature walks, collecting shells on the beach. Since then I have had fun learning something new each day and becoming more creative. I became much happier once I made having fun a top priority.

Dr. Gottman reminds us that in order for a marriage to be happy, the wife must be happy. This may seem obvious, until we think about all the women who sacrifice their happiness for their families. Remember that you have the right to be happy, as long as you are thoughtful and considerate of others. I have a client who lovingly says to her new stepfamily, "Just remember, as long as I'm happy, we are all happy." Although, of course, other factors also influence her stepchildren's happiness, they enjoy hearing her make this comment, and often tease her about whether they are doing enough to keep her happy.

Do you need to add more fun to your life? More than likely, you are so preoccupied with juggling all the tasks that make up your day that you don't give much thought to having fun. Perhaps you need to reprioritize so that you include some time in your schedule every week for pleasure. Here are some activities that can make you smile:

- **Read.** Reading transforms your daily existence, and expands your awareness of the world.
- **Dance.** Whether it's moving around on your living-room floor or taking a class, dancing is fun—and, as an added bonus, you'll burn a few calories.
- **See a movie**, preferably a comedy or something inspiring.
- **Spend time outdoors** and appreciate the beauty of nature.
- **Have dinner** with friends, especially those who are encouraging and accepting.
- **Visit an art gallery or museum.** Appreciate the creativity of others, and you may be inspired to create, too.
- **Get a makeover of your hair, clothes and makeup.** This can help you feel like a new person, and you'll find that others will respond differently to you, as well.

Of course, you can't give up the many responsibilities of adulthood, but they don't have to take up all your time. While we don't have complete control over our destinies, we can choose our priorities. Having fun deserves to be a priority for you.

Pleasures with Partners

Having fun is vital to the health of any relationship. How much fun do you have with your partner? Has your relationship become stale due to boredom, too many chores or a lack of trying? Perhaps you need to refocus your priorities and concentrate on adding more fun in the mix. After all, why be in a relationship if fun isn't part of it?

Stepmothers in the online chat room encourage each other to set aside one night a week for "date night," where couples can spend time alone.

"STEPMOTHERS SPEAK"

I wish we could go out to dinner and the movies once a week, but we can't always afford a babysitter, and our kids are too young to be left alone. Instead, we create our own fun. We made an agreement to tell each other one joke a day to ensure that we laugh together. It's not that easy to find a good joke each day—I can spend fifteen minutes online before finding one I like—but the time spent is worth it because laughing with my husband is one of the joys of my life. Try it, you might really like it!

—Wickedly Funny Stepmom

When was the last time you and your partner laughed together? Here are a few suggestions on how to have more fun with your partner.

- **Exercise** with each other. Go for a bike ride, walk in the park or play tennis as a couple.
- **Play** board, computer or card games together.
- **Exert** your minds by cooperating on jigsaw puzzles, crosswords or quiz books.
- **Redecorate** a room together or build furniture, such as a coffee table or shelves.
- **Have a picnic** in a park, a meadow or your own backyard.
- **Pamper** each other by sharing massages.
- **Learn** a language together.
- **Take** an enjoyable class together, on wine tasting, film or crafts.
- **Join** a coed bowling or volleyball league with your partner.

Keeping romance alive in your relationship is very important. Don't forget that affectionate gestures express love, and can put a smile on your partner's face. For instance:

- **Tell** him at unexpected moments that you love him.
- **Give** him plenty of hugs.
- **Leave him a love note** in his briefcase, on the TV or on his computer screen.
- **Flirt** with him.
- **Surprise** him with his favorite treats of cookies, cigars or anything else he enjoys.
- **Keep in touch** during the day through text messages, e-mails or phone calls (as long as it doesn't distract him from his job). Of course, you should work this out between you, because you may not have the same idea of how much contact with each other is appropriate throughout the day.

Fun with Stepchildren

Life goes by quickly. Instead of being overly burdened by the tedious chores associated with parenting, try to enjoy the time you spend with your stepchildren.

"STEPMOTHERS SPEAK"

I have an ongoing joke with my stepchildren; whenever I insist they do something, like chores, they smile at me and tell me that "Walt [Disney] had it right." I then chase them around the house with a broom, and we all have a good laugh. It is important to laugh. Honestly, they will be gone before you know it, and you will miss them.

—ALL IN THE STEPFAMILY

Having fun sounds simple, yet many of us find it difficult to do. Often, it seems that there's never enough time in the day to accomplish everything, and we may have to make difficult choices about what to put off for another time. You may need to choose, for example, between cleaning the bathroom or playing cards with your husband and stepchildren. While a clean home is important, consider that you may be better off if you choose to play a game, which would be good for your emotional health and your relationship with your stepchildren.

Develop common interests with your stepchildren. For example, I love pets, and can't imagine life without the fun and intimacy they provide. My husband and I gave my stepdaughter a kitten for her fifth birthday. His antics brought us all joy, and the times he was ill drew us closer together. Choose a puppy or kitten from a shelter with your stepchildren, and spend time grooming, feeding and playing with your pet. If having a cat or dog is not a realistic option for you, consider a bird or fish. It doesn't matter what kind of pet you have—caring for it and giving it love can bring your family together.

It's possible that your stepchildren have limited free time. They may be busy with extracurricular activities or seeing their friends. This is entirely normal, and while you don't want them to sacrifice their other activities, you can make sure the time they spend with you is fun and interesting.

Mealtimes are a special opportunity to bond and have fun together. My stepdaughter was quiet when she was young. To draw her out, we played "my most embarrassing moment" at dinner. We took turns around the table, each sharing an embarrassing moment we'd had. This was a funny, entertaining way to talk about our lives and develop intimacy. My stepdaughter got to know me by hearing about experiences that made me blush. We also played the "rose and thorn" game at dinner. We each shared the best thing that had happened to us that day, along with the worst. This game can be very enlightening and a real eye-opener, challenging our assumptions about each other.

Without a doubt, having fun is easier when you have some money. Wealthier stepfamilies have a greater choice of activities to select from. However, having limited financial resources is no excuse for not having fun, and there are plenty of activities that are free or reasonably priced. Many people who grew up during the Depression have fond memories of the fun their families had with no money at all. Fun is a state of mind, and the possibilities for it are endless. For example, you can:

- **Ride** bikes as a family.
- **Assemble** a complicated jigsaw puzzle together.

- **Play** hide and seek, tag and Red Rover outdoors.
- **Build** sand castles at a nearby beach.
- **Make** popcorn and watch a video or DVD.
- **Have** a scavenger or treasure hunt.
- **Play** card games or learn card tricks to amaze each other.
- **Garden** together. Grow houseplants if you don't have a yard.
- **Bake** and decorate cookies together.
- **Go** to the zoo or library.
- **Create** a family Internet blog.
- **Put together** a scrapbook.
- **Decorate** a T-shirt or your blue jeans together, or start some other craft project.
- **Teach** each other to play board games, chess, Scrabble or backgammon.
- **Learn** and perform magic tricks together.
- **Assemble** a family album, with information and pictures about each family member.
- **Attend** free classes together at your community center or place of worship.
- **Go fly** a kite!
- **Pitch** a tent in the yard, have a campfire and tell ghost stories.
- **Write and direct** a play to perform before other family members.
- **Sing** songs together.
- **Build** a tree house together in your backyard.
- **Tell** jokes to each other.
- **Play** sports, like basketball, soccer and volleyball as a group, or volunteer to coach a kids' team.
- **Take a hike** through the countryside.
- **Start a collection** of rocks, shells, coins or stamps together.

- **Volunteer** at a homeless shelter or other nonprofit organization.

These are just a few of the activities you can enjoy with your stepchildren. I am sure you can come up with many more. Remember, it's never too late to start having fun. So start right now!

Chapter Twelve

Step 10: Create a Support Network

Peer support is an important ally on your journey toward self-acceptance and a satisfying life, and it is one of the most effective and easily accessible forms of help you can get for emotional issues. Your problems may not be solved immediately, but by talking to a peer, you will feel understood by someone who is walking in your shoes, a very powerful experience that can help immeasurably. Realizing the importance of peer support was the inspiration for this book.

Online chat rooms are a modern version of in-person peer support groups, and they may be just as effective, if not more so. Peer support groups are simply networks of individuals who share common concerns and interests. Also called *self-help groups,* they provide a safe environment where members can explore their feelings.

The Value of Peer Support

I witnessed the value of this approach during the fourteen years I spent doing peer support training for the New York City Police Department. Police officers have incredibly stressful jobs, and often feel they have nowhere to turn for emotional support. They don't want to burden their families with their problems or cause them to worry excessively, and they often distrust mental health professionals, believing that therapists could not possibly understand what they go through. In some cases, peer support programs for law enforcement personnel have saved the lives of officers in distress. I have been privileged to train several peer support officers who later rescued colleagues from the brink of suicide.

While other peer support groups may not share such life-or-death struggles, they do have many other similarities. "Twelve-step" programs are probably the most notable and successful example. Alcoholics Anonymous was the first of these programs, founded in 1935 by "Doctor Bob," an Ohio surgeon, and Bill Wilson, a New York stockbroker, both of whom had struggled with alcoholism. Bill W. and Dr. Bob believed that the best way to achieve and maintain their sobriety was to attend support groups with peers who shared a common goal. Following the success of AA, other twelve-step programs were started, such as Al-Anon (for family members of alcoholics), Narcotics Anonymous and Gamblers Anonymous.

Twelve-step programs differ from professionally run therapy groups, where a mental health professional leads the group and ensures the group's effectiveness. Since everyone who attends a twelve-step meeting has equal standing, no one has greater authority than anyone else, and no one is considered more knowledgeable. All participants share responsibility for the content of the meeting, and giving and receiving help is a two-way street.

"STEPMOTHERS SPEAK"

Because nobody knew. Because nobody else has been where you are, or where most of us on this board have been. And the people who might have had the imagination to say something might have seen how much you loved your man and not have wanted to scare you away.

—Fifth Wheel

"STEPMOTHERS SPEAK"

Why didn't someone tell me that I would always be second in line? Why didn't someone tell me that I would never have my husband completely to myself? Why didn't someone tell me that dealing with my husband's baggage sucks? Why didn't someone tell me that I'd feel so alone and alienated because it's difficult to share these feelings with friends/family who just don't understand? Why didn't someone tell me that the next ten years of my life would be controlled by a woman I dislike greatly? She will influence when I take vacations, and she will affect my financial situation. Why didn't someone tell me that I would feel so resentful? Why didn't someone tell me that these feelings will wash over me like waves when I least expect it and think I can handle everything? Why didn't someone tell me?

—Tired of It All

Other types of peer support or self-help groups have also been quite useful to members who share particular challenges, such as cancer or Parkinson's disease, and other serious illnesses. Doctors frequently recommend support groups as part of a treatment plan.

Using these groups as a model, the Steps for Stepmothers on-line chat room began in May of 2004 as a grassroots effort to provide stepmothers with support, advice and encouragement. The following is a typical exchange between members:

The Steps for Stepmothers online chat room has been a haven and a godsend for many of us stepmothers. It is a place to brainstorm, release stress, seek advice and get reality checks, and it is a place of catharsis for many of us who are dealing with extraordinary levels of negative emotion. Stepmothers discuss their problems with women in similar circumstances without having to leave their homes or offices. Without any formal training in counseling or group dynamics, members instinctively know how to support each other.

Online peer support provides members with a broader perspective than they might get from local peer groups, and for those who might be reserved or shy about discussing their problems in front of strangers, it offers the anonymity of an online community. It doesn't matter that these women are often separated from each other by thousands of miles. Access to the Internet provides them with instant companionship and assistance from other stepmothers who share their concerns. In a nonjudgmental atmosphere, they discuss their specific situations, along with ways to improve relationships with partners and stepchildren. Many of the voices of experience and encouragement in this book come from the peer support chat room.

There are only three basic rules you need to follow when you join an online chat room or any peer support group:

(1) *Be respectful of other members.*

(2) *Maintain confidentiality. It is imperative that what is discussed in the support group is not shared with outsiders.*

(3) *Be nonjudgmental. Many stepmothers feel isolated, misunderstood and judged by family members, and need a place where they can finally feel understood and supported. To ensure this, all members must be careful to respond to each other in a nonjudgmental and caring manner.*

A Note of Caution

Most members of support groups try their utmost to respect each other, be nonjudgmental and give constructive advice. Occasionally, someone may respond harshly to a comment, or perhaps offer an unhelpful suggestion. Therefore, when participating in a support group, carefully consider if the suggestions you receive are beneficial to your situation before you follow any advice.

Also, keep in mind that online chat rooms are public forums. Anyone can read posts, including family members or strangers with serious emotional problems. To avoid being harassed, it is important to protect your identity by choosing an online screen name that others will not associate with you. For instance, if you care about maintaining your privacy, don't select Minnesota Bowling Champion 2008 or Harvard Grad Stepmother—names that can give away your identity to family and friends. For further protection, slightly alter personal information, such as the ages and gender of your stepchildren, or the city where you live. This can prevent predators from violating your personal space.

Unfortunately, participation in a peer support group cannot always guarantee the happiness or successful relationships that you seek. A few participants joined the online chat room in last-ditch efforts to save their marriages, but left their partners after discussing their problems with the other stepmothers. They concluded that they had exhausted all options to improve their situation, and that separation was the best solution. However, they did get strength, confidence and valuable friendship as members of the online chat room.

"STEPMOTHERS SPEAK"

I just want to thank all of you for all the love and support you've given me this past summer. I want to apologize for not telling you sooner how I was doing because frankly, I wasn't okay. It was hard to pack up and leave my partner, to be the one to hand back the keys, and drive far away from a situation that was destroying me.

For all of you, words can't express my thankfulness. Before joining this community of women, I truly felt alone with my worries, fears, frustrations and upsets. Here I didn't feel like the sideshow freak. If there is ANYTHING I can do to help or repay you, please let me know.

—RECOVERING SLOWLY

Peer support can change your outlook on life. As one stepmother said on the message board, "It has been really helpful [even after the fact] to know that my feelings and my reactions to situations are perfectly normal."

If you think you might benefit from talking to other stepmothers, please look for a local support group in your area or join one of the many stepmother online sites. Your input will be appreciated by other members of the community, and, perhaps most important, you will be embraced with enthusiasm and compassion by others who know what you are going through. You will receive the guidance and encouragement you need from those who have "been there" as you embark on your journey toward a life of greater serenity and fulfillment.

Afterword

Let your mind start a journey through a strange new world.
Leave all thoughts of the world you knew before.
Let your soul take you where you long to be...
Close your eyes, let your spirit start to soar,
and you'll live as you've never lived before.

~ ERICH FROMM

The future looks brighter than ever for us stepmothers. We no longer have to be victims of unfortunate circumstances. By following the steps in this book, you can achieve greater perspective, stability and contentment, even though your stepfamilies may still experience problems.

We stepmothers are the true romantics of the world. We bravely commit to relationships that are fraught with potential difficulties. We take bigger gambles than most women by shouldering additional burdens, caring for stepchildren, dealing with complicated family dynamics, coping with ex-wives and ex-in-laws, and struggling against an unfair stereotype that blames us for problems we did not create. We are admirable and courageous people living our conviction that love and hard work will override our problems. We are tenacious, persistent and devoted to the principles of love and family. If we can work this hard for our families, we can put similar efforts into our own personal growth and development.

We deserve to have fulfilled lives. Be assured that this goal is attainable, as long as you are willing to invest time and effort in the process. I hope you are as excited about the ideas and exercises outlined in this book as I am. The sooner you put them into practice, the sooner you can start to feel happier and more invigorated about living your best possible life.

While a great deal of information and many exercises are contained in this book, please don't feel pressured to memorize the contents of each chapter, or to complete every single exercise, in order to derive all of this program's benefits. Some stepmothers choose to follow the guidelines in sequential order, while others prefer to work it one step at a time, selecting what is most relevant to their current problems. Later, they may pick other steps to work on. Whatever your approach, keep *The Happy Stepmother* handy as a reference guide for the future. You can use it as often as necessary to gain emotional support, reassess your priorities and refocus your efforts.

After reading this book, I hope you realize that you are not alone in your struggles, and that many other women are facing similar challenges. This realization is important for two reasons: It can help you overcome any misplaced blame you may feel for the problems in your stepfamily, and it can encourage you to reach out to other stepmothers for acknowledgment, support and help. Even if your circumstances are dire, the knowledge that others understand what you are going through can make all the difference in helping you get through the day. Being listened to may not seem like such a big deal, but the opportunity to be heard comes up far less frequently than most of us need. Feeling understood and accepted by others is one of the most powerful and meaningful of all human experiences. All too often, family members and friends are unable to help us with this. As stepmothers, however, we can satisfy this important need for each other. If you don't know any other stepmothers in your community, you can join the Steps for Stepmothers online chat room.

Keep in mind that every moment of our brief lives is precious. Since there are never any guarantees about the future (our stepfamily relations can improve or can worsen, just like other aspects of our lives), we need to focus on what we can control. Experience, explore and participate in as many activities and social interactions as you can. Embrace each day with gusto. Don't wait until your stepchildren move out of your home before seeking your own happiness. If you let time slip away from you, you will never be able to recapture those moments.

This book shows you the pathways for achieving your dreams, but taking the steps to get there is up to you. You must choose to focus on your own priorities, first and foremost, and not expect a spouse or other family members to do it for you. You have the support of all of us, but you are the only one who can fulfill your own needs. Best of luck to you on your journey!

Appendix A

About the Web site Questionnaire

You may be interested in knowing more about how I gathered the information for this book. In May 2004, I launched a Web site, stepsforstepmothers.com, to gather data about stepmothers. The Web site includes an online questionnaire consisting of 120 questions asking stepmothers to evaluate their partnerships, relationships with stepchildren and feelings about being a stepmother, by selecting the most appropriate responses to questions on a seven-point scale. They also are asked to write about their most difficult experiences as stepmothers, and to share advice they would give to other women.

More than three thousand women answered the questionnaire over a two-year period from 2004 to 2006. This was a self-selected group of stepmothers who use the Internet for information and assistance and were drawn to this particular Web site for a variety of reasons. While these women do not represent all stepmothers, they do represent a very diverse population.

Respondents to the questionnaire came from a wide variety of races, religions, socioeconomic levels and age groups, although the majority were Caucasian, college graduates, and in their early thirties. The ages of those responding ranged from as young as twenty-one to their mid-fifties. They lived throughout the United States in cities, suburbs and rural areas, and each of the fifty states was represented. Approximately 25 percent of the women were cohabiting with partners and considering marriage. The average respondent had been married for three years, and had dated her partner for three years prior to her marriage.

Almost all the stepmothers who participated in the study were actively involved with their stepchildren. One-third cared for them full-time, another third had joint responsibility, with stepchildren spending every other week in their homes, and most of the remaining stepmothers had every other weekend with their partner's kids. A handful of the respondents lived hundreds or thousands of miles away from their stepchildren, and spent time with them only during vacations and holidays.

Half of the stepmothers who filled out the questionnaire had at least one biological child. The majority of these women also had one or two stepchildren, and a small number had more than five. Most of the stepchildren ranged in age from toddlers to teenagers; a small number were adults. A handful of these adult stepchildren resided with their fathers and stepmothers because they were unemployed or recently divorced.

Each of the stepfamilies was unique, with varying numbers of stepchildren, ex-wives and their male or female partners, biological children, and multiple sets of in-laws. The variety of experiences that these stepmothers encountered was also great, and their problems ranged from daily irritations to major crises.

Despite the unique experiences encountered by each step-mother, several common themes emerged from responses to the questionnaire. All these women tried, to the best of their abilities, to create happy, loving stepfamilies and hoped that, over time, they would succeed. Every single one of the three thousand respondents complained of mental and physical exhaustion as a result of trying to achieve this goal, as well as self-blame, a sense of failure and heartache.

Many of the respondents also said that they felt misunderstood by family and friends, and had stopped confiding in them after being met with criticism. They were tired of being blamed by others for problems they did not create. These women openly discussed feeling fragile and depressed due to the conflicts in their stepfamilies, and were seeking online assistance and information to help them before they cracked under the strain, or before their marriages were beyond repair. Some had tried couples counseling, and the results were mixed. While some stated that they had been helped, others said that they had not experienced any tangible benefits from psychotherapy.

The burdens some of these women endure, and the ways their lives have been compromised by difficult stepfamily experiences, are staggering. Their problems are far more challenging than I had ever imagined, and this awareness has intensified my passion to help stepmothers lead more satisfying lives. They confirmed and reinforced my belief that stepmothers are an underserved group who do not deserve to be overlooked and ignored. Their experiences—along with my own as a stepmother, and the knowledge I gained in my psychotherapy practice—helped me to formulate the advice found in this book.

Appendix B

Stepmothers Speak:
Advice from Stepmothers to Other Stepmothers

One of the questions on the online questionnaire asks stepmothers what advice they would give to others—the following suggestions are from their responses.

A good sense of humor and a strong sense of self are absolute musts for anyone who is considering becoming a stepmother. And the knowledge that everything we do for our stepfamilies will be taken for granted and unappreciated. If you accept this, then you will never be disappointed.—CS

Know what you are walking into. All stepmothers join previously existing families that have been torn apart by separation and divorce. Family members often are angry, confused and hurt. Sometimes, adults are vindictive. The safe world that the children had experienced with Mommy and Daddy no longer exists, and they are unjustly exposed to the darker sides of human behavior. Children of divorce have loyalty issues, no matter how well step-parents treat them or how badly a biological parent has treated them. It's little wonder that the lives of stepmothers are not easy. Initially there will be lots of problems: emotional, financial, vengeful. Over time, with prayer and sacrifice, it gets better.—TM

Sometimes venting in a safe environment is enough to keep going on. As the expression goes, "Misery loves company." But let's not forget, "Shared happiness equals double happiness."—JB

Be civil, and pretend you are on the set of *Leave It to Beaver* when in the presence of your partner's ex. This tactic also works well with in-laws. This will keep you from saying a lot of things that you will *really* want to, but know you shouldn't.—RH

Try to get along with your partner's ex-wife. If you can be civil during those times you have to be together, then your life will be easier. That means biting your tongue and trying to react normally when things are chaotic. You don't have to go overboard and be her friend or sounding board. If you or she cannot be civil, then don't have contact of any kind. I have chosen this route. But for the first couple of years I gave it my best shot. And that is all I can ask from myself and all my husband could ask of me.—WN

Move slowly and intelligently when building relationships with stepchildren, especially if there's the slightest hint of resentment, anger or emotional problems. Encourage your husband to be a parent without you sometimes. They are *his* children, after all. I'm convinced that relationships that are carefully built (instead of rushed into) have the strongest foundations. And accept that there are some things you just have no control over. Those are the things you cannot allow to consume too much of your life. Use your head to think more than your heart, and be practical. You have to be realistic about your own limitations and your own tolerance levels. Don't do too much or you can find yourself overwhelmed and in trouble. You have to realize that if your stepchildren cause you to lose yourself, your husband will realize he's not married to the same person anymore.—TT

Always remember that you are important in your stepchildren's lives and they need you, regardless of what anybody says. It is harder to be a stepparent than a biological one. Hold your head up high and know that you are not alone. You have other stepmothers to lean on for support.—OS

Patience, patience and more patience.—NS

You have to concentrate on what you *can* control, not on what you cannot. Stand up firmly for the fights that you cannot lose. Don't ever give up your dreams.—CB

Immediately discuss and agree to household rules and regulations with your husband. This includes chores, schedules, discipline and child support.—DT

Know from the beginning that you are not your stepchildren's mother and you don't have to be in order to enjoy a good and loving relationship with them. The more people who love a child, the better off he or she will be. Be supportive to your stepchildren and when they lash out at you, know that it is most likely not about you; it is about them. Being a single mother is also very difficult. There are many burdens, guilt and bitterness that single moms deal with on a daily basis, and they will often take these feelings out on you, even though you don't deserve it. Don't let them run over you and don't let them bring you down. Pray for them and for guidance in dealing with them. It is the only way you will endure.—AC

Never abandon your daily regimen of exercise and proper diet, and get plenty of rest, no matter what's going on. Make a list of the great things you bring to your household if your partner or stepchildren ever challenge you. Also, keep a journal and each week write about your stepfamily. Changes in family life can be fast and furious, and sometimes it all seems a blur. It's easy to overlook progress.—VW

Communicate openly with your partner about *everything!* You two must have a united front and a set of house rules to be followed by your stepchildren and biological children! When your husband is able to stand by you and back you up when situations arise, it makes it so much easier! Remember, they aren't your kids. Don't try to change them or raise them as you do your own. Learn to let your partner parent them! Don't let his ex-wife get to you, *never* feed into her tricks and games and they'll soon fade away. Let her know up front that she or your stepchildren will not ever be able to come between you and your partner!—JK

Don't do things because others expect you to be the perfect step-mother. I dove headfirst into being a stepmom. From day one, I went to dance recitals, PTA meetings and every other activity you can imagine. I didn't realize that my stepdaughter already had a caring mother. She didn't need me to ask her 100 questions about school and ballet classes. I got so caught up in being the instant stepmother that I stopped being me. I started to fret over every word I said and if it sounded "motherly." My stepdaughter didn't ask for that. My parents, my in-laws and my husband's friends expected that of me. I wish I wasn't concerned about what they thought of my maternal skills and followed my gut instincts.—HG

If you are doing more for your stepchildren than either their biological mom or dad, then you are doing too much and you should stop *immediately*. Treat your stepchildren the way you would treat a scared, adopted pet. Help them to feel safe in a contained (emotional) space. Let them show you what they want and need. As trust grows—and it will—you can reach out to them more readily. In the beginning, though, I would let them come to you and just be available for that.—VM

Don't expect to have a happy family at first. Let things take their own course and eventually you will establish your own unique family. Expect rejection.—ST

Remember to hire a sitter or have Grandma babysit for your stepchildren so you and your partner can go out for a quiet dinner once in a while. Couples need to spend some time apart from children.—AB

For heaven's sake, don't listen to any advice from someone who's not a stepparent. They don't know what they are talking about! Being a stepparent is something you don't truly understand until you are one.—NA

At first I would say *run*, but in all honesty, being a stepmother can be a rewarding experience. It is not for the weak at heart because there are so many people and all of their baggage to deal with. At times you can feel like a juggler on the high wire. First, define your role with your husband. Make sure he agrees to support you if his ex-wife tries to undermine your efforts. If he is on your side, your life will be much easier. Encourage your husband to reassure his children that you want a good relationship with them. This will calm any fears they may have of not being loyal to their mother.—SD

Discuss with your partner how you as parents will handle discipline, but do not be the one to enforce it. Leave it to him as the biological parent to enforce the discipline and give the consequences. Your input should be a part of that.—MJ

Have clear "rules of the house." Discuss them with your husband *before* they become an issue. You can add rules to the list as you need them. This way, everybody knows what is expected of them. This is important because stepchildren need to know the rules in each household. We go over our house rules every time they come over to make sure we are on the same family page. Clear house rules also eliminate any room for your stepchildren to question your authority in your own home.—KW

Don't try to be the child's mother. Even if she is the biggest train wreck in the world, she is still the child's mother and you can't replace her.—OP

Quality time with stepchildren is more important than money and gifts. You want your stepchildren to know you care about them and value the time you are together.—HF

You are not perfect; you shouldn't expect to be perfect. *Do not* try to be superwoman; you will only make yourself miserable if you do. Don't get sucked into doing everything so your partner can relax. This will come back to haunt you at a later time, and you will have a hard time giving up all the responsibilities you've taken on.—HJ

Remember that you are important, too. Try to make time for yourself as well as time alone to be with your partner. A healthy, happy family starts with the two of you. Hopefully, you can convince your husband of that.—LR

Appendix C
Resources for Stepmothers

Support Groups

Unfortunately, stepmother support groups are not as common as those for twelve-step programs and ones for grief and bereavement and illnesses, such as cancer and diabetes. To find if one exists in your area, check your local papers, such as the *Penny Saver,* for listings, or call your local chapter of the American Association of Marriage and Family Therapists.

Monthly Steps for Stepmothers support groups are held in New York City. If you live close by, check the Web site, www.stepsforstepmothers.com for the exact location and specific times of meetings.

You are welcome to participate in the Steps for Stepmothers online chat room. Go the posting board page to sign up. It's simple and free to do.

Helpful Web sites

American Association for Marriage and Family Therapy (www.aamft.org)
This organization provides a nationwide online registry of marriage and family counselors, as well as links to marriage education resources.

National Stepfamily Resource Center (www.stepfamilies.info)
This organization's Web site includes links to resources for

stepfamilies, frequently asked questions and research summaries. The NSRC also publishes *Your Stepfamily* online magazine, which offers articles on stepfamily life.

National Council on Family Relations *(www.ncfr.org)*
NCFR is a forum for family researchers and educators who develop materials to aid and promote healthy families. They also publish two professional journals, *Family Relations* and *The Journal of Marriage and Family.*

The Gottman Institute *(www.gottman.com)*
This is the official Web site of marriage expert Dr. John Gottman, and it contains information about his work, books, videos and workshops.

About Our Kids *(www.aboutourkids.org)*
The Web site for New York University's Child Study Center includes many articles on parenting, growth and development, and school and learning issues.

I Do Take Two *(www.idotaketwo.com)*
This Web site is filled with practical information about getting married the second time around.

Here is a sampling of the many resources available on yoga, mindfulness and meditation. Feel free to explore further.

Yoga

Yoga Journal magazine (www.yogajournal.com) offers many resources, including a section on "basics," online video yoga classes and a signup for its free e-mail newsletter.

Moving Toward Balance: 8 Weeks of Yoga with Rodney Yee (Emmaus, Pa.: Rodale Press), contains three hundred color photographs and a music CD. You can order it through www.8weeksofyoga.com. Many other DVDs with Rodney Yee are also available.

The Healing Path of Yoga: Alleviate Stress, Open Your Heart and Enrich Your Life, with Nischala Joy Devi (New York: Three Rivers Press, Random House). Her CDs are available at www.abundantwellbeing.com.

Laughter Yoga, developed by Dr. Madan Kataria, is an energizing practice of laughter and yoga breathing that has become a worldwide movement. Information at: www.laughteryoga.com.

Meditation

www.learn-to-meditate.com. This Web site offers samples of meditation practices from Eastern and Western traditions. This is a good starting place.

How to Meditate: A Guide to Self-Discovery, by Lawrence LeShan, PhD (New York: Macmillan). A classic introduction by a psychologist; straightforward and clear. CDs and audiocassettes also available.

Meditation: Achieving Inner Peace and Tranquility in Your Life, by Brian L. Weiss, M.D. (includes CD) (Carlsbad, Calif.: Hay House, www.hayhouse.com).

Meditations to Heal Your Life, by Louise Hay (Hay House, www.hayhouse.com).

Mindfulness

Some books on mindfulness meditation (tapping into the riches in the present moment) include Thich Nhat Hanh: *Peace is Every Step: The Path of Mindfulness in Everyday Life; The Miracle of Mindfulness: A Manual of Meditation;* and *Teachings on Love* (Parallax Press, www.parallaxpress.org).

Books by Rachel Remen, *Kitchen Table Wisdom: Stories That Heal* (New York: Riverhead Books, 1996) and *My Grandfather's Blessings:*

Stories of Strength, Refuge and Belonging (New York, Riverhead Books, 2000) are excellent. Information on audiocassettes and DVDs can be found at www.rachelremen.com.

Endnotes

Why I Wrote This Book

(x) *Studies from the U.S. Census Bureau*
http://www.harrisfamilylaw.com/pdfs/us-divorce-statistics.pdf,
60 percent of remarriages failed in 1997;
http://www.usattorneylegalservices.com/divorce-statistics.html,
75 percent of all divorced people remarry, half of them within three
years. Sixty-five percent of all second marriages fail.

Chapter 2
Our Emotional Challenges and How the Ten Steps Can Help

(19-20) *In her book* Constance Ahrons, *We're Still Family: What
Grown Children Have to Say About Their Parents' Divorce* (New York:
HarperCollins, 2004), p. 101.

(20) *Parent alienation syndrome happens* Richard A. Gardner,
*The Parental Alienation Syndrome: A Guide for Mental Health and
Legal Professionals* (Cresskill, N.J.: Creative Therapeutics, Inc.,
1992), pp. 73-126.

(28) *A recent study* by Lisa Strohschein, "Parental Divorce and Child
Mental Health Trajectories," *Journal of Marriage and Family* 67
(2005): 1286-1300.

(29) *In a longitudinal study of divorce* E. Mavis Hetherington and
John Kelly, *For Better or Worse: Divorce Reconsidered* (New York:
W. W. Norton, 2002), p. 232.

Chapter 3
Step 1: Understand the Facts

(37) *"better a serpent than a stepmother"* This quote by Euripides, the
Greek playwright who lived between 480 and 406 BC, appears in
his play, *Alcestis*. The quote can be found at
http://www.bartleby.com/66/74/21774.html.

(38) *Fairy tales are not the only way* Stephen Claxton-Oldfield and Bonnie Butler, "Portrayal of Stepparents in Movie Plot Summaries," *Psychological Reports* 82 (1998): 879-882.

(39) *Dr. Claude Steele* Claude M. Steele, "A Threat in the Air: How Stereotypes Shape the Intellectual Identities and Performance of Women and African-Americans," *American Psychologist* 52 (1997): 613-629.

(39) *In a similar experiment* Joshua Aronson et al., "When White Men Can't Do Math: Necessary and Sufficient Factors in Stereotype Threat," *Journal of Experimental Social Psychology* 35 (1999): 29-46.

(44) *In her twenty-five-year study* Judith S. Wallerstein, Julia M. Lewis, and Sandra Blakeslee, *The Unexpected Legacy of Divorce: A 25-Year Landmark Study* (New York: Hyperion, 2000).

(44) *"Children of divorce need more time"* Wallerstein et al., 2000, p. 37.

(45) *While stepchildren may take longer to grow up* Wallerstein et al., 2000, pp. 186-194.

(45) *Dr. E. Mavis Hetherington conducted* Hetherington and Kelly, 2002, pp. 241-242.

(46) *While some children exhibit obvious problems* Elizabeth Marquardt, *Between Two Worlds: The Inner Lives of Children of Divorce* (New York: Crown, 2005), pp. 19-76.

(46) *a term coined by* Constance Ahrons, *The Good Divorce: Keeping Your Family Together When Your Marriage Comes Apart* (New York: HarperCollins, 1994).

(48) *Dr. Wallerstein found* Wallerstein, 2000, p. 249.

(48) *Divorce often lives on* Wallerstein, 2000, pp. 150-151.

(49) *As mentioned earlier* Hetherington and Kelly, 2002, pp. 241-242.

(53) *After divorce, the economic well-being* Timothy S. Grall, "Custodial Mothers and Fathers and their Child Support: 2005," *U.S. Census Bureau Current Population Reports*, http://www.census.gov/prod/2007pubs/p60-234.

(55) *Balancing the demands of a job, home, child care* Jenn Yuen Tein, Irwin Sandler and Alex Zautra, "Stressful Life Events, Psychological Distress, Coping, and Parenting of Divorced Mothers: A Longitudinal Study," *Journal of Family Psychology* 14 (2000): 27-41.

(58) *According to* U.S. Census Bureau *Current Population Reports*, August 2007. "Custodial Mothers and Fathers and Their Child Support: 2005," by Timothy S. Grall. http://www.census.gov/prod/2007pubs/p60-234.

(61) *Dr. E. Mavis Hetherington found* Hetherington and Kelly, 2002, p. 249.

(72) *Despite the best efforts of everyone involved* Ahrons, 2004, p. 150.

Chapter 4
Step 2: Revise Unrealistic Expectations

(77) *Cognitive therapy, founded by* Aaron Beck, *Love Is Never Enough: How Couples Can Overcome Misunderstandings, Resolve Conflicts, and Solve Relationship Problems Through Cognitive Therapy* (New York: HarperCollins, 1988), pp. 197-212.

Chapter 5
Step 3: Your First Priority: Self-Care

(88) *"You, yourself, as much as anybody in the entire universe, deserve your love and affection."* This quote by Buddha, the Hindu Prince Gautama Siddharta, who lived from 563 to 483 BC, can be found in http://www.famousquotes.com/show.php?_id=1054269.

(89) *Contrast this with* Tal Ben-Shahar, *Happier: Learn the Secrets to Daily Joy and Lasting Fulfillment* (New York: McGraw-Hill, 2007), p. 37.

(90) *Dr. Martin Seligman, a cognitive psychologist* Martin E. P. Seligman, *Authentic Happiness: Using the New Positive Psychology to Realize Your Potential for Lasting Fulfillment* (New York: Free Press, 2002), p. 102.

(90) *In one study* Ed Diener and Martin E. P. Seligman, "Very Happy People," *Psychological Science* 13, no. 1 (2002): 81-84.

(95) *Recent studies by* Paul Ekman et al., "Buddhist and Psychological Perspectives on Emotions and Well-Being," *Current Directions in Psychological Science* 14 (2005): 59-63.

(96) *Dr. Richard Davidson found* Richard J. Davidson et al., "Alterations in Brain and Immune Function Produced by Mindfulness Meditation," *Psychosomatic Medicine* 65 (2003): 564-570.

(101) More information about laughter yoga can be found on the Web site, http://www.laughteryoga.org/.

(103) *The positive psychology* Seligman, 2002, p. 134.

(103) *According to Dr. Seligman* Martin E. P. Seligman, Acacia C. Parks, and Tracy A. Steen, "A Balanced Psychology and a Full Life," in *The Science of Well-Being*, F. Huppert, B. Keverne and N. Baylis, eds. (Oxford: Oxford University Press, 2006).

(103) *In a study of people who* Martin E. P. Seligman, Tracy A. Steen, Nansook Park, and Christopher Peterson, "Positive Psychology Progress: Empirical Validation of Interventions," *American Psychologist* 60, no. 5 (2005): 410-421.

(104) *Research conducted by* Robert A. Emmons, Michael E. McCullough, and Jo-Ann Tsang, "The Assessment of Gratitude," in *Handbook of Positive Psychology Assessment*, S. Lopez & C. R. Snyder, eds. (Washington, D.C.: American Psychological Association, 2003), pp. 327-342.

(104) *The results of this study* Ben-Shahar, 2007, p. 122.

(104) *Keeping a daily gratitude list* Robert A. Emmons and Michael E. McCullough, "Counting Blessings Versus Burdens: Experimental

Studies of Gratitude and Subjective Well-Being in Daily Life," *Journal of Personality and Social Psychology* 84 (2003): 377-389.

(107) *In his book* Frederic Luskin, *Forgive for Good: A Proven Prescription for Health and Happiness* (New York: HarperCollins, 2002), p. 68.

(107) *Dr. Robert Enright, who pioneered* Robert D. Enright, *Forgiveness Is a Choice: A Step by Step Process for Resolving Anger and Restoring Hope* (Washington, D.C.: APA Books, 2001), pp. 46-47.

(107) *Dr. Luskin's definition* Luskin, 2002, p. 68.

(107) *Numerous studies have found that forgiveness*

Suzanne R. Freedman and Robert D. Enright, "Forgiveness as an Intervention Goal with Incest Survivors," *Journal of Consulting and Clinical Psychology* 64, no. 5 (1996): 983-992.

Gayle L. Reed and Robert D. Enright, "The Effects of Forgiveness Therapy on Depression, Anxiety, and Posttraumatic Stress for Women after Spousal Emotional Abuse," *Journal of Consulting and Clinical Psychology* 74, no. 5 (2006): 920-929.

Wei-Fen Lin, et al., "Effects of Forgiveness Therapy on Anger, Mood, and Vulnerability to Substances Among Inpatient Substance-Dependent Clients," *Journal of Consulting and Clinical Psychology* 72, no. 6 (2004): 1114-1121.

Rahdi H. Al-Mabuk, Robert D. Enright, and P. A. Cardis, "Forgiveness with Parentally Love-Deprived College Students," *Journal of Moral Education* 24, no. 427 (1995): 427-444.

Chapter 6
Step 4: Make Your Relationship Your Second Priority

(115) *Dr. Judith Wallerstein, the psychologist who* Judith S. Wallerstein and Sandra Blakeslee, *The Good Marriage: How and Why Love Lasts* (New York: Warner Books, 1995), pp. 327-338.

(116) To gain a more thorough understanding of the research find-ings of Dr. John Gottman, consider reading one or all of his excellent books, including:

John Gottman, Julie Schwartz Gottman, and June DeClaire, *10 Lessons to Transform Your Marriage: America's Love Lab Experts Share Their Strategies for Strengthening Your Relationship* (New York: Crown, 2006).

John Gottman and Joan DeClaire, *The Relationship Cure: A 5 Step Guide to Strengthening Your Marriage, Family, and Friend-ships* (New York: Crown, 2001).

John Gottman and Nan Silver, *Why Marriages Succeed or Fail: And How You Can Make Yours Last* (New York: Fireside, 1994).

———, *The Seven Principles for Making Marriage Work: A Practical Guide from the Country's Foremost Relationship Expert* (New York: Crown, 1999)

(118) *Good marriages are not free of* Gottman and Silver, 1999, pp. 129-155.

(118) *Often, Dr. Gottman notes, when couples are struggling* Gottman and Silver, 1999, 68-70.

(119) *Dr. Gottman also found that happily married* Gottman et al., 2006, pp. 136-139.

(120) *Dr. Gottman observes that couples in unhealthy* Gottman and Silver, 1999, pp. 27-34.

(123) *According to Dr. Elaine Eaker,* Elaine D. Eaker et al., "Marital Status, Marital Strain and the Risk of Coronary Heart Disease or Total Mortality: The Framingham Offspring Study," *Psychosomatic Medicine* 69 (2007): 509-513.

(125) *When you are talking about difficult topics with* Gottman and Silver, 1994, pp. 181-185.

(126) *Dr. Gottman recommends that, instead* Gottman and Silver, 1999, pp. 159-170.

(127) *The University of Utah study found* Timothy W. Smith et al., "Hostile Personality Traits and Coronary Artery Calcification in Middle-Aged and Older Married Couples: Different Effects for Self-Reports versus Spouse-Ratings," *Psychosomatic Medicine* 69 (2007): 441-448.

(129) *Dr. Gottman draws a crucial distinction* Gottman and Silver, 1999, pp. 27-29. Also in Gottman and Silver, 1994, pp. 189-195.

(130) *If you have to choose just one way to improve* Gottman and Silver, 1999, pp. 29-31.

(131) *In his research, Dr. Gottman has found* Gottman and Silver, 1999, pp. 170-176.

Chapter 7
Step 5: Balance Love and Money

Many books are available to help you gain financial independence, including:

Jean Chatzsky, *The Ten Commandments of Financial Happiness: Feel Richer with What You've Got* (New York: Portfolio, 2005).

———*Make Money, Not Excuses: Wake Up, Take Charge, and Overcome Your Financial Fears Forever* (New York: Crown, 2006).

Suze Orman, *The Money Book for the Young, Fabulous & Broke* (New York: Penguin Group, 2007).

———*Women and Money: Owning the Power to Control Your Destiny* (New York: Spiegel & Grau, 2007).

Chapter 9
Step 7: Provide and Receive Respect and Compassion

(192) Wendy Liebman made this comment during her appearance on the *Tonight Show with Jay Leno* on January 16, 2006.

(200) Caroline Myss, *Why People Don't Heal and How They Can* (New York: Crown, 1997), pp 31-35.

Chapter 11
Step 9: Make It Fun!

(234) *Dr. Gottman reminds us that* Gottman and Silver, 1999, pp. 99-127.

References

Ahrons, Constance. 1994. *The good divorce: Keeping your family together when your marriage comes apart.* New York: HarperCollins.

———. 2004. *We're still family: What grown children have to say about their parents' divorce.* New York: HarperCollins.

Al-Mabuk, Rahdi H., Robert D. Enright, and P. A. Cardis. 1995. Forgiveness with parentally love-deprived college students. *Journal of Moral Education* 24: 427-444.

Amato, Paul R. 2000. The consequences of divorce for adults and children. *Journal of Marriage and the Family* 62 (4): 1269-1287.

———. 2001. Children and divorce in the 1990s: An update of the Amato and Keith (1991) meta-analysis. *Journal of Family Psychology* 15: 355-370.

Aronson, Joshua, Michael J. Lustina, Catherine Good, Kelli Keough, Claude M. Steele, and Joseph Brown. 1999. When white men can't do math: Necessary and sufficient factors in stereotype threat. *Journal of Experimental Social Psychology* 35: 29-46.

Aronson, Joshua, Claude M. Steele, Moises F. Salinas, and Michael J. Lustina. 1998. The effects of stereotype threat on the standardized test performance of college students. *Readings about the Social Animal* 8th ed., ed. Aronson, E. New York: Freeman.

Beck, Aaron. 1988. *Love is never enough: How couples can overcome misunderstandings, resolve conflicts, and solve relationship problems through cognitive therapy.* New York: HarperCollins.

Ben-Shahar, Tal. 2007. *Happier: Learn the secrets to daily joy and lasting fulfillment.* New York: McGraw-Hill.

Bray, James H., and John Kelly. 1999. *Step families: Love, marriage, and parenting in the first decade.* New York: Broadway Books.

Chatzsky, Jean. 2005. *The ten commandments of financial happiness: Feel richer with what you've got.* New York: Portfolio.

———. 2006. *Make money, not excuses: Wake up, take charge, and overcome your financial fears forever.* New York: Crown.

Claxton-Oldfield, Stephen, and Bonnie Butler. 1998. Portrayal of stepparents in movie plot summaries. *Psychological Reports* 82: 879-882.

Cole, Charles Lee, and Jessica R. Broussard. 2006. The social context and history of divorce in the U.S. *Family Therapy Magazine* 5:(3) 6-9.

Davidson, Richard J., et al. 2003. Alterations in brain and immune function produced by mindfulness meditation. *Psychosomatic Medicine* 65: 564-570.

Davis, Shannon N., Theodore N. Greenstein, and Jennifer P. Gerteisen Marks. 2007. Effects of union type on division of household labor: Do cohabiting men really perform more housework? *Journal of Family Issues* 28: 1246-1272.

Diener, Ed, and Martin E. P. Seligman. 2002. Very happy people. *Psychological Science* 13 (1): 81-84.

Eaker, Elaine D., et al. 2007. Marital status, marital strain and the risk of coronary heart disease or total mortality: The Framingham Offspring Study. *Psychosomatic Medicine* 69: 509-513.

Einstein, Elizabeth, and Linda Albert. 2006. *Strengthening your stepfamily.* Atascadero, Calif,: Impact.

Ekman, Paul, Richard J. Davidson, Mathieu Ricard, and Alan B. Wallace. 2005. Buddhist and psychological perspectives on emotions and well-being. *Current Directions in Psychological Science* 14: 59-63.

Emmons, Robert A., and Michael E. McCullough. 2003. Counting blessings versus burdens: Experimental studies of gratitude and subjective well-being in daily life. *Journal of Personality and Social Psychology* 84: 377-389.

Emmons, Robert A., Michael E. McCullough, and Jo-Ann Tsang. 2003. The assessment of gratitude, in *Handbook of positive psychology assessment,* ed. Lopez, S., and C. R. Snyder, 327-342. Washington, D.C.: American Psychological Association.

Enright, Robert D. 2001. *Forgiveness is a choice: A step by step process for resolving anger and restoring hope.* Washington, D.C.: APA Books.

Freedman, Suzanne R., and Robert D. Enright. 1996. Forgiveness as an intervention goal with incest survivors. *Journal of Consulting and Clinical Psychology* 64 (5): 983-992.

Gardner, Richard A. 1992. *The parental alienation syndrome: A guide for mental health and legal professionals.* Cresskill, N.J.: Creative Therapeutics, Inc.

Gottman, John, and Joan DeClaire. 2001. *The relationship cure: A 5 step guide to strengthening your marriage, family, and friendships.* New York: Crown.

Gottman, John, Julie Schwartz Gottman, and Joan DeClaire. 2006. *10 Lessons to transform your marriage: America's love lab experts share their strategies for strengthening your relationship.* New York: Crown.

Gottman, John, and Nan Silver. 1994. *Why marriages succeed or fail: And how you can make yours last.* New York: Fireside.

———. 1999. *The seven principles for making marriage work: A practical guide from the country's foremost relationship expert.* New York: Crown.

Harra, Carmen. 2005. *Everyday karma.* New York: Ballantine.

Hetherington, E. Mavis, and John Kelly. 2002. *For better or worse: Divorce reconsidered.* New York: W. W. Norton.

Kasser, Tim, and Aaron Ahuvia. 2002. Materialistic values and well-being in business students. *European Journal of Social Psychology* 32: 137-146.

Kiecolt-Glaser, Janice K., et al. 2005. Hostile marital interactions, proinflammatory cytokine production, and wound healing. *Archive of General Psychiatry* 62: 1377-1384.

Leon, Kim, and Erin Angst. 2005. Portrayals of stepfamilies in film: Using media images in remarriage education. *Family Relations* 54: 3–23.

Lin, Wei-Fen, Robert D. Enright, David Mack, Dean Krahn, and Thomas W. Baskin. 2004. Effects of forgiveness therapy on anger, mood, and vulnerability to substance use among inpatient substance-dependent clients. *Journal of Consulting and Clinical Psychology* 72 (6): 1114-1121.

Luskin, Frederic. 2002. *Forgive for good: A proven prescription for health and happiness.* New York: HarperCollins.

McLanahan, Sara. 1999. Father absence and children's welfare. In *Coping with Divorce, Single Parenting, and Remarriage: A Risk and Resiliency Perspective.* ed. Hetherington, E. M. Mahwah, N.J.: Erlbaum.

McLanahan, Sara, and Gary Sandefur. 1994. *Growing up with a single parent: What hurts, what helps.* Cambridge, Mass.: Harvard University Press.

Marquardt, Elizabeth. 2005. *Between two worlds: The inner lives of children of divorce.* New York: Crown.

Myss, Caroline. 1997. *Why people don't heal and how they can.* New York: Crown.

O'Brien, Laurie, and Mary Lee Hummert. 2006. Age self-stereotyping, stereotype threat, and memory performance in late middle-aged adults. *Social Cognition* 24: 338-358.

Orman, Suze. 2007. *The money book for the young fabulous and broke.* New York: Penguin Group.

———. 2007. *Women and money: Owning the power to control your destiny.* New York: Spiegel & Grau.

Papernow, Patricia L. 2006. Therapy for people who live in step-families. *Family Therapy Magazine:* 5 (3): 34-41.

Reed, Gayle L., and Robert D. Enright. 2006. The effects of forgiveness therapy on depression, anxiety, and posttraumatic stress for women after spousal emotional abuse. *Journal of Consulting and Clinical Psychology* 74 (5): 920-929.

Rosen, Sydney, ed. 1991. *My voice will go with you: The teaching tales of Milton H. Erickson, M.D.* New York: W. W. Norton.

Salwen, Laura. 1990. The myth of the wicked stepmother. *Women and Therapy* 10: 117-125.

Seligman, Martin E. P. 1990. *Learned optimism.* New York: Knopf.

———. 1993. *What you can change and what you can't: The complete guide to successful self-improvement.* New York: Knopf.

———. 2002. *Authentic happiness: Using the new positive psychology to realize your potential for lasting fulfillment.* New York: Free Press.

Seligman, Martin E. P., Acacia C. Parks, and Tracy A. Steen. 2006. A balanced psychology and a full life. In *The science of well-being,* eds. F. Huppert, B. Keverne, and N. Baylis, 275-283. Oxford, UK: Oxford University Press.

Seligman, Martin E. P., Tracy A. Steen, Nansook Park, and Christopher Peterson. 2005. Positive psychology progress: Empirical validation of interventions. *American Psychologist* 60 (5): 410-421.

Smith, Timothy W., et al. 2007. Hostile personality traits and coronary artery calcification in middle-aged and older married couples: Different effects for self-reports versus spouse-ratings. *Psychosomatic Medicine* 69: 441-448.

Steele, Claude M. 1997. A threat in the air: How stereotypes shape the intellectual identities and performance of women and African-Americans. *American Psychologist* 52: 613-629.

Steele, Claude M., and Joshua Aronson. 1995. Stereotype threat and the intellectual test performance of African-Americans. *Journal of Personality and Social Psychology* 69: 797-811.

Strohschein, Lisa. 2005. Parental divorce and child mental health trajectories. *Journal of Marriage and Family* 67: 1286-1300.

——. 2007. Prevalence of methylphenidate use among Canadian children following divorce. *Canadian Medical Association Journal* 176 (12): 1711-1714.

Tein, Jenn Yuen, Irwin Sandler, and Alex Zautra. 2000. Stressful life events, psychological distress, coping, and parenting of divorced mothers: A longitudinal study. *Journal of Family Psychology* 14: 27-41.

Wallerstein, Judith S., and Sandra Blakeslee. 1995. *The good marriage: How and why love lasts.* New York: Warner Books.

Wallerstein, Judith S., Julia M. Lewis, and Sandra Blakeslee. 2000. *The unexpected legacy of divorce: A 25 year landmark study.* New York: Hyperion.

Whiteside, Mary F., and Betsy Jane Becker. 2000. Parental factors and the young child's postdivorce adjustment: A meta-analysis with implications for parenting arrangements. *Journal of Family Psychology* 14: 5-26.

Williams, Redford, and Virginia Williams. 1993. *Anger kills: Seventeen strategies for controlling the hostility that can harm your health.* New York: HarperCollins.

Zeig, Jeffrey K. 1985. *Experiencing Erickson: An introduction to the man and his work.* New York: Brunner/Mazel.

Index